Dictators as Gatekeepers for Europe

Dictators as Gatekeepers for Europe

Outsourcing EU Border Controls to Africa

Christian Jakob and Simone Schlindwein

Daraja Press

2019

Published by Daraja Press
https://darajapress.com

© Christoph Links Verlag GmbH, Berlin 2017
All rights reserved

German edition first published by Christoph Links Verlag GmbH, 2017
New English edition published by Daraja Press, 2019

Library and Archives Canada Cataloguing in Publication
Title: Dictators as gatekeepers for Europe : outsourcing EU border controls to Africa / Christian Jakob and Simone Schlindwein ; translated by Lydia Baldwin and Emal Ghamsharick.
Other titles: Diktatoren als Türsteher Europas. English
Names: Jakob, Christian, 1979- author. | Schlindwein, Simone, 1980- author. | Baldwin, Lydia, 1972- translator. | Ghamsharick, Emal, 1985- translator.
Description: New English edition. | Translation of: Diktatoren als Türsteher Europas : wie die EU ihre Grenzen nach Afrika verlagert. | Includes bibliographical references.
Identifiers: Canadiana (print) 20190049200 | Canadiana (ebook) 20190049219 | ISBN 9781988832272 (softcover) | ISBN 9781988832289 (ebook)
Subjects: LCSH: European Union countries—Relations—Africa. | LCSH: Africa—Relations—European Union countries. | LCSH: European Union countries—Emigration and immigration—Government policy. LCSH: Africa—Emigration and immigration—Government policy. | LCSH: Emigration and immigration—Political aspects. | LCSH: European Union countries—Foreign economic relations—Africa. | LCSH: Africa—Foreign economic relations—European Union countries. | LCSH: Economic assistance, European—Africa. | LCSH: Border security—European Union countries. | LCSH: Border security—Africa.
Classification: LCC JZ1570 .J3513 2019 | DDC 327.406—dc23

The translation of this work was supported by a grant from the *Goethe-Institut*. The translation was also sponsored by the *Rosa Luxemburg Stiftung* with funds of the Federal Ministry for Economic Cooperation and Development of the Federal Republic of Germany. This publication or parts of it can be used by others for free as long as they provide a proper reference to the original publication.

Cover image: REUTERS/Mohamed Nureldin Abdallah
Cover design: Kate McDonnell

Contents

EUROPE'S NEW BORDERS IN AFRICA

OPENING THE MARKETS

CONCLUSION

Acronyms

AECID Agencia Española de la Cooperación Internacional de Desarrollo

AEI Afrique-Europe-Interact (transnational migration advocacy network)

AfD Alternative für Deutschland (Alternative for Germany; far-right German political party)

AFIC Africa-Frontex-Intelligence Community

AG Rück Bund-Länder-Arbeitsgruppe Rückführungen (Federal- and State-level Workgroup on Repatriations)

AHK Außenhandelskammer (German Chambers of Commerce Abroad)

AI Amnesty International

AME L'Association Malienne des Expulsés (Malian Association of Deportees)

AQM al-Qaida in the Maghreb (Islamist militia and branch of the global terrorist network in North Africa)

ASD Aerospace and Defence Industries Association of Europe

AU African Union

BAMF Bundesamt für Migration und Flüchtlinge (Federal Office for Migration and Refugees)

BKA Bundeskriminalamt (Federal Criminal Police Office)

BMVg: Bundesministerium für Verteidigung (Federal Ministry of Defence)

BMZ Bundesministerium für wirtschaftliche Zusammen¬arbeit und Entwicklung (Federal Ministry for Economic Cooperation and Development)

CDU Christlich Demokratische Union (Christian Democratic Union; conservative German political party)

CIGEM Centre d'Information et de Gestion des Migrations (Euro-Malian agency for migration management)

CSU Christlich-Soziale Union (Christian Social Union; conservative political party in Bavaria)

DG ECHO Directorate-General for European Civil Protection and Humanitarian Aid Operations

DIE Deutsches Institut für Entwicklungspolitik (German Development Institute)

DW Deutsche Welle (Germany's public international broadcaster)

EAC East African Community

EADS European Aeronautic Defence and Space; European corporation since renamed Airbus

EBCG European Border and Coast Guard

ECCHR European Center for Constitutional and Human Rights:

ECHR European Court of Human Rights

ECOWAS Economic Community of West African States

EDF European Development Fund

EEAS European External Action Service

EIRR Eritrean Initiative on Refugee Rights

EMN European Migration Network

EOS European Organisation for Security

EPA Economic Partnership Agreement

ERMCE Enhancing the Response to Migration Challenges in Egypt (EU-funded migration policy program in Egypt)

ESF European Security Fencing (Spanish fencing producer)

ESI European Stability Initiative

ESSN Emergency Social Safety Net (EU program for supporting Syrian refugees in Turkey paid from the FRT)
EU: European Union

EU-LISA European Agency for the operational management of Large-Scale IT Systems

EUBAM European Union Border Assistance Mission (EU training mission in Libya)

EUCAP EU Capacity Building Mission (EU military mission in Niger and Sahel)

EURODAC European Dactyloscopy (fingerprint identification system which records the fingerprints of all registered asylum seekers)

EUROPOL European Union law enforcement agency

EUROSUR European Border Surveillance System

EUTF EU Emergency Trust Fund (European emergency fund for Africa)

EUTM European Training Mission

FDP Free Democratic Party (liberal German political party)

FRA EU Fundamental Rights Agency

FRT Facility for Refugees in Turkey (EU program to support Syrian refugees in Turkey)

GIZ Deutsche Gesellschaft für Internationale Zusammen¬arbeit (German Corporation for International Cooperation)

GNA Government of National Accord (provisional government in Libya)

HRW Human Rights Watch

IBM Integrated Border Management

ICAO International Civil Aviation Organization

ICC International Criminal Court

ICJ International Court of Justice

IGAD Intergovernmental Authority on Development (peace-keeping and development association between Northeast African states)

IOM International Organization for Migration

IPA Instrument for Pre-accession Assistance (EU financing instrument for membership candidates)

IS Islamic State (Islamist terrorist organization)

IWI Israel Weapon Industries

JEM Justice and Equality Movement (Sudanese rebel organization)

KfW Kreditanstalt für Wiederaufbau (German state-owned development bank)

LIBE Committee on Civil Liberties Justice and Home Affairs

MINUSMA United Nations Multidimensional Integrated Stabilization Mission in Mali (UN mission in Mali)

NATO North Atlantic Treaty Organization

NCCHF National Committee to Combat Human Trafficking (Sudan)

NDR Norddeutscher Rundfunk (North-German public broadcaster

NGO Non-Governmental Organization

NIS Nigeria Immigration Service

NISS National Intelligence and Security Service (Sudan)

NRC Norwegian Refugee Council

NSS National Security Sector (Egypt's security service)

OECD Organization for Economic Co-Operation and Development

RABIT Rapid Border Intervention Teams of Frontex (police officers from all over the EU deployed to the external borders)

ROCK Regional Operational Centre in support of the Khartoum Process and AU-Horn of Africa Initiative

RSF Rapid Support Forces (Sudan's border protection unit)

SADC Southern African Development Community

SPD Social Democratic Party of Germany

SPÖ Social Democratic Party of Austria

UEMOA Union Economique et Monétaire Ouest Africaine (West African Economic and Monetary Union)

UN United Nations

UNECA United Nations Economic Commission for Africa

UNEP United Nations Environment Programme

UNHCR United Nations High Commissioner for Refugees (UN refugee agency)

UNODC United Nations Office on Drugs and Crime

UNOWAS United Nations Office for West Africa

USA United States of America

WAPIS West Africa Police Information System

WDR Westdeutscher Rundfunk (public broadcaster for Western Germany)

WHO World Health Organization

WTO World Trade Organization

Preface:
Rediscovering Africa

The world's greatest superpower is paralyzed. The USA is divided around the wall President Trump wants to build along the Mexican border. The conflict has escalated into a deep crisis of government around the question of whether building this wall would be treason against what the West claims to stand for – open-mindedness, liberal values, multi-culturalism.

Europe has long answered this question at its own southern border: Put up that wall! (Just do not let it look like a wall.) In recent years, the EU has built a defense system against migration from the south, which – unlike Trump's wall – is not limited to its own borders. Today, it goes straight through the Sahara all the way to the equator. And there is no government crisis in Europe; the public just accepts it, as right-wing populists have demonized migration for too long.

For a long time, Europeans cared little about their southern neighbor continent. Africa stood for wars, climate change, diseases like the deadly 2014 Ebola epidemic in West Africa, or disasters like the 2017 famine in East Africa. But now the continent is back at the center of attention; there is talk of a 'new era of partnership.'

It started when the situation along the Balkan route escalated in summer of 2015. Hundreds of thousands of unrestrained refugees, including a few thousand Africans, were heading to Central Europe. Shortly thereafter, the European Union (EU) invited 33 African heads of state to a summit in Malta. Billion-euro aid and cooperation programs were drafted. 'A situation like in the summer of 2015 cannot and must not repeat,'[1] said German Chancellor Merkel at the time. Europe projected its panic caused by the uncontrolled movement of refugees along the Balkan route onto Africa, and that is where Europe now plans to solve its migration problem – through broad interventions in the countries south of the Mediterranean.

Europeans have been shaping Africa according to their own demands since colonial times. The map of Africa that hung on the wall of the conference room at the German Reich Chancellery in 1885 was over 16 feet high. Representatives of 13 European states, the USA and the Ottoman Empire had followed Chancellor Otto von Bismarck's invitation to the so-called Congo Conference in Berlin in order to negotiate the trading rights along the Congo and Niger rivers.

When the conference ended on 26 February 1885, the colonial masters had split up the continent among themselves, drawing many of the African borders that are now the target of EU migration control efforts. Nobody consulted its inhabitants.

A lot has changed since. What has remained are the colonial borders and the old fear of the "Black man." Once the Europeans feared deadly tropical diseases, today right-wing extremists are fanning the fear of an 'invasion' or 'population exchange' (*Umvolkung* in German).

This goes along with a growing fear of terrorism, triggered by the attacks in Paris in November 2015, in Brussels in March 2016 and on the Berlin Christmas market in 2016. The attackers pledged allegiance to the so-called Islamic State (IS), which is also active in Libya and the Sahel Zone these days. Europe treats refugees and migrants as the usual suspects, which is why the domestic measures against terrorism – surveillance and control, biometrization and data collection – resemble the external measures used to fight irregular migration.

Every few years, the World Bank publishes how many people worldwide migrate from one country to another. It records the 30 largest 'migration corridors' between two countries.[2] There is just one Sub-Saharan nationality on the list: Burkinabés who leave their home country Burkina Faso for Côte d'Ivoire. The share of Sub-Saharan Africans in Europe among all of the world's migrants is so small that they do not even make the Top 30, although the continents lie just a few miles apart.

In 2017, 132,750 Africans submitted their first asylum application in Europe[3] – the population of a small European city, like Amiens (France) or Newport (UK). Compared to the EU's half-billion inhabitants, the number is negligible. For Germany alone, a recent study set the annual demand for immigration from outside the EU at 146,000.[4]

However, the figure of annual arrivals from Africa has increased sixfold from 2010 to 2017, and many fear it could go on like this. The United Nations (UN) expect Africa's population to reach 2.5 billion by 2050,[5] and only thereafter is this population growth expected to stagnate. In June 2017, just before the federal election campaign, German Development Minister Gerd Müller (CSU) claims: 'Up to 100 million people'[6] could come heading north from Africa, if we fail to slow down climate change. This figure is not verified and shockingly exaggerated, most likely in order to stoke fears.

After all, those people are Black. Carlos Lopes, until recently the UN's chief economist for Africa, reminds us that hundreds of thousands of labor migrants from Bolivia, Ecuador, Colombia and Peru have come to Spain in the last decade – the same period when Spain, which lies just a few miles from Africa, implemented the *Plan África* to stop immigration from West Africa. Lopes calls Spain's simultaneous admission of Latin American migrants a 'cultural choice': 'There was no fear of migrants, but fear of Africans.'[7]

This fear, as with Islamophobia, is one of the drivers behind the right-wing swing, which has shaken the political structure of many European states. It is probable that the debate around immigration, open borders and asylum have affected the EU as a project more than the European sovereign debt crisis of 2010.

Law professor Ralph Weber claims that working-age Germans risk becoming 'a minority in their own country within less than a generation.' At the state assembly elections in the East German state of Mecklenburg-Vorpommern, he won 35 percent of the vote in his district of Vorpommern-Greifswald III along the Baltic coast.[8] It was the best result for the far-right Alternative for Germany (AfD) thus far. Weber does the math and estimates that 3.5 million 'illegal immigrants' have entered the country as of 2017. Should they 'spread with the life-embracing proliferation strategy particular to these peoples, which means four or five children in ten years,' there would soon be 'eleven to twelve million illegal immigrants and their offspring.' Utterly or completely unfounded arguments of this sort are common among the far right. Weber, however, claims these were just the issues the people brought up at his many campaign events in Germany's northeastern corner.

The fear of African and Muslim immigrants is rarely voiced as candidly as in Ralph Weber's election campaign, but it is spreading. It drives the increasing attempts to get migration in a globalized world back under control – especially migration from and within Africa. Most of the immense migration corridors on the World Bank list make no noise at all. Most of the people on the move are accepted without concern – as long as they are not Africans heading towards Europe.

In 2004, the United Nations Educational, Scientific and Cultural

Organization (UNESCO) held a conference which referred to Africa as 'the forgotten continent.' This used to be a near-synonym for Africa, but these times are over. Africa is now the center of Europe's attention.

This is basically good news and could be used to talk about food crises, land and resource grabbing, infrastructure, democratization or healthcare. But these topics are secondary to the European public and many politicians; they care about how to fend off refugees.

The multi-billion EU-Turkey deal is intended as a blueprint. It also has many critics, who say that Europe and Turkey's leader Recep Tayyip Erdoğan had begun a new, appalling form of isolationism. In fact, however, the EU has long been paying off migration source countries through 'neighborhood policies,' 'working arrangements' and 'partnership frameworks.' Unlike the deal with Turkey, these treaties have rarely caused an outcry. The only exception was the 2008 deal between Italian Prime Minister Silvio Berlusconi and Libyan dictator Muammar Gaddafi. Berlusconi offered Gaddafi billions of euros as a compensation for alleged 'colonial injustice' in a trade he later described as 'less refugees – more oil.'[9]

Today the EU as a whole is trying to close many such deals with African states, making it harder and harder for refugees to find protection and more dangerous for labor migrants to reach places where they can earn an income. This is not the only effect, though. The more Europe tries to control migration from Africa, the harder it becomes for many Africans to move freely through their own continent, even within their own countries.

While this book is about the new approach to Africa, it describes Europe's domestic affairs.

As the EU integrates, its borders are growing faster than its territory. First it acted like a nation state by controlling the access points to its own territory, but after a while, this was not enough. Following the collective failure to regulate immigration from outside among its members, the EU switched to trying to cut off migration streams outside its territory, especially in Africa. First the transit states, then the countries of origin were supposed to stop as many people as possible from entering the Schengen Area – a plan full of hubris.

The EU is upping the bid – while it paid around €2 billion from 2000–2015, it plans to spend another 15 million by 2020. The EU is paying for the costs caused by its own migration management: providing for intercepted refugees, jeeps or ships for the border police, deportations, 'improved' detention centers. As a bonus, it offers extra development aid for the border guards of its 'coalition of the willing.'

This is why some African states, like Tunisia, have made the attempt to emigrate to Europe without valid documents a punishable offense.[10] Others skip the legal process and jail migrants arbitrarily – like Libya. Some build border posts out of the blue, like Sudan. Others introduce biometric passports which their citizens cannot afford, like the Democratic Republic of Congo. The DRC demands $185 for its new high-tech passports, which are produced by a Belgian-Arabic consortium.[11] Some take back deportees from Europe, even if they are citizens of other countries – like Morocco. Some states deploy soldiers to block the migration routes – like Egypt. Some states simply prohibit the transportation of migrants and abolish freedom of movement – like Niger. Others allow European officers to take over – like Senegal. And others yet close the borders not just for transit migrants, but even for their own citizens, if they try to get to Europe irregularly – like Algeria. They are doing exactly what is still – rightfully – considered one of the gravest sins of former Communist bloc states in Central and Eastern Europe.

Increasingly, the money Europe pays for migration control is declared as official development assistance (ODA), more widely known as development aid – a misappropriation of funds intended for poverty and emergency relief. This also violates the principles of development aid, because labor migration is a blessing for poor countries – the money remitted by expatriates is spent directly with small traders and farmers.

This mix-up of development aid and migration control will increase. 'Tackling the root causes of migration' is the new development paradigm, although the African public hears very little of it, since most of the negotiations are held in secret.

Germany is the powerhouse of the EU's new Africa policy. The Federal Government's latest event was a conference in October 2018, which hosted more than a dozen African leaders in Berlin. Egypt's military ruler al-Sisi was also invited. At a press conference, Merkel praised the general: 'Egypt secures its maritime borders so well that there is effectively no migration from Egypt to Europe, although many refugees live in Egypt. This is worthy of great recognition [...]and we are supporting Egypt with an untied loan of €500 million.'

That is exactly how Europe's migration diplomacy works.

In autumn 2016, Merkel traveled to Africa for the first time in a long while. After her trip, a series of African leaders and delegations came to Berlin. The same happened in Brussels. Suddenly the continent had all the attention it would have needed during the 2014 Ebola epidemic. When Chancellor Merkel took over the presidency of the G20 states, one of her program's pillars was 'accepting responsibility – especially for Africa.' The series of Africa conferences in Berlin continued until summer 2017; even German Africa pundits were losing track.

The agenda sounded as if written in a fair-trade shop: 'Africa is not poor – we made it poor.' Statements like these herald Development Minister Müller's 'Marshall Plan with Africa,' which has no lesser goal than stopping 'post-colonial exploitation.'[12] In November 2018, Müller reported to the *Bundestag* about his Marshall Plan – and in all seriousness referred to the notorious Congo Conference: 'The Chancellor – I had the honor of attending – organized the largest Africa conference since 1884 three weeks ago.'[13]

While the government's concern for Africa, including the term 'continent of opportunity,' is not new, the sudden concentration of diplomatic activity signalizes a shift.

This new policy is more disposed to use military means. 'The past two years' events were a wake-up call, which we have understood,'[14] said Defense Minister Ursula von der Leyen (CDU) in March 2017 at a conference in Berlin, which she organized with Development Minister Müller. Her statement was obviously tailored to the migration crisis Europe has witnessed on the Balkan route, claiming that a repetition of such a situation was to be avoided at all cost. If Africa's problems were left unsolved, people would 'start moving when they are threatened,' said von der Leyen. She added that the ministries of development and defense had often seen each other as 'antagonists in the past.' This would have to stop, since Germany's development and defense policies for Africa were now going hand in hand.

Müller referred to Nigeria, soon to be the world's third most populous state, which would be 'in flames' if the Islamist Boko Haram militia advanced further. 'Imagine the dramatic effects on all of us,' said the Minister, 'Africa's future also determines our future.'

The 'war on jihad' really is one of the greatest overlaps between European and African interests. The EU helps, while also exploiting the situation. For example, it sends about €100 million[15] in equipment and training to the G5 Sahel Joint Force (G5S), which brings together military units from Mali, Mauritania, Niger, Burkina Faso and Chad. The G5S is deployed to fight the jihadist groups, which in fact pose a great problem for these states. Hence, they gladly accepted the European support. However, the unit's mandate is not limited to counter-terrorism, but also spans 'human trafficking' – a EU propaganda term for all types of irregular migration.

Whether more troops in the Sahel will pacify the region remains doubtful. The G5S committed grave violations against Mali's civilian population in 2018,[16] causes tension between the involved states[17] and supports policies that strongly disadvantage the Tuareg, which might severely destabilize states like Niger.[18]

Just how Africa's future might look is something Günter Nooke, Personal Representative of the German Chancellor for Africa, has thought about. In October 2018, he suggested that African states should give up parts of their territory for payment, so the EU could settle refugees. 'Maybe some African heads of government would be willing to lease out a piece of their territorial sovereignty and permit free development there for 50 years. These areas could become special economic zones for settling migrants, with the support of the World Bank, the EU or individual states.'[19]

Statements and policies like these are one major strain on Europe and Africa's relationship. African public opinion increasingly finds that the Europeans prefer having the Africans drown in the Mediterranean instead of letting them in. This impression was solidified when CNN published a video of a slave auction in Libya in November 2017. Many Africans changed their social media profile pictures to 'Stop Slavery' images. They saw Europeans as the main culprits, since they are the ones equipping the Libyans to hunt migrants.

This is also one reason the November 2017 summit of the African Union and the European Union ended in a diplomatic scandal, without a final resolution. Olawale Maiyegun, Secretary of the AU, said during the summit that the European migration policy was to keep the Africans out at all costs. The results, he said, could be seen in the Sahara or the Mediterranean, and added that he found it inconceivable that the EU, a professed champion of human rights, was deporting Africans under these conditions.

Europe, on the other hand, is promoting the notion that migration happens only in reaction to an evil. There has to be a 'push factor,' something driving people away. These factors should be identified and addressed by political means, such as development aid. If this succeeded, people would stay at home. This opinion also finds supporters in the EU Commission, the liberal Free Democratic Party (FDP) or the far-right Alternative for Germany (AfD). The political left also tends to interpret these evils as arms exports, unfair trade relations, resource grabbing, colonialism or climate change. They all want to 'tackle the causes of migration' to prevent displacement. This armchair approach reduces migration to armed conflict, poverty, hunger or global warming. However, migration is a fact of human history and as easy to stop as globalization. On a world scale, migration has been a routine social process, whether in Europe, Africa, Asia or the

Americas. People migrate whether the climate changes or not, whether trade is equitable or unfair, whether Germany stops or continues its arms exports. Many parts of the world accept this.

The AU is also promoting this stance. 'We all immigrated from somewhere, and migration will always continue,' says its secretary, Olawale Maiyegun.

Europe will have to deal with it – in a way that prevents suffering and promotes development. There is no other solution to the migration problem.

More than three years of intensive European migration diplomacy in Africa show that few countries are willing to collaborate. Migration is too important for Africa.

In three years of talks, only one state – Ethiopia – signed a readmission agreement with the EU as a whole. In February 2019, the AU proposed a resolution prohibiting its members from setting up the 'regional disembarkation platforms' demanded by the EU on their territory. The EU wants to detain refugees and migrants who are rescued in the Mediterranean at these camps. A draft joint position paper by the AU states: 'The setup of "disembarkation platforms" would be tantamount to de facto "detention centres" where the fundamental rights of African migrants will be violated and the principle of solidarity among AU member states greatly undermined. The collection of biometric data of citizens of AU Members by international organisations violates the sovereignty of African Countries over their citizens.'[20]

Africa has formulated its own vision of the future, particularly the AU's 50-year plan of 2013, the Agenda 2063. Drafts for a common African passport were presented at the AU summit in Addis Ababa in February 2019.[21] Africa's strategy is more integration and more migration – all Africans should be able to work and travel throughout the continent without a visa.

This is exactly where Europe's and Africa's interests part ways – the demand for more border controls is incompatible with the goal of free movement throughout Africa. Europe is ignoring this and once again tries to force its own ideas on Africa.

Berlin/Kigali, March 2019

Notes

1. *Spiegel Online* (2016) 'Eine Situation wie im Sommer 2015 darf sich nicht wiederholen', 6 December | http://bit.ly/2g5soyo

2. World Bank Group, (2016) *Migration and Remittances Factbook 2016, Third Edition*, Washington DC, World Bank

3. Eurostat

4. Bertelsmann Stiftung (2019) 'Deutscher Arbeitsmarkt auf außereuropäische Zuwanderung angewiesen', 12 February | http://bit.ly/2GEk08y

5. Unicef (2017) 'Generation 2030 Africa 2.0.' *Unicef Online Publication*, November 2017 | https://bit.ly/2z9e7gr

6. *Spiegel Online* (2017) 'Müller warnt vor 100 Millionen Flüchtlingen aus Afrika', 18 June | http://bit.ly/2tfNxw4

7. Personal interview on 1 June 2017

8. Election results for Mecklenburg-Vorpommern, final result for District 30, 4 September 2016 | http://bit.ly/2vlIajl

9. *Corriere* (2008) 'Berlusconi da Gheddafi, siglato l'accordo: "Uniti sull'immigrazione,"' 01 September | https://bit.ly/2TuUSDM

10. Badalic, V. (2018) 'Tunisia's Role in the EU External Migration Policy: Crimmigration Law, Illegal Practices, and Their Impact on Human Rights', *Springer*, February 2019 | http://bit.ly/2SwYolH

11. Lewis, D. (2017), 'Special Report: Congo's pricey passports send millions of dollars offshore', *Reuters*, 13 April | http://reut.rs/2VRVpkN

12. *Stern* (2017) 'Entwicklungsminister Müller erwartet "gewaltigen Migrationsdruck Richtung Europa" - CSU-Politiker will "Marshall-Plan" für Afrika', 18 January | http://bit.ly/2URfasx

13. BMZ (2018) 'Rede von Bundesentwicklungsminister Dr. Gerd Müller zum Haushaltsgesetz 2019.' | https://bit.ly/2WipZEn

14. Jakob, C. (2017) 'Die Wiederentdeckung Afrikas', *taz*, 11 June | http://www.taz.de/!5416153/

15. EEAS (2018) 'The European Union's partnership with the G5 Sahel countries', 18 June | http://bit.ly/2TwZcaC

16. Ladurner, U. (2018) 'Killer im Auftrag Europas.' *Die ZEIT*, 14 November | http://bit.ly/2tZz4G5

17. Schnabel, S. (2018) 'Mehr Sicherheit für den Sahel? Warum die Initiative der G5 Sahel Joint Force mehr Zweifel als Hoffnung aufwirft.' Prif Blog, 7 September 2018 | http://bit.ly/2F2rJM8

18. DGAP (2019) 'Angst vorm Aufbruch.' March/April | http://t.co/bey34V9tkk

19. Ruppel, U. (2018) 'Wir haben lange Zeit zu viel im Hilfsmodus gedacht.' *BZ*, 7 October | http://bit.ly/2Nw397m

20. Boffey, D. (2019) 'African Union seeks to kill EU plan to process migrants in Africa', *The Guardian*, 24 February | http://bit.ly/2NWsh9p

21. African Union (2018) New Year's Message of the Chairperson of the African Union Commission, Moussa Faki Mahamat, 31 December | http://bit.ly/2UwzzTP

Closing the borders

Europe's deals with a wanted war criminal

'I'll say it straight: The refugees are no threat to us. These people are heading for Europe,'[1] explains the commander of Sudan's Rapid Support Forces (RSF) in August 2016 at a press conference in Sudan's capital of Khartoum. Here he proudly presents to the journalists more than 800 arrested 'illegal migrants': Eritreans, Ethiopians, and Sudanese; among them women and children. Like livestock, they have been hauled on trucks from prison to the press conference. When the RSF captured them, they were on their way to Europe. '[We are working] on behalf of Europe,' says Major General Mohamed Hamdan Daglo to the cameras.

Daglo is notorious under his nom de guerre Hametti. Sudan's chief border guard is suspected of war crimes and has a bloody past. Hametti's uncle is a tribal chief in war-torn East Darfur. His clan traditionally roamed the desert border regions as camel drivers and traders. Sudan's regime set up his mounted assault troop in 2003 to fight the rebels in East Darfur. Known as 'Janjaweed,' Hametti's militia is accused of cruel war crimes by international human rights groups.[2] UN investigators have presented evidence of torture, rape, and mass executions.[3]

In Sudan, however, Hametti is considered a hero. Just in April 2016, right before the elections, Sudan's president Omar al-Bashir promoted him to major general and handed out bravery medals to his fighters. Hametti had won the decisive victory in Darfur's civil war and smashed the rebel group JEM (Justice and Equality Movement). While Bashir eulogized Hametti from the back of a pick-up truck, bloated corpses were rotting behind him in the desert sand.[4] Amnesty International's 2016 report on Darfur mentioned poison gas attacks by the government against its own people – as in Syria.[5] The International Criminal Court had issued the first arrest warrant against President Bashir back in 2009; the second followed a year later. The charge: genocide in Darfur.[6]

Hametti is also doing Bashir's dirty work in other civil war regions, such as South Kordofan and Blue Nile. In 2013, his units brutalized demonstrators in the capital. He boasts of being known as the guardian of Bashir's power. In 2014, he speaks to the cameras of Australian channel ABC at his headquarters in Darfur.[7] His fighters present heavy weapons. To Sudanese-born ABC reporter Nima Elbagir, Hametti brags that he's been taking direct orders from Bashir ever since their first meeting in 2006. In 2013, the National Intelligence and Security Service (NISS) took over his militia to control the border between Darfur and Chad and cut off the JEM's retreat routes. Hametti hired his clan members to do the job. In return he asked for power, influence, and – most of all – equipment.[8]

The latest constitutional amendment of 2015 allows Sudan's NISS to maintain its own troops. Article 151 expands its tasks from 'collecting and analyzing information and data,' placing the NISS on equal footing with the armed forces.[9] In January 2017, Sudan's parliament passed a law placing the now 30,000 RSF soldiers under direct orders of President Bashir and made the troops part of the army.[10] Hametti is now officially Bashir's personal henchman: When people across Sudan start protesting against rising inflation and bread prices in December 2018 and demand that Bashir step down, he call Hametti's RSF to the capital to secure his regime. Hametti claims he 'did not come to terrorize anyone' but 'will be on the lookout for terrorists and agents.'[11] A few days later, plainclothes snipers start shooting at protesters in Khartoum from rooftops. Amnesty International report 37 protesters killed by the end of 2018.[12] At the same time, it emerges that Hametti's paramilitary mercenaries are also fighting the war in Yemen alongside the Saudi-led coalition. The UN rightfully named the Yemen war the worst humanitarian disaster of 2018. Among the 14,000 RSF fighters stationed in Yemen, 'at least 20 percent' are child soldiers, most from Darfur.[13]

As Bashir's personal guard unit, the RSF are better equipped than the regular army because they fight wherever Bashir's power needs upholding;[14] this includes the war on migrants. The RSF guard the strategically important borders with Libya, Egypt, and Chad[15] as Bashir's fight against illegal migration on behalf of the EU keeps earning him credit on the international scene. Hence, RSF commanders repeatedly face the cameras in Khartoum to declare the arrest of migrants. In January 2017, they once again arrested 1,500 people trying to flee over the border.[16] The wave of arrests went on in 2018. At a press conference in August 2018, RSF General Murtada Osman Abu al-Gasim declared that most of those arrested were Sudanese citizens from Darfur. He guaranteed that the RSF would meet its duty to protect the national borders to ensure security and stability.

To the regime, all refugees from Darfur are public enemies; the RSF have been fighting them since the civil war. The chaos in Sudan's northern neighbor state of Libya has also attracted former rebels from Darfur. The trade in gold from their home region has made them rich. They are now recruiting more Darfurian refugees crossing Libya on their way to Europe and are gearing up along the border against Sudan's government. Hametti's task is to create a buffer zone for catching the refugees before the enemy can recruit them. So he is trying to build a coalition with the Libya Dawn militia, which sits in the National Transitional Council (NTC) in the capital of Tripoli and receives support from Sudan and Qatar.

At the press conference in August 2016 mentioned above, Hametti's spokesman tells international reporters that 25 of his soldiers were killed, 315 were injured and 151 cars were lost while arresting the migrants. 'Fighting against [illegal] migration and human trafficking has inflicted on [our forces] heavy loss of life and destroyed [our] vehicles during chasing operations in the Libyan desert, nevertheless, nobody even thanked us [for sacrifices we made],'[17] Hametti complains. This comment is aimed at the EU, from which he expects more equipment as a sign of gratitude.

Merkel discovers Africa

'Africa's well-being is in our interest,' declares German Chancellor Angela Merkel in October 2016 before stepping on the plane. Her trip takes her to Mali, Niger, Ethiopia – three countries in three days, and the prelude to a new Africa policy.

On 9 October 2016, Merkel first treads Malian ground for a few hours to shake President Ibrahim Boubacar Keïta's hand on the runway of Bamako-Séno International Airport. She cites 'protecting the borders' as one of the goals, alongside security and stability.[18] The next day in neighboring Niger, she visits an immigration center of the International Organisation for Migration (IOM) near the capital of Niamey. The desert state is along the main route for migrants from Western and Central Africa heading for the Mediterranean. For many, their journey to Europe ends in this EU-funded camp. Merkel has a message to Africans and warns them against false hopes: 'Often very young people risk a life-threatening journey without knowing what awaits them, or if they are even allowed to stay,'[19] she says the next day in the Ethiopian capital of Addis Ababa, just after inaugurating the new building of the Peace and Security Council (PSC) of the African Union (AU), which was funded by Germany.

The Chancellor has not been to Africa in five years. Her 2016 visit makes it seem as if Berlin were rediscovering Europe's southern neighboring continent. In the preceding months, Development Minister Gerd Müller (Christian Social Union (CSU)) visited Eritrea, Rwanda, Senegal, Benin and Togo, and invited African partners to Berlin. Federal Defense Minister Ursula von der Leyen (Christian Democratic Union (CDU)) went to Mali in April 2016 to visit German soldiers of the UN peacekeeping mission MINUSMA. Foreign Minister Frank-Walter Steinmeier (Social-Democratic Party (SPD)) also went on several trips to Africa in 2016, including one to Nigeria in October

Just after coming back, Merkel received two African heads of state at the Chancellery. Idriss Déby, the first Chadian president to visit Germany, said: 'I hope the door will be open now and we will be coming to Berlin many more times.'[20] A few days later, Merkel welcomed Muhammadu Buhari, president of Nigeria. Africa's most populous state is among Germany's closest partners on the continent. Nigerian asylum applicants in the EU are second only to Eritreans. Merkel emphasized Germany's willingness to create prospects for young Nigerians in their own country through jobs and training opportunities and more local involvement by German companies. Today, this is seen as tackling the causes of migration. Emigrants, however, would have it harder, warns the Chancellor. The same month, Nigeria enters talks with the EU Commission about a readmission agreement for illegal immigrants from Nigeria.[21]

So much Africa in Berlin is no coincidence. Scarcely ten days after Merkel's trip, the EU member states meet in Brussels. Their main issues: Migration, guarding the EU's external borders and reforming EU asylum laws. New 'Migration Partnerships' between the EU and African states are set up. The European Commission picks five 'priority countries,' Niger, Nigeria, Senegal, Mali and Ethiopia, to 'tackle the root causes of migration.' Four months later, the partnerships have started to yield results, states an EU press release: 'Furthermore, the 24 projects of the EU Emergency Trust Fund for Africa signaled initial success, so that the EU Commission proposed to increase funds to €500 million.'[22]

The Migration Partnerships are just the next step in a wider EU policy towards Africa which hardly anyone understands anymore:

Agenda of Migration, Action Plan on Return, Marshall Plan with Africa, Compacts with Africa, Processes of Valletta, Khartoum, Rabat ... Yet, this bureaucratic labyrinth has one final goal: Stopping migration from Africa.

From the start, Merkel's activism gave the EU's Africa policy a distinctive German note – better yet, her personal note. This urgency is also related to the upcoming federal elections in autumn 2017. Low number of refugees would help the Chancellor get re-elected. Germany's *Willkommenskultur* lasted only about a year.

Most deals between the EU and African states aim to better secure African borders, which were drawn up by European powers in the 19th century. Migrants are not meant to reach the Mediterranean anymore. The EU is hiring Africa's leaders as gatekeepers. Those who make it to Europe anyway still risk immediate deportation – even to authoritarian states like Sudan, Eritrea or Ethiopia.

One diplomatic cable of the German Foreign Office speaks of 'tailored country packages' which should 'not reach the public under any circumstances.' The reason being that 'the EU's reputation is at stake if it gets too involved in this country.'[23] This unidentified country is Sudan.

Ethiopia, Eritrea, Sudan, Somalia, Niger, Chad, Mali, Gambia, Senegal, Ghana, Ivory Coast, Tunisia, Algeria, Morocco or Nigeria – the EU has made 'tailored country packages' for each of these states since 2016. EU negotiations with African partners comprise strategy papers for readmission agreements and increasing the number of deportations. Another cable of the Foreign Office states that easier labor market access for African migrants could not be part of the package, since the German job market is too tense.[24] This turns the Chancellor's statement upside down: Germany's well-being is in Africa's interest.

A few days before the Chancellor jets from Western to Eastern Africa, a few dozen Ethiopians, Sudanese, Malians and Nigerians gather in front of the building of the EU Commission at the Brandenburg Gate to protest Merkel's new Africa offensive. They inflate a rubber dinghy and use bricks to theatrically build a wall. Their banner reads 'EU: No deals with war criminals!' atop the logo of the Society for Threatened Peoples (*Gesellschaft für bedrohte Völker* (GfbV)), which has organized this rally.[25] A poster held up by two Ethiopians of the Oromo minority reads 'Stop the genocide in Ethiopia and Sudan.' Just one day before Merkel's visit, Ethiopia declares a state of emergency and shuts off the Internet. Protests during the traditional Thanksgiving celebrations of the Oromo people were brutally suppressed by police and military forces. Many people were killed. The government counted 52, the opposition claimed more than 500.

'Supporting dictators in Ethiopia does not improve living conditions there, but creates refugees and supports crimes against humanity,' warns Seyoum Habtemariam, director of the Ethiopian Human Rights Committee in Germany, speaking through a megaphone. The bystanders applaud. Some have made masks with the faces of Chancellor Merkel and Sudan's President Bashir. The masked protesters shake hands. 'No pact with war criminals!', the protesters chant.

War criminal extorts the EU

For its new migration policy towards Africa, the EU had to choose Sudan, of all countries, as its main partner. Why? It is the 'main transit country' for migrants heading from the Horn of Africa towards the Mediterranean, as stated in an internal document of the German Foreign Office.[26] President Bashir is the only head of state in the world with an outstanding arrest warrant – the EU, and Germany especially, had pushed for it. Ever since, Sudan has practically been isolated. But none other than Hametti is now a key player the new EU migration policy.

After years of icy silence, jets are now flying frequently between Khartoum, Brussels and Berlin. In early October, just before Merkel's trip to Africa, German members of the *Bundestag* went to meet Sudan's Minister of Interior, Lieutenant Esmat Abdul-Rahman. At the same table with the members of the *Bundestag* Committee on Economic Cooperation and Development sit two agents of the National Intelligence and Security Service (NISS), who follow the talks. The previous day, the Germans had met Bashir's advisor Ibrahim Mahmoud Hamid – this time without NISS agents. This close confidant maintains Bashir's international ties to the West, as the international arrest warrant prevents him from doing this himself.[27]

Hamid is the official Sudanese contact in the Khartoum Process, a dialog platform for the EU to negotiate with states along the route of migrants from the Horn of Africa to Europe. Both Germany and Sudan sit on the Steering Committee. At the same time, the Rabat Process was set up for West Africa. Both deals aim to tackle 'people smuggling and human trafficking,' as stated in the Khartoum Process.[28] They claim to give victims better protection against exploitation and abuse and – most importantly – intend to curb the uncontrolled migrant flows on the continent, which the new EU Foreign and Security Policy considers a threat.[29]

To achieve this, the EU wants to support Africa's border security agencies with training, technical aid and supplies of suitable equipment to implement the migration policy, as stated in the description of the Better Migration Management (BMM) project, which is part of the Khartoum Process. European advisors will go to train their African colleagues so they can stop migration to Europe.[30]

German border guards run similar 'empowerment projects' in other countries, such as Tunisia or Mali. For example, a project description of the German Ministry of Defence for Tunisia lists 'procurement of electronic surveillance systems.'[31] The security forces of border agencies usually report to the police, the army or the secret service. Sudan's Minister of Interior sent a list of all items he would need for capacity building, although it was not considered further. It included equipment, internment cells, fences and combat helicopters for the border police.[32]

Germany and Sudan's historical ties

Sudan was the main recipient of German development cooperation funds in Africa for a long time. In the 1980s, the state of Lower Saxony maintained a partnership with Sudan. To this day, Lower Saxony takes in a higher rate of asylum seekers from Sudan than other German states. Official ties were cut when the current ruler Bashir seized the power in a coup in 1989, but many personal contacts to Khartoum remain, which still influence the German government's perception of Africa's third largest country by area.

The Sudan department of the German Foreign Office treats the country as part of the Arab region due to its language and Islamic religion. Hence, Berlin interpreted internal conflicts as cultural or religious in nature: 'Arabic' or 'Muslim' against 'Christian' or 'Black African.' Bashir's rule fostered this into a genocidal, racist ideology to massacre and displace parts of the population of Darfur and other internal conflict zones. This is one reason South Sudan declared its independence in 2011.

The German government helped to arm the racist police and military dictatorship suppressing the other minorities. Even before Bashir's seizure of power, German development cooperation in Sudan in the 1980s focused on training the security forces. The first batch of Sudanese police officers was trained by the Federal Criminal Police (*Bundeskriminalamt*) in Wiesbaden. Gun manufacturer Heckler & Koch from the southern state of Baden-Württemberg supplied its G3 assault rifle, Daimler-Benz sold military unimogs and the former state-owned corporation Fritz Werner built an ammunitions factory for the Sudanese people.[33]

German armament supplies went on until the EU imposed an arms embargo against Sudan in 1994. German aid has made Sudan Africa's third-largest arms producer, and Sudan's soldiers drive German military trucks to this day. In 2011 and 2012, Germany exported over 3,000 military trucks to the Netherlands and to Belgium, before being shipped on to Sudan. These trucks have been sighted in warzones there.[34] Even today, the standard-issue rifle of the German *Bundeswehr* is killing people in the civil war in Darfur. The investigators who drafted the arrest warrant against Bashir also found evidence of German arms.[35] So Sudan's minorities are fleeing from German weapons.

Ulrich Delius of the GfbV therefore thinks that partnerships with regimes like Sudan's are an 'unsuitable means, because the policies of these states are producing more and more refugees.'[36] His demonstration at the Brandenburg Gate in October 2016 was intended to raise awareness on this issue.

A young refugee from Darfur also spoke at this rally. The 22-year-old Abdulman, who does not want to give his real name for fear of the worldwide network of Sudan's secret service, has been living in Germany for one year. He goes to a vocational school in Lower Saxony and speaks decent German. 'My escape to Europe was very expensive, complicated and dangerous,' he reports.[37] After his mother, father and brothers were killed by Hametti's horseback militia, he first escaped to Khartoum. Here he organized protests against the government and was arrested multiple times. To escape the country, he had to get a passport with a fake name. The reason: 'Our passports also show where we come from – and anyone who tells the authorities that he is from Darfur or has a typical Darfurian name, will not get a passport,' says Abdulman. His travel document with an Arabic pseudonym allowed him to cross the border to Egypt. From Cairo, he took a Turkish Airlines flight to Istanbul, from where he went to Greece by boat. Together with hundreds of thousands of Syrians, Afghans and other nationalities, he marched the Balkan route to Germany by foot in 2015. His journey cost more than €2,500. He borrowed the money from an uncle and came to Europe heavily indebted. 'It would have been much cheaper to take a plane from Khartoum to Frankfurt, but how could I get a visa from the German embassy with a fake passport?' he asks.

Today, more and more people like Abdulman from Darfur are fleeing Bashir's dictatorship to Europe. More than 11,000 people arrived in 2015. But only half received protection in an EU member state. The others are under threat of deportation. However, the return rate for Sudan is 'particularly low,' as stated in an EU strategy paper for the planned readmission agreement of March 2016.[38] The rate for Sudan is only about 12 percent; for other countries it is about 40 percent. As to the reason, the paper states 'a complete lack of cooperation on readmission from the Sudanese side.' To improve Sudan's willingness, the EU paper goes on to promise 'capacity-building measures' and makes an offer the rogue regime cannot resist: readmission as a 'partner' to the international community.[39] The EU also considers forgiving all of Sudan's debts to EU states and wants to speak to the USA about striking Sudan from the list of state sponsors of terrorism and to the World Trade Organization (WTO) about starting new negotiations. The EU is clearly reaching out to the dictator.

The EU's total financial involvement is huge. Under the Khartoum Process, it provided €40 million for the BMM project at the Horn of Africa. Sudan is one of eight partner governments in this process. Germany is chipping in another €6 million. From the total sum of the Africa-EU Migration and Mobility Dialogue (MMD), €17.5 million are allocated to Sudan. On top of that, the German government guaranteed €35 million in refugee aid as a one-off measure. The largest EU package comprises €100 million over two years from the Emergency Trust Fund (EUTF) to meet the challenges of climate change, poverty or neglect. This fund had been set up in 2015 prior to the migration summit in the Maltese capital of Valletta for the African partners to fight the causes of migration.[40]

Italy, which is most affected by migrants and refugees, wants the EU talks to move faster. The Italian police signed a bilateral agreement with Sudan in August 2016. Most notably, it governs the cooperation of security forces in border controls, fighting drug trafficking, terrorism and migration and better collaboration in repatriation procedures.[41] Three weeks later, a plane takes off from Turin Airport to Khartoum with 48 deported Sudanese citizens on board.[42] A few days later, General Hametti faces the cameras and demands the promised equipment. Italy reacts flexibly: The IOM gets a contract from the Italian development agency to give border management training to Sudanese police forces.[43]

So the German government starts approaching Khartoum as well. Just one week after Merkel's return from Africa in autumn 2016, a Sudanese police delegation visits Berlin. The chief of Sudan's immigration agency, Lieutenant General Awad Dahiya, wants to introduce biometric passports and ID cards to better meet the EU's demand to control migration, so he visits the government printing office in Berlin. Then he shakes hands at the headquarters of the Federal Police. The press office declares that it is just a 'meet and greet,' emphasizing that 'no agreements were made between the

Sudanese police and the Federal Police during this visit.'[44] Sudan's Ministry of Interior states that the talks in Berlin were about technical and logistical equipment and training measures, and that the head of the German Federal Police gladly accepted the invitation to visit Khartoum.[45]

Just after getting the €100million offer, Sudan's Minister of Foreign Affairs, Ibrahim Ghandour, visited Berlin and Brussels. There he told the public broadcaster ARD: 'We have been asking for devices like GPS and other border protection equipment for a long time.' He cited talks with Germany and the EU and said he expected a mutual understanding. Asked whether Sudan was ready to take back refugees, he replied: 'The migration commissioner in Brussels told me "We have 12,000 illegal migrants from Sudan in the EU. Are you ready to take them back?" I told him: "Immediately. Stand by your promise, and they are more than welcome."'[46]

'It's a disgrace'

'The EU should carefully consider its reputational risks in its engagement with Sudan,' states an EU strategic paper on Sudan, which is why the EU channels any direct involvement through NGOs.[47] However, Germany's official agency for international cooperation, GIZ, also directly handles projects on the ground. 'After the discussion with the EU, we set down very clear human rights principles,' says Martin Weiß, who is the GIZ manager in charge of the project, mentioning that they were included in the introduction to the project. The text reads: 'Activities will be conducted in full respect of the human rights of migrants [...].'[48]

Weiß thinks training measures for Sudan's border guards could be an option, because 'refugees are criminalized there.' The training would not take place in Sudan, however, but in Ethiopia and would be open to Sudanese participants. EU trainers would teach humane treatment of migrants – to normal police pursuing human-rights compliant investigations, as the GIZ emphasizes. The RSF would be explicitly excluded from attending. Weiß underlines: 'We will not work with people who are on sanctions lists due to crimes against humanity,' and 'we will not supply any equipment that is listed on applicable sanctions lists.' The only exception: Office supplies (up to and including laptops).

Weiß traveled to Africa often in 2016. Talks had to be started with new governments that were to join the Khartoum Process, and with partners like the IOM or the United Nations Office on Drugs and Crime (UNODC). Offices were rented and staffed in Kenya,

Ethiopia and Sudan. A meeting with all project partners took place in October 2016, including Italian, French and British nationals, Weiß reports. Five to ten measures per country were planned. For Ethiopia, the GIZ developed 'training for judges and public prosecutors on how to prosecute human trafficking, with a focus on human rights-compliant treatment of the victims.' In Sudan, 'safe houses' for victims of human traffickers to seek shelter and counseling were planned. 'Prisons in Sudan are full of migrants. Our task is to promote awareness for their situation.' As refugees and migrants are sentenced for not having papers, the GIZ stresses, the agency intends to train border guards and police officers – but only those who report to the Ministry of Interior, not the military.

'It's a shame for the GIZ to make a deal like this,' criticizes the former UN special investigator for Sudan, Jérôme Tubiana, who now is a researcher for an NGO called Small Arms Survey and frequently visits the Sudanese border. 'It's often not clear who is who – even if they are wearing a uniform,' says Tubiana, and warns against working with the local security agencies, especially with Hametti: 'He is clearly a war criminal.'

BMM is not the only European training project for Sudanese border guards. The EU is also funding the setting up of the ROCK operational center at the police academy of Khartoum. It is intended for East African states to gather and exchange information about smuggling networks and migration routes[49]. In response to a parliamentary inquiry, the German government stated that the Federal Police had given introductory courses on ID document verification to Sudanese border police officers responsible for ID controls at airports in January and February 2016. The courses took place at the training academy of the Sudanese police in Khartoum.[50]

Eritrea: One of the world's top refugee makers

News about the training assistance from the EU have spread throughout Africa. Eritrean refugees who fled their country over the Sudanese border in summer 2016 told the Eritrean Initiative on Refugee Rights (EIRR) that they had seen heavily armed special units patrolling in German military trucks. 'They say Sudan's units were equipped by Germans, that's why they no longer dare to cross the border,' said EIRR director and journalist Meron Estefanos.[51] The Eritrean exile in Sweden assumes that these rumors spread after the cooperation between Sudan's border units with Germany became public. But rumors alone are enough, she says, to cause Eritreans to prefer fleeing to Ethiopia over Sudan. Since Sudan's border units have started targeting refugees for arrests, no one feels safe anymore.[52]

Yahia al-Adi Suleiman, police commander of the Sudanese province of Kassala, which borders on Eritrea, confirmed in a January 2018 interview that his units were working with other forces, such as the military and secret service, to guard the borders. He also has a request to the EU: 'I've always said, as long as European countries are the destination and suffer from this illegal migration, they will have to pay by sending transportation, modern surveillance gear, modern vehicles, even airplanes to guard the long borders to Ethiopia and Eritrea.' So far, he says, all he got from the EU were a couple of motorcycles.

Sudan's neighbor Eritrea, with its 5.4 million inhabitants, is among the smallest and also the poorest of African countries – and one of the world's largest producers of refugees. The World Bank estimates that more Eritreans are living outside than inside their own country. The cause is President Isayas Afewerki's regime, which has been in power since independence from Ethiopia in 1991; his rule has become increasingly autocratic. In 2005 he treated the opposition with particular brutality, so the EU cut his development aid by 70 percent, costing his government almost €190 million per year. Germany officially froze its cooperation in 2007. The UN Security Council passed some measures in 2009, which included an arms embargo. Members of the regime were struck with travel bans. In 2011, the UN accused Afewerki of using tax money to fund the Islamist al-Shabaab militia in Somalia, which is close to the international terrorist network al-Qaeda. In 2015, UN investigators appealed to all countries to stop forcing Eritrean asylum seekers to return, since the regime punished anyone trying to leave the country without permission.[53]

Asmara's dictatorship, however, is profiting from its huge diaspora. Eritreans must pay two percent of any income earned abroad to their home country – the so-called Recovery and Rehabilitation Tax (RRT). No matter if they live on welfare or have a job, even if they take on a different nationality. Until 2011, Eritreans in Germany had to pay this tax every month at the embassy in Berlin or at the consulate in Frankfurt. The German government banned this practice in 2011. Now Afewerki's officials are collecting this tax from relatives who stayed in Eritrea. The government does not publish its budget, but it's assumed to be funded mostly by remittances from Eritrean refugees all over the world.[54]

Afewerki's rule rests on a massive security and secret service apparatus with activities worldwide. 'Information gathered through the pervasive control system is used in absolute arbitrariness to keep the population in a state of permanent anxiety,' states the latest UN report on human rights. 'It is not law that rules Eritreans, but fear,' concluded the investigators led by Australian expert Mike Smith.[55]

The Eritrean government had refused to work with the UN investigators and banned them from entering, because they accused the army of crimes against humanity, systematic sexual abuse of women and exploitation of their own population as forced laborers.[56] Eritrean human rights organization EIRR also sees the regime's crimes as the main reason why the citizens are fleeing in masses.[57]

With good cause, one of the worst dictatorships on earth has not been receiving aid money for a while. This will change now; while Eritrea is the 43rd largest country by population in Africa, it is Africa's number one source of asylum applicants in Europe. Some 5,000 people flee the country every month. Most seek a new home in Africa – Ethiopia, Kenya, Uganda, Sudan or even in civil war-torn South Sudan. In 2016, only 20,000 came to Germany.[58] The large Eritrean exile community in Frankfurt started in the 1980s; there even is an Orthodox church. It attracts many refugees who already have family in Germany. German Development Minister Müller visited Eritrea's capital Asmara in December 2015 – as the first German minister in 20 years – to meet President Afewerki: 'We want to support Eritrea in stopping the exodus of the youth,' he said, 'by improving the living situation here and also opening opportunities for returnees.' Müller was said to be considering aid in areas such as vocational training and energy supply under the condition that Eritrea's government start economic and political reforms and improve the human rights situation.[59]

Müller's visit to Asmara ushered in the end of the regime's isolation. Just a few weeks later, an Eritrean government delegation flew to Berlin and Brussels. On 28 January 2016, Eritrea and the EU signed a deal that promised €200 million from the 11th European Development Fund (EF) through 2020. This fund was set up in June 2013 with a budget of €30 billion to finance development projects in Africa through 2020. Another €13 million were promised to Eritrea for supplying energy to small businesses – to create jobs and get people to stay.[60]

The main reason young people are fleeing is the 'national service.' All men and women are drafted into this military service after leaving school. The constitution limits it to two years, but this can easily become half a lifetime. Recruits work as soldiers along the long border to neighboring Ethiopia, on road construction projects, in quarries or on mega projects like the hydroelectric dams being built right now. They perform heavy physical labor for less than $30 a month – outright slavery.[61]

In a strategy paper from March 2016 on the planned readmission agreement with Eritrea, the EU names reform of the forced national service as a 'key interest,' because it drives young people out of the country. This reform is a condition for Eritrea to receive the €200 million from the EDF.[62] One month later, the German government responds to a parliamentary inquiry: 'The Eritrean government seems to make efforts to limit the duration of the national service to the official limit of 18 months, but cannot offer alternative employment opportunities to the young people afterwards. Jobs and employment opportunities are therefore a key prerequisite for the government to reduce the service time throughout the country. By providing support in the areas of vocational training and employment promotion, Germany can provide an important contribution.'[63]

Berlin and Brussels are apparently ready to trust in the regime's promises and hope for a positive turn. Christian Manahl, head of the EU delegation to Asmara, says that the EU asked no preliminary demands from Afewerki's regime, but hoped that the cooperation would 'improve governance.' As an example, Manahl names the national service, where he says the EU was exerting 'pressure' to have the reform 'realized.'[64]

Apparently, the German authorities are hoping that more freedom in Eritrea will cost its citizens their right to asylum. Germany's Federal Office for Migration and Refugees (BAMF) and the Swiss State Secretariat for Migration sent a joint delegation to Asmara in the first half of 2016. The officials sought to find out how dangerous Eritrea really is. Their closing report states: '[Guards] do not systematically shoot at illegal emigrants at the border, but shots may occur.'[65]

'The government is doing the utmost that it can do, under the circumstances,' Information Minister Yemane Ghebremeskel told Reuters on 25 February 2016, saying 'salaries would rise but there were no plans to scrap or cut national service.' He added: 'Demobilization is predicated on removal of the main threat [from Ethiopia].'[66] The Eritrean exile organization ERRI speaks of a double game. 'Afewerki made this promise to the EU, not to us Eritreans. He is just fooling the West,' says EIRR director Estefanos.

Afewerki got what he wanted: after more than a decade of isolation, Eritrea will join the Khartoum Process, the mentioned EU dialog round with the Horn of Africa countries. The EU strategy paper mentions the country's 'constructive role.'[67] In 2019, Eritrea will even take over the chair of the Khartoum Process.

Some of the funds for the BMM project will also go to Asmara. Manahl assures that these funds will not be transferred to Eritrean accounts, but rather spent locally by European and international

NGOs. 'We can't change the problem by looking away, that's why we have to cooperate,' says the Austrian. While many EU states still had 'concerns' about a possible cooperation with Eritrean security forces, 'this is not excluded' for the future, says Manahl.

Launched in July 2017, the GIZ's BMM project focuses on three measures: First, it supports the Eritrean government's ratification of the Palermo Protocol. Eritrea's challenge is to find 'human rights-compliant' ways to combat human trafficking, says the GIZ. Second, the GIZ is preparing courses for Eritrean judiciary officials. The GIZ claims these courses are explicitly closed to members of the police, border guard, military or secret police and merely intended to train judges on 'how to handle these offenses in court.' After all, there had been no proper legal basis against human trafficking, which is why the judiciary lacked knowledge and legal means.

The Eritrean government has formed a committee drawn from the Ministry of Foreign Affairs and the Ministry of Information as well as civil society organizations. It is tasked with coordinating questions surrounding migration; the GIZ claims to be working with this committee for its BMM project.

But what if refugees voluntarily seek help to cross borders? 'We do not prevent people from escaping,' the GIZ states curtly. Asked how it intends to respond to the government's alleged involvement in human trafficking, the GIZ replies that its 'mission' was to get partner states to 'prosecute criminal elements and human traffickers,' but that it was 'not tasked with investigating' whether 'criminal government agencies could be involved.'

Finally, the GIZ works on a third measure with the Ministry of Information, called the 'information and consulting component.' Its purpose is 'education about possible threats from human trafficking and trade in human beings.' The GIZ states that it would not 'develop any determent campaigns.' Instead, it aimed to help people who are planning to migrate to find 'viable alternatives' in Eritrea. What about those who do not consider life-long military service an acceptable outlook? 'We are talking about these issues and have made it our goal to sensitize the government to the issue of human rights,' responds the GIZ.[68]

On 24 May 2016, Eritrea celebrated the 25th anniversary of its independence from Ethiopia with pomp and parades. A few European journalists were allowed to enter and take photos. The UN world heritage agency UNESCO just declared Asmara a world cultural heritage. The parades celebrated President Afewerki as a liberator. Thousands of conscripted soldiers, both male and female, marched in line, followed by school children. Many of them probably toyed with the thought of fleeing, maybe even to Europe. Afewerki's omnipotence is unchallenged. Being courted once again by Europeans certainly helped the dictator, as well as the expected funds from Brussels that are meant to keep Eritreans at home.

The opposite happened: In 2018 more Eritreans fled their country than in any of the preceding years. The EU agency ECHO counted 27,500 Eritrean asylum applicants in Ethiopia from the opening of the borders to the end of December.[69] 'I just sometimes wonder who is left inside the country,' Naser Haghamed, head of one of the largest international NGOs, Islamic Relief Worldwide (IRW), is quoted saying in December 2018.[70]

The backdrop is the fast and undeniable political rapprochement between Eritrea and its former arch-enemy Ethiopia. On 9 July, Ethiopian Prime Minister Abiy Ahmed signed a joint declaration with President Afewerki which stated that the 'state of war' was over.

It was almost like the fall of the Berlin Wall in 1989, when in September 2018, after more than two decades of conflict, Africa's best secured border was suddenly opened. From one day to the next, free movement replaced fire trenches and deadly border patrols. Hundreds of Eritreans flowed across the border with fully loaded cars and donkey carts. Ethiopian Airlines resumed daily connections to Asmara after 18 years. An advertisement called the maiden flight in July 2018 a 'bird of peace.' Flights were booked out at once.

The EU continues to hope that the regime will limit the national service, since the Ethiopian threat is over now. But most Eritreans in exile have little faith in the internal political developments. 'The only thing that's changed so far is that even more Eritreans are fleeing now,' says the director of the Eritrean refugee organization Africa Monitors in December 2018. Just after opening the border, he says, Afewerki had ordered the reserve units back to the barracks – old people and invalids, who had returned home after half a lifetime of slave labor. They were to undergo renewed training. The government says that people would now have to work even harder to make up for underdevelopment. 'If he [Afewerki] again promised the EU to reduce the service, that's a flat-out lie,' says Africa Monitors.

Surveys by this international organization have found that only a small number of Eritreans have stayed in Ethiopia. The camps are overcrowded; asylum applications were suspended until November for Ethiopia to decide whether to accept the refugees. Still most fear that they will be deported. Hence most Eritreans sought protection in neighboring Kenya and Uganda. 'More and more Eritreans are arriving every day,' reports Africa Monitors from Kampala.

The EU also fears swelling numbers of Eritrean refugees. When in 2018 Ethiopian Airlines announced plans for stopover flights from Addis Ababa via Asmara straight to the EU – to London, Oslo, Rome and Milan – a confrontation between the EU and Addis ensued in the background. A few weeks later, the airline corrected its announcement.

Notes

1. *Sudan Tribune* (2016) 'Sudan says it is combating illegal migration "on behalf of Europe"', 30 August

2. *Human Rights Watch* (2015) Men with no Mercy – Rapid Support Forces attacks against civilians in Darfur', September 2015 | http://bit.ly/2vfkZpW

3. *Report of the International Commission of Inquiry on Darfur to the United Nations Secretary-General* (2005) Geneva, 25 January | http://bit.ly/1V9W2nr

4. *Sudan Tribune* (2015) 'Hametti and his president: war as a livelihood', 9 May | http://bit.ly/2ucinVw

5. *Amnesty International* (2016) El Gizouli, Magdi: 'Scorched Earth, Poisoned Earth, Sudanese Government Forces Ravage Rebel Marra, Darfur.' September 2016 | http://bit.ly/2vfH9Z4. Later investigations by other NGOs and secret services indicate that other, non-chemical weapons were used, which nevertheless cause comparable injuries.[footnote]see Loeb, Jonathan: 'Did Sudan use chemical weapons in Darfur last year?' *Bulletin of the Atomic Scientists*, 17 January 2017 | http://bit.ly/2vlvxoe

6. Both warrants published on the ICC website | http://bit.ly/2vfKkA5

7. Elbagir, Nima (2008) 'Meet the Janjaweed', *ABC News*, 3 June | http://ab.co/2tX2JSC

8. *Enough Report* (2014) 'Janjaweed Reincarnate – Sudan's New Army of War Criminals', June 2014 | http://bit.ly/2tWKwVz

9. *Dabanga* (2015) 'Constitutional amendments demise of Sudan's Bill of Rights: Opposition', 8 January

10. *Sudan Tribune* (2017) 'Sudanese parliament passes RSF Act integrating militiamen in the army', 17 January

11. *Sudan Tribune* (2018) 'Sudan's militia leader urges government to provide services', 25 December | http://bit.ly/2TbvXoW

12. *Associated Press* (2018) 'Sudanese police clash with anti-government protesters', 31 December | http://bit.ly/2R7ioKP

13. *New York Times* (2018) 'On the Front Line of the Saudi War in Yemen:

Child Soldiers from Darfur', *New York Times*, 28 December |
http://nyti.ms/2VfJcqF

14. *Sudan Tribune* (2018) '28 illegal migrants arrested on Sudan-Libya
    border: RSF', 19 August | http://bit.ly/2PO8tVY

15. *Sudan Vision* (2016) 'Rapid Support Forces Working to End Human
    Trafficking', 13 November

16. *Sudan Tribune* (2017) 'Sudan's RSF militia arrests 1500 illegal migrants
    near Libyan border', 8 January

17. *Sudan Tribune* (2016) 'Sudan says it is combating illegal migration "on
    behalf of Europe"', 30 August

18. *ZIB 8:00* (2016) 'Afrikareise der deutschen Bundeskanzlerin', 10
    October

19. *Tagesschau um 17:00 Uhr* (2016) 'Falsche Vorstellungen von Europa –
    Merkels Appell an Afrika', 11 October | http://bit.ly/2uQw6U8

20. Transcript of press conference of Chancellor Merkel and Idriss Déby,
    President of the Republic of Chad, in Berlin | http://bit.ly/2tREvVO

21. Press meeting of Chancellor Merkel with Nigerian President
    Muhammadu Buhari, Berlin 14 October 2016 | http://bit.ly/2ucumlR

22. 'EU zieht erste Bilanz der Migrationspartnerschaften mit Afrika',
    Press release of the EU Commission's Permanent Representation in Germany,
    Berlin, 18 October 2016 | http://bit.ly/2vbhGAj

23. Communication no. 1273 from Brussels to the German Foreign Office.
    23 March 2016; (authors' archive)

24. Internal cable of the German Foreign Office in Berlin, 2 March 2016,
    (authors' archive)

25. This quote and the following ones are cited from interviews with
    protesters. Berlin, 5 October 2016

26. 'Sachstand Sudan', Internal paper of the German Foreign Office. June
    2016

27. Background conversation between the authors and members of the
    Committee, Berlin, 12 October 2016

28. *Europäischer Treuhandfonds für Stabilität und Bekämpfung der
    Fluchtursachen in Afrika, Aktionspapier für die Umsetzung des Horn-von-
    Afrika-Fensters: T05 – EUTF – HoA – REG – 09*, (authors' archive)

29. *Shared Vision, Common Action: A Stronger Europe – A Global Strategy for
    the European Union's Foreign And Security Policy*, June 2016 | http://bit.ly/
    2uNC1e2

30. *Europäischer Treuhandfonds für Stabilität und Bekämpfung der
    Fluchtursachen in Afrika, Aktionspapier für die Umsetzung des Horn-von-
    Afrika-Fensters: T05 – EUTF – HoA – REG – 09*, (authors' archive)

31. *Projektliste Ertüchtigung des BMVg und AA* (2016) Berlin, 13 May, (authors' archive)

32. *Europäischer Treuhandfonds für Stabilität und Bekämpfung der Fluchtursachen in Afrika, Aktionspapier für die Umsetzung des Horn-von-Afrika-Fensters: T05 – EUTF – HoA – REG – 09*, (authors' archive)

33. Deckert, Roman (2008 'Deutsches Kriegsgerät im Sudan', 1 July |http://bit.ly/2uO0tfy

34. *Dabanga* (2015) 'Germany restricts Dutch export after providing army trucks to Sudan', 15 June | http://bit.ly/2tRFuoY

35. Deckert, Roman (2007) 'Internationaler Strafgerichtshof: Haftbefehl wegen G3-Lieferungen an Janjaweed', *Kleinwaffen-Newsletter des BITS*, June 2007

36. Interview with Ulrich Delius, Berlin, 5 October 2016

37. Interview with Abdulman, Berlin, 5 October 2016

38. *EU Strategy Paper Sudan* (2016) 17 March | http://bit.ly/2wqWgzq

39. *Ibid.*

40. EU Commission *The EU Emergency Trust Fund for Africa.*| http://bit.ly/1MWApno

41. *Rom* (2016) 'Polizeiabkommen Italien und Sudan', 3 August | http://bit.ly/wbIEIF

42. *No-Racism.net* (2016) 'Italy: Deportations to Sudan!', 27 August 2016 |http://bit.ly/2vfC8Q7

43. 'IOM Trains 19 Police Officers on Passport Examination in Khartoum', *IOM press release*, Khartoum, 17 November 2016 | http://bit.ly/2vfp3GO

44. Inquiry and response by e-mail to press office of German Federal Police, 21 October 2016

45. *Sudan Tribune* (2016) 'Sudan, Germany agrees to promote cooperation to combat illegal migration', 16 October

46. Interview quoted according to: 'Report Mainz: Flüchtlingsdeal mit Despoten: Die EU will afrikanische Regime mit Sicherheitstechnik ausrüsten', 17 May 2016 | http://bit.ly/2tROkmK

47. *EU strategy paper on Sudan*, Brussels, 17 March 2016 | http://bit.ly/2wqWgzq

48. Introduction in: 'Annex I to the Delegation Agreement CRIS No. [EUTF05 – HoA – REG – 20] – Description of the Action, Better Migration Management', October 2016 | http://bit.ly/2AI6EUR

49. Regional Operational Centre in support of the Khartoum Process and AU-Horn of Africa Initiative (ROCK); Action Fiche for the implementation of the Horn of Africa Window | http://bit.ly/2tWuyuy

50. *Deutscher Bundestag 18/12275* (2017) Berlin, 4 May | http://bit.ly/2fI09aH

51. Phone interview with Meron Estefanos, 30 September 2016

52. *IRIN* (2016) 'Sudan and Eritrea crackdown on migrants amid reports of EU incentives', 25 May | http://bit.ly/1VioQce

53. *Human Rights Council* (2015) 'Report of the commission of inquiry on human rights in Eritrea', 4 June

54. Freidel, Morten (2016) 'Von wegen Freiheit', *FAZ*, 12 May | http://bit.ly/2ucycM4

55. *Human Rights Council* (2016) 'Detailed findings of the commission of inquiry on human rights in Eritrea', 8 June | http://bit.ly/1MhB1i3

56. 'UN Inquiry finds crimes against humanity in Eritrea', *UN press release*, Geneva, 8 June 2016 | http://bit.ly/2tX3iMe

57. Phone interview with Meron Estefanos, director of ERRI, 30 September 2016

58. Schlindwein, Simone 'Länderinfo Eritrea: Mit EU-Hilfe in die Weltgemeinschaft', *tageszeitung* | http://bit.ly/2vaLLfs

59. 'Reise nach Eritrea', *Press release of the German Ministry for Economic Cooperation and Development*, Berlin, 17 December 2015 | http://bit.ly/2ucdL1N

60. Dept. of International Cooperation and Development: *Country overview for Eritrea by EU Commission* | http://bit.ly/2uQSdtu

61. Hellge, Anna; Jakob, Christian; Schlindwein, Simone (2017) 'Ein Fall für das Fluchtursachenbekämpfungsministerium', *tageszeitung*, 28 January | http://bit.ly/2vlJ1K6

62. *EU strategy paper on Eritrea* (2016) Brussels, 17 March | http://bit.ly/2wqWgzq

63. *Bundestags-Drucksache 18/8216* (2016) Berlin, 25 April | http://bit.ly/2RnOPon

64. Phone interview with EU delegation leader in Eritrea Christian Manahl, 3 October 2016

65. *Focus Eritrea – Update Nationaldienst und illegale Ausreise* (2016) Report of the *Swiss State Secretariat for Migration (SEM)*, Bern-Wabern, 22 June

66. *Reuters* (2016) 'Eritrea won't shorten national service despite migration fears.' 25 February | http://reut.rs/2IY2CNj

67. *EU strategy paper on Eritrea* (2016) Brussels, 17 March | http://bit.ly/2wqWgzq

68. Interview with Africa Monitors, Kampala, 23 November 2018

69. *The Independent* (2018) '27.000 Eritreans "seeking refugee status" in Ethiopia', 23 December

70. *InfoMigrants* (2018) 'Eritrea: "I just sometimes wonder who is left inside the country"', 26 December | http://bit.ly/2LNWGFP

A brief history of Europe's gatekeepers

Speaking of a 'flow' or 'influx' of migrants is considered inappropriate, as it sounds like a broken dam, a looming disaster. But there is no better image than a river to describe what happens if you try to stop migration: If you block the route, there will be a jam. People will seek the path of least resistance around the blockage. And just like water flowing downhill, they will find it. Here they will try to keep moving. If you block their way again, the whole story repeats. That is the history of European migration control. The movements of people are blocked for a while, only for them to find new paths. The attempts at containment follow them. The high-profile deal between the EU and Turkey was just one step in this containment policy.

It started in Ceuta and Melilla, the two Spanish enclaves in Morocco, where Europe's direct border with Africa extends over 12 miles. It is the shortest path from one continent to the other. For a long time, anyone was free to cross this border, there was nothing but a boundary marker. Moroccans and other Africans crossed the border to work and were able to board ships to Andalusia – until June 1991. That was when Spain joined the Schengen Agreement. Upon taking effect in March 1995, the agreement was to make Spain part of a new borderless community – the EU. It also required Spain to protect the new external borders of the Schengen Area. At the time, 'The March' by British author William Nicholson ran on television. In this movie, a 'desperate army of miserable people'[1] (as described by *Der Spiegel*) boards boats from Tangier to Spain. Just past Algeciras, they are stopped by a 'European Army.' The movie was fictional, but the pressure on Spain's military was real: some

European partners doubted its ability to protect the EU's external border.

On 15 May 1991, Spain's social-democratic president, Felipe González, decided that Moroccans would now need a visa for Spain. He ordered the chief commissioner of Algeciras, José Cabrera, to let 'absolutely nobody' pass the Strait of Gibraltar. Lieutenant Colonel Mariano Ortiz of the Guardia Civil in Algeciras expressed awareness for Spain's responsibility for Europe, but also said 'we can't rebuild the Berlin Wall here at the beach.'[2]

Nonetheless, the old migration route from the Maghreb to Andalusia was cut off. North Africa's freedom of movement was traded in for Europe's. To keep the doors open for a few of his subjects, Morocco's King Hassan II had to sign the first in a series of readmission agreements. Morocco now had to take back all rejected migrants, because it would be too much trouble for Spain to deport them back to their original countries. Morocco was also required to guard Spain's border fortifications against migrants. Over time, Madrid and Brussels started paying up for this service. Between 2007 and 2010 alone, Rabat received €654 million in 'neighborhood assistance.'[3]

The Integrated System of External Vigilance (*Sistema Integrado de Vigilancia Exterior* (SIVE)) was created – a blueprint for the satellite-assisted EU border monitoring network EUROSUR. Cameras, radar systems, helicopters and headquarters in Madrid now watch the Spanish coast around the clock. When construction began, SIVE was estimated to cost €260 million for the period from 2000 to 2008.[4]

Moreover, Spain built the first fence around the enclave of Melilla; the EU paid three quarters of the costs. At first the fence was easy to scale. The government has upgraded it five times now. People like Sambo Sadiako from Senegal left their lives here. On the morning of 6 March 2009, the Spanish border police Guardia Civil found his bled-out body hanging in the razor wire. At first, the Spanish government claimed that 'adverse weather conditions' had caused Sadiako to fall to his death during the night. But this was false. The pathologists found his death to be caused by 'massive loss of blood due to severed arteries.'[5] Sadiako was only 30 years old.

Merely 'psychological and visual effect'

The fence was built using razor wire type Concertina 22,[6] which is intended for protecting nuclear power plants, ammunitions depots and airports. This wire has sharp blades at intervals of 38 mm (1.5

in) – 22 mm (1.2 in) long, 15 mm (0.6 in) high. This is enough to sever tendons, nerves and blood vessels. Antonia Mora heads the company that makes this razor wire, European Security Fencing (ESF), part of the Mora Salazar metalwork group. He stated that the wire had a 'psychological and visual effect.' While there could be 'cuts and scratches' when 300 people at once climb the fence one over another,' the 'purpose of the fence is not to injure anyone, but to deter.'[7]

Sadiako is not the only case; a four-digit number of people have suffered severe injuries. Now six meters high, the double fence is a trap for humans. Those who are not deterred get caught in the razor wire. Those who fall or jump down the other side are greeted by criss-crossing wires which are nearly impossible to escape.[8] A steel wall and an underwater fence to catch swimming intruders are also being planned.

Due to the many severe injuries and deaths, the razor wire was taken off for a while. But in October 2013, the Spanish government decided to install ESF razor wire once more. 'This fence is not just Melilla's fence. It's the fence for all of Europe,'[9] stated the president of Melilla, Juan José Imbroda. Construction for the first section was completed in November 2013; further ones are to follow.

This build-up is controversial in Spain. The country's largest daily paper, El País, posted a video showing a heavily bandaged Cameroonian man lying in a hospital after trying to climb the fence. 'The doctors needed twelve hours to stitch my wounds,'[10] he explains, adding that he feels ashamed to show his skin with all the scars.

The socialist delegate Antonia Trevín brought a piece of the wire to a parliamentary session in December 2013. He wore a leather glove to show the piece and proposed to instead use drones against undocumented migrants. 'Our problem is not finding them,' replied Interior Minister Fernández Díaz. 'The problem is how to stop them.'[11] Prime Minister Mariano Rajoy then decided to keep the razor wire.

EU Home Affairs Commissioner Cecilia Malmström also demanded an explanation. Díaz traveled to Brussels, explained that the fence was a 'passive element of dissuasion' covered by the law, and invited the Commissioner to come and see for herself.[12] Malmström was satisfied with the explanation.

In the end, it might be the Guardia Civil who prevents further deaths: on 16 November 2013, the police and border guard union stated that the officers were 'fed up with seeing people dying' while trying to cross the border. 'We don't want to find more [Africans] bleeding and entangled in the razor wire,' read the statement, as the confrontation with these preventable deaths exposed the border guards to 'unnecessary stress.'[13]

Dead bodies on the beach

The second-shortest path from Africa to Europe is by boat via the Moroccan-occupied West Sahara territory to the Canary Islands. The 240 km (150 mi) sea route takes around 12 hours – if the vessel is seaworthy. The harder the Ceuta/Melilla route became, the more people took this route. Not all of them made it. Since 2000, more and more dead bodies have washed ashore of the volcanic islands – drowned Africans along European holiday beaches. Today it is normal; back then it was not. Spanish newspapers printed photos of the bodies. Eventually, Spain got Morocco to block the beaches in West Sahara. So the migrants moved south and started from Nouadhibou in Mauritania. Now their sea route stretched to 900 km (560 mi) – and became more dangerous – but the package tourists would no longer have to look at capsized migrants.

People like Cheikh Ould Baya joined the game. The mayor of the northern Mauritanian town of Zouérat used to be a border guard commander. Now he is advisor to the Fisheries Minister, who is also responsible for his country's maritime borders. 'We are the founders of this process,' he says, 'we are one of the first countries to act against illegal migration.'[14]

Back in 2003, Mauritania signed an agreement that was an all-inclusive package for Spain. Mauritania would now take back anyone who was found or suspected to be heading for Spain, whether they were citizens of Mauritania or any other state. But this did not yet mean that Mauritania would stop migrants on their way, so the number of arrivals continued to increase. In 2006, around 30,000 people crossed the Mauritanian desert on their way to the Canaries. 'It used to be legal, we had hardly any laws against human trafficking,' says Baya.

Baya expanded the coast guard. 400 men, ten radar stations along 700 kilometers (435 mi) – he sounds like a general reporting after a successful battle. 'Our aid came from Germany and Spain.'[15] The program targeted both illegal fishery and irregular migrants.

They called it 'Guantanamito'

The Guardia Civil donated patrol boats to the Mauritanian navy and stationed a reconnaissance plane, a helicopter and ships there.

Anyone caught by the Guardia Civil on the way to the Canaries was pushed back to Mauritania. Police officers from both countries went on joint patrols along the Mauritanian coast to stop boats from embarking. Spain also funded an internment camp in a former school in the Mauritanian town of Nouadhibou. The locals called it 'Guantanamito.'[16] Fences were installed atop the earthen walls; the captives got uniforms consisting of white T-shirts and synthetic sweatpants. There was no legal basis for their detention, and the Spanish Red Cross supplied them with food. In 2008, a delegation from Amnesty International counted 35 imprisoned Africans having to share 17 beds in one cell measuring 16×26 ft.[17] From here, Mauritanian soldiers drove them southwards through the desert on trucks.

In 2006 alone, Mauritania dumped 11,000 Africans, most arrested by the Spanish, at the red-hot southern end of the Sahara, near Gogui on the Malian border. Sometimes the Red Cross picked up the migrants, sometimes not. If no one came to get them, they had to walk through the desert for hours – after being driven through the Sahara for days. Many people died of thirst.

Now the North Atlantic route had become so hard that migrants again started heading for the upgraded fence in Ceuta and Melilla. Thousands of people tried to climb over in the summer and fall of 2005. They used plastic bags and tree branches to make ladders, rolled over the barbed wire and dropped down the other side, dragging along more ladders for the second fence, until they reached the path patrolled by the Guardia Civil. At least 14 people died,[18] but the fence could not resist the onslaught.

What Europe now invests billions to achieve for half of Africa took its blueprint from Spain's neighborhood policy under the Socialist government of José Luis Rodríguez Zapatero. 'We believe that it makes sense to link the increase in development aid to the drafting of readmission agreements,'[19] former justice minister and current Socialist MEP Juan Fernando López Aguilar said frankly in 2006.

Plan África

'Traditionally Spain had little presence in or institutional relations with Black Africa. In some cases, they were virtually non-existent,'[20] admitted former Socialist Foreign Minister Miguel Ángel Moratinos. The so-called Plan África (2006 to 2008, followed by a second plan from 2009 to 2012) changed this. In 2006, Spain opened embassies in Cape Verde, Mali and Sudan; one year later it followed suit in Niger, Guinea-Bissau and in Conakry in the Republic of Guinea. From 2006 to 2008, Spain finalized twelve agreements with West African countries. The University of the Basque Country studied how heavily Spain relied on development aid to get African countries to cooperate.[21] From 2004 to 2008, Spain nearly quadrupled its aid for the region. Official Development Assistance (ODA) focused especially on West Africa, the crucial region for transit migration. In the same period, the funds invested here increased more than fivefold, from €35 to €219 million. The funds for police cooperation with nine West African states increased from €83,000 to around €4.8 million between 2004 and 2007. This made the cooperation profitable for West African countries.[22]

After the run on the fences in Ceuta and Melilla in the fall of 2005, Madrid opened the first embassy in Mali's capital of Bamako. A German diplomat described its tasks as follows: 'They have a very large department for internal security. Border control, border police, fighting human traffickers – that's what it's about.'[23] Mali became a priority country for the Spanish development assistance agency AECID (*Agencia Española de la Cooperación Internacional de Desarrollo*). In return, Mali was to keep Central African transit migrants from crossing the country northwards.

But the cooperations always affected citizens of the transit countries as well. They could no longer cross the border just like that, and Europe hardly ever kept its promises to grant them visas.

'A menace to Mali's society'

In 2008, former EU Development Commissioner Louis Michel opened the Centre for Migration Management and Information (CIGEM) in Mali's capital of Bamako under such an agreement. This EU liaison office was pompously announced as a 'Job Center for Africa.' 'Instead of demonising the migration phenomenon, it should be supported, structured and managed optimally as a positive human element for both Africa and Europe,'[24] said Michel, claiming that the CIGEM paved the way for Mali to make 'greater use of the development opportunities provided by migration.' One year later, in 2009, only 29 Malians were admitted to the EU – as seasonal vegetable pickers on the Canary Islands.[25] The CIGEM's real priority was to spread propaganda to dissuade people from migrating. On the way to the Mauritanian border, the EU set up warning signs that read 'Stop irregular migration. It is a menace to Mali's society!' with the EU's logo underneath.

In 2009, migrants were already boarding ships in Senegal, 1,500 kilometers (930 miles) from the Canaries. The Guardia Civil stationed ships, an airplane and a helicopter in Dakar. Senegal introduced tougher laws against human trafficking and allowed the Guardia Civil to patrol its coast, as long as a Senegalese officer was on board. Fishing boats on their way north were forced to turn back within Senegal's maritime territory – while ironically, regional overfishing by Spanish fleets was forcing them to venture further out to sea.[26] Senegal's government claimed that the coast guard did so to avert threats to the well-being of Senegalese citizens.

Today, the North Atlantic route is closed. In 2017, only 421 refugees arrived on the Canaries.[27] Mayor Baya is proud. 'We're an example, we were pioneers,' he says. On 8 February 2017, Baya is sitting in a grey suit, snacking on wasabi nuts at the bar of the fancy Westin Dragonara Resort in St Julians, Malta, plotting how to get back into the game. Hundreds of high-ranking officials from Africa and Europe are meeting at this conference hotel to negotiate the EU Emergency Trust Fund (EUTF) for Africa, which the EU established one year earlier to combat illegal migration. From the total of €3.2 billion at the time, the EU planned to advance only €38 million to Mauritania. (As of January 2019, the fund has grown to €4.1 billion, of which €81 million are intended for Mauritania.)[28] Not enough, if you ask Baya. He thinks that what the EU and Africa are negotiating in Valletta has one easily stated goal: 'Zero illegal migration. We already have that in Mauritania – almost.

'We're currently convincing them to buy us a new airplane.'

But he thinks it does not have to stay this way. Baya is a bit worried about the development in Niger and Libya, the Central Sahara route, which today is taken by most of the people heading for Europe. Soon, Baya fears, this route could be closed. And then, he is 'one hundred percent sure,' people will take the Atlantic routes again. He has come to Malta to make this clear to the Europeans. His country wants more money for coast guards, training, equipment, jeeps, boats – just what states like Niger are getting right now. 'We're currently convincing them to buy us a new airplane,' he says – with infrared cameras and night vision. He says it would cost €6 million. 'That's nothing compared to what we could do with it.'

Mauritania has done everything the Europeans wanted: built internment camps, taken back refugees, allowed European border police to patrol its waters. As a result, the migration route shifted away. In his view, Baya has become a victim of his own success. 'Brussels forgot about Mauritania, because we are not having any problems, because we've done our homework.'

The more internal borders Europe took down, the more it set up elsewhere. This outsourcing has clear advantages for Europe: Every migrant who never makes it over will not cost money to deport back, so the focus slowly moved from transit to source regions. On 19 January 2012, Ilkka Laitinen, then head of the EU border control agency Frontex, signed a so-called working arrangement with Rose Uzoma, head of the Nigerian Immigration Service (NIS). He expressed 'great pleasure to conclude this working arrangement with such an important partner.' Nigeria is more than 2,200 mi from the Schengen Area, but Laitinen was sure that 'the mutually beneficial exchanges of information and expertise are an important element of Frontex's approach.'[29]

Lampedusa – Libya, one-way

Europe did what it could to block the Western Mediterranean and Atlantic routes by sea and by land, reaching all the way into Africa's heart. But this didn't keep people in place. Instead, the migration movements along the Central Mediterranean route to Italy via Libya and Tunisia increased. Before, many shied away from this route, because it required them to cross the Sahara at its widest extent. So Italy's government got involved in Libya, just as Spain had done in West Africa.

Ethnologist Silja Klepp has researched the history of this cooperation. It goes back to the time when Libya was still officially seen as a 'rogue state'. After the bombing of the *La Belle* discothèque in Berlin in 1986 and the explosion of the Pan Am flight over the Scottish town of Lockerbie in 1988, which was linked to Libyan dictator Gaddafi, the country was politically isolated. Nevertheless, the Italian government entered informal preliminary talks with Gaddafi in the late 1990s. In December 2000, they signed an initial agreement in Rome. Besides fighting terrorism and crime, it dealt with curbing migration.

High-ranking Italian and Libyan politicians would meet continually over the following years. Rome was clearing the way for Gaddafi's rehabilitation. Finally, in 2003, the UN lifted its sanctions against Libya. The EU followed suit in 2004. Collaboration started taking off. Klepp writes: 'Deportation flights with migrants from Libya, detention centers for migrants, technical support for better monitoring of the Libyan border and training support for security officers in Libya were funded by Italy.'[30] In 2004 and 2005, Italy deported over 4,000 migrants from the island of Lampedusa back to Libya by plane.

Migrants on the sea route were treated brutally. South African political scientist Richard Pithouse describes the treatment:

'If they are intercepted by the Italian navy the migrants are forced off the boats, often with clubs and batons that dispense electric shocks, and taken to prisons in Tripoli. [...] From Tripoli they are taken to European funded migrant detention centres in places like the tiny village of Al Qatran out in the dessert near the border with Chad and Niger. Al Qatran is a thousand kilometres from Tripoli and it may take three days for captured migrants to be moved across that distance in trucks. In the detention centres there may be more than 50 people in a room. They sleep on the floor. [...] There are beatings, rapes and extortion. Suicides are a common response [...]'[31] Italy's Interior Minister Roberto Maroni, however, called the cooperation with Libya a 'historical step'.[32]

Dublin – a convenient solution

This tragedy is not just Italy's fault. 'What Italy has done was only trying to pass the buck,'[33] writes law professor Gregor Noll of Lund University. 'So the reprehensible pact trading in migrants' lives between Berlusconi's and Gaddafi's governments is but a logical consequence of reprehensible EU legislation in the form of the Dublin Regulation.' This EU agreement assigns the asylum procedure to the Schengen Area country which failed to prevent the illegal border crossing. For countries in the middle of Europe, like Germany, this is a convenient solution. For southern periphery states it is a huge problem.

This is why Berlusconi pushed for the cooperation with Libya. In March 2009, he met Gaddafi in the Libyan town of Sirte to close the Treaty of Friendship, Partnership and Cooperation.[34] Claiming reparations for colonial injustice, Italy was to send over $5 billion through 2025, mostly for infrastructure projects.[35] Italian companies won large contracts from Tripoli – and Libya ramped up its gatekeeping efforts for Italy, including the acceptance of pushed back migrants *en masse*.

Similar measures were taken at the EU level. In December 2004, the Commission published a report stating that Gaddafi was ordering 'arbitrary' arrests of migrants, locking them up in detention centers, separating children from their parents and not protecting women against rape. But the EU did not act on these findings. In 2006, EU Commissioner for Justice and Home Affairs Franco Frattini sent the first €3 million in border control aid to Tripoli.

The freshly created EU border control agency Frontex soon joined the scene. Klepp cites a letter by Gil Arias, then Deputy Executive Director of Frontex, asking for permission to patrol Libyan waters and push back migrants captured at sea.[36] Arias' request was rejected. In 2007 Frontex wrote a report to the EU with the purported goal of swaying Tripoli. 'This report made clear that Libya did not intend to sign the Geneva Refugee Convention. And unlike earlier EU papers, this report did not comment on the human rights situation in Libya or the unacceptable conditions under which migrants were imprisoned there,'[37] says Klepp. Instead, Frontex enclosed Gaddafi's wish list: To protect the borders, he asked Brussels for 10 ships, 12 reconnaissance planes, 18 helicopters, 22 fully equipped command centers, 28 patrol boats, 80 pick-up trucks, 86 trucks, 100 speedboats and 240 off-road vehicles.

Deals with Gaddafi

Brussels decided to negotiate an all-inclusive package with Gaddafi. Talks for a framework agreement began in 2008. This agreement was not just about political relations, but also about energy policy and trade. The EU was planning a free-trade zone in the medium run. Fighting off refugees was the first priority though. In September 2009, the deputy director-general of the EU Commissioner for External Relations, Hugues Mingarelli, informed the EU Parliament about the state of the negotiations in a closed meeting. Franziska Brantner, member of the *Bundestag* for the Greens, was horrified: 'The Commission wanted to close a refoulement deal with Gaddafi so they could return unwanted migrants from all over Africa back to Libya.'[38]

In 2010, Libya and the Commission closed a Memorandum of Understanding. Brussels offered Libya technical aid and cooperation for the period from 2011 to 2013. The priority of this cooperation was to share the responsibility of 'managing migration.'[39] Gaddafi was to receive €50 million from Brussels to further seal off his borders to African migrants.

Shortly before, Gaddafi had thrown the UN Refugee Agency (UNHCR) out of the country, because it had criticized conditions in Libyan deportation camps. The Commission was not concerned – the Memorandum was signed in June 2010.

Arab Spring changes the game

Four months later, in October 2010, EU Commissioner for Home Affairs Cecilia Malmström and EU Commissioner for Enlargement and European Neighbourhood Policy Štefan Füle traveled to Tripoli. Füle was enthusiastic about the good development of relations with Gaddafi in recent years and their shared interests.[40] Malmström added that good cooperation with Libya in all issues related to migration had a high priority for the EU.[41] The two wanted to find out how to best declare the funds sent to Gaddafi without provoking too much criticism. Their solution was to give the staff at Libyan deportation camps workshops on human rights and on how to register refugees – so they could take over the same job which the UNHCR had handled until the previous summer.

This meant factually rewarding Gaddafi for throwing out the UN agency, stated Brantner, who was then MEP for the Greens. 'Not a single euro should have been spent on this.'[42] To keep the European Parliament from interfering, the Commission had split the sum intended for Gaddafi into three separate budget items. This way, the split funds fell below the Parliament's veto threshold.

In January 2011, the EU Parliament called the planned readmission agreement absolutely unacceptable. A unanimously accepted report by Portuguese MEP Ana Gomes stated that such an agreement violated the values of the EU Charter of Fundamental Rights. But at a hearing, the Commission remained steadfast. One representative cited 'massive political pressure' from the European Council. 'They wanted this deal at any cost,' said one observer of the hearing[43].

After brutal attacks on protesters in Libya at the start of the Arab Spring in 2011, German Federal President Christian Wulff called Gaddafi a 'state terrorist' and 'psychopath.'[44] Merkel designated him a 'despot.' NATO General Secretary Anders Rasmussen found him cruel and brutal. The EU could not be fazed. As late as 15 February 2011, Gaddafi's closest confidant, Libyan Interior Minister Abdul Fatah Younis, was received in Brussels. It was not until shortly after his visit, when the news about the fighting in Libya became more dramatic, that EU Foreign Affairs Commissioner Catherine Ashton froze the funds.

The Arab Spring in 2011 swept away dictators in Cairo, Tripoli and Tunis and gave migrants access to the sea. Within a few weeks in early 2011, thousands of boats arrived in Italy. Young North Africans, but also people from sub-Saharan Africa and the Middle East used their newfound freedom to travel. Shortly thereafter, the EU convinced Tunisia and the Libyan rebel government to close the beaches to emigrants. Ashton managed to get this promise from the Libyan rebels in the coastal town of Benghazi before they had even defeated Gaddafi. They stood by their word and just kept running the gruesome migrant prisons built by Gaddafi.

'Worse than Dante's *Inferno*'

Now the story from the Atlantic repeated in the Mediterranean: The migrants moved elsewhere, this time to the east. First Israel, and from 2009, the Aegean region become migration hot spots. Some nights, hundreds of people arrived on isles such as Lesbos on rubber dinghies. They came from all over the world: Gambians, Eritreans and Afghans arrived at the Greek beaches all at once. Turkey, insulted by the stalled EU accession talks, let them pass. Greece followed a hard line and locked people in makeshift prisons under conditions that even Greek Deputy Interior Minister Spyros Vouyias called 'worse than Dante's *Inferno*.'[45] On Lesbos, a crowd including minors and pregnant women was locked into an old factory building in the village of Pagani. Some stayed there for months in burning heat without knowing when they would be set free. More than 100 people had to share one toilet and a faucet. Diseases broke out and doctors rarely visited.

This caused yet another shift in the migration route, this time to the north, through the tripoint between Turkey, Bulgaria and Greece. One reason was Bulgaria's accession to the Schengen Area. In 2011, 55,000 people illegally crossed the Evros river, which forms the border. It is not even 200m (650ft) wide and has a calm flow, but still many people drowned. In summer, when it carries less water, some underestimated its depth and tried to wade through; many people did not know how to swim. In winter, when the water runs higher, people fell out of overloaded boats.

Still the route stayed attractive – until 4 December 2013. 'This is a historic day for the Turkish people,' said Turkish Foreign Minister Ahmet Davutoğlu, who would later play a decisive role in the so-called EU-Turkey Deal.[46] Back in 2013, he had already negotiated a deal in Brussels requiring Ankara to accept rejected asylum seekers who enter the EU via Turkey. In return, Brussels joined talks about easier visa requirements for Turkish citizens. Frontex guards on the Greek side were now able to alert their Turkish colleagues by radio whenever they saw migrants heading for the border. The Turks would stop them and take them back to the country's interior. The following year, only 24,000 refugees made it to Greece.

In the meantime, Libya had fallen into chaos. The old militias, once paid for stopping migrants, now turned into traffickers and literally took the last shirts off refugees' backs for a space on a boat to Southern Italy. The route was expensive and murderous; yet it was the first choice in 2014, especially for those escaping from Syria.

Then something happened: Turkey had taken in two million Syrians since the start of the war in 2011. Now it opened the gates. Anyone was free to hop on a dinghy along the western Turkish coast and head for Greece. The deal signed in 2013 by Davutoğlu was suspended – for now.

In 2014 the EU found out that migration could not be stopped, just slowed down. It was the first year when large numbers of migrants started coming by land, not by sea – along the Balkan route.

Notes

1. *Der Spiegel* (1991) 'Krieg des dritten Jahrtausends', 19 August 1991, p. 130

2. *Der Spiegel* (1992) 'Bestrafung der Armen', 16 November 1992, p. 226

3. Eerste EU-Marokko top in teken van economische samenwerking (2010) *Europa Nu*, 5 Oktober | http://bit.ly/2wekLwy

4. Johnson, Dominic (2004) 'Boat people', *tageszeitung*, 28 December

5. *El Diario* (2009) 'Una persona murió desangrada en 2009 por cortes con el alambre de cuchillas de la valla de Ceuta', 22 November | http://bit.ly/2vlNSl4

6. *ESF* (2013) 'Valla fronteriza de Melilla' | http://bit.ly/2uNKwFP

7. *20 minutos* (2013) 'El fabricante de las concertinas de Melilla: "La finalidad no es ni cortar ni pinchar a nadie"', 29 November 2013 | http://bit.ly/2f1Ioq8

8. *El Mundo* (2006) 'El Gobierno presenta la tercera valla de Melilla, que impide que los inmigrantes se lesionen al saltar', 22 March | http://bit.ly/2weDoR4

9. *La Razon* (2013) 'Juan José Imbroda: "El pobre de solemnidad no salta la valla, tiene que pagar a las mafias"', 3 November | http://bit.ly/2hh61KP

10. *El País* (2013) 'Tardaron doce horas en coserme las heridas después de saltar la verja', 1 December | http://bit.ly/1cymxud

11. *El País* (2013) 'El Congreso rechaza retirar las cuchillas de las vallas de Ceuta y Melilla y todas las alternativas', 18 December | http://bit.ly/2uNy496

12. *El País* (2013) 'Interior: "La concertina es un elemento pasivo de disuasión, no es agresivo"', 26 November | http://bit.ly/2vh43PH

13. *EL País (2013)* '¿Pero quién defiende las cuchillas en la valla de Melilla?', 16 November | http://bit.ly/2hipc6M

14. Personal interview, Malta, 8 February 2017

15. *Gesellschaft für internationale Zusammenarbeit* 'Nachhaltige Bewirtschaftung der Fischereiressourcen' Projektbeschreibung, | http://www.giz.de/de/weltweit/17009.html

16. *Jeune Afrique* (2008) 'Meunier, Marianne: "Bienvenue à "Guantanamito"', 7 July | http://bit.ly/2vZwSy2

17. *Amnesty International* (2008) 'Mauritania: "Nobody wants to have anything to do with us"', Report, 1 July | http://bit.ly/2ueohCF

18. *n-tv* (2005) 'Tote nach Flüchtlingsansturm', 6 October | http://bit.ly/2uRO08F

19. *tageszeitung* 'Datenbank Migration Control', Länderreport Spanien | http://bit.ly/2hih7yU

20. *Ibid.*

21. *Entreculturas y ALBOAN* (2011) 'Nerea Azkona: Políticas de control migratorio y de cooperación al desarrollo entre España y África Occidental durante la ejecución del primer Plan África', Madrid, 2011 | http://bit.ly/2uOG75x

22. *Ibid.*

23. Personal interview, Bamako, January 2011

24. *EU Commission (2008)* 'The European Commission and Mali join forces to improve the management of migration', Brussels, 6 October | http://bit.ly/2M4HvIA

25. *UNDP* 'Mali 2015 Migration Fact Sheet' | http://bit.ly/2uTwUHI

26. Jakob, Christian (2011) 'Der europäische Raubfisch', 9 February 2011 | http://bit.ly/2vgZLIb

27. *Frontex (2018)* Risk Analysis for 2018, Warsaw | http://bit.ly/2CMIBFQ

28. *EU Commission* 'EU Emergency Trust Fund for Africa', | http://bit.ly/2h4hmch; Mauritania | http://bit.ly/2CObJMU

29. *Frontex (2012)* 'Frontex signs Working Arrangement with Nigeria', 19 December | http://bit.ly/2uRHdfm

30. Klepp, Silja (2011) 'Europa zwischen Grenzkontrolle und Flüchtlingsschutz: Eine Ethnographie der Seegrenze auf dem Mittelmeer (Kultur und soziale Praxis)', Bielefeld, transcript

31. Pithouse, Richard (2011) 'The World Remade', *The South African Civil Society Information Service*, 23 February | http://bit.ly/2vbIqAR

32. *Il Giornale* (2009) 'Clandestini, la Libia riprende i barconi Maroni: passo storico', 8 May | http://bit.ly/2uQWAow

33. Noll, Gregor and Giuffré, Mariaguillia (2011) 'EU migration control: made by Gaddafi?', *Lund / Trento*, February 2011 | http://bit.ly/2voUdhQ

34. *Camera dei deputati* N. 2041 (2008) Rome, 23 December | http://bit.ly/1IwZD9C

35. *Corrierre della sera* (2008) 'Berlusconi da Gheddafi, siglato l'accordo: "Uniti sull'immigrazione"', 20 August | http://bit.ly/1KQY2YH

36. Klepp, Silja (2011) 'Europa zwischen Grenzkontrolle und Flüchtlingsschutz: Eine Ethnographie der Seegrenze auf dem Mittelmeer (Kultur und soziale Praxis)' Bielefeld, transcript, 2011

37. Personal interview, Bremen, March 2012

38. Personal interview, Berlin, October 2009

39. *EU Parliament* (2011) 'EU-Libya Framework Agreement', 20 January | http://bit.ly/2uR5Rgh

40. *EU Commission* (2010) 'Commissioners Malmström and Füle visit Libya to reinforce EU-Libya cooperation', 4 October | http://europa.eu/rapid/press-release_IP-10-1281_en.htm

41. *Ibid.*

42. Phone interview, March 2010

43. Personal interview, October 2011

44. *Saarbrücker Zeitung* (2011) 'Bundespräsident Wulff nennt Gaddafi einen "Psychopathen"', 24 February | http://bit.ly/2tWVLx6

45. *Pro Asyl Newsletter* (2010) no. 154, January 2010 | http://bit.ly/2vP5jeV

46. *Die Welt* (2013) 'EU und Türkei einig über Rücknahme von Flüchtlingen', 4 December | http://bit.ly/2udg2cO

Diplomacy:
Monsieur Vimont's last job
A deal with Africa

People who spend their professional lives moving big things have a hard time letting go. Just like Pierre Vimont, who did not retire to the Côte d'Azur or a small chalet in the Alps, but to a cream-colored Art Nouveau mansion at Rue de Congrès in downtown Brussels. The lower floors of the US security policy think tank Carnegie Endowment for International Peace (CEIP), ranked fifth among the world's most influential of its kind in 2017, are occupied by young analysts, political advisors, media experts. On the third floor, at the end of a stairway laid out with thick, red carpet, Pierre Vimont is sitting at a smoked glass desk. Even in midsummer, he wears his white shirt buttoned up, his red tie sitting tightly. The wave in his grey hair makes him resemble a British lord. He was *Chef de Cabinet* in Paris and has been France's ambassador to Washington and Brussels. Later, when the EU began opening embassies and pursuing a foreign policy of its own – like a real state rather than a wobbly compromise – the Commission named Vimont Secretary-General of its shadow foreign ministry, the European External Action Service (EEAS). Vimont worked six years to build this crossbreed between the EU Commission and the Council, until retiring as a Senior Fellow at the CEIP in February 2015. But his exit was brief. After just two months, end of April 2015, his phone rang. It was the Polish President of the EU Council, Donald Tusk. 'Could you come back?' he asked. Vimont could.[1]

Five weeks earlier, during the night from 18 to 19 April 2015, a refugee boat had capsized on the way from Libya to Italy. 28

passengers were rescued; around 500 drowned. In the previous week, around 1,000 people had died in several smaller incidents. Carlotta Sami, speaker of the UN refugee agency UNHCR, called it 'one of the worst tragedies involving refugees and migrants in the last 12 months'.[2] Four days later, the EU heads of state meet for an extraordinary Council summit in Brussels. Most of the 28 EU states do not feel affected by the crisis. At the time, the Balkan route is still fairly quiet. In Brussels, they mostly want to talk about whether extra euros to Rome could soften the shock. As usual.

One participant wants more: German Chancellor Merkel. Attendants report her saying to the gathered leaders: 'This will keep going, it won't stop'.[3] Merkel's idea is a summit with Africa. After all, that is where the refugees are coming from. So Africa must be the key to stopping them. Italy and Spain had the same idea in the past. The other member states have not pursued this thought so far. The EU and the African Union (AU) meet every four years anyway, so the other states prefer waiting until the next scheduled meeting in November 2017. Merkel does not want to wait. She senses that the Mediterranean situation will get worse. Maltese Prime Minister Joseph Muscat supports her: 'I'll organize the summit.' 'Any objections?' asks Council President Donald Tusk, who chairs the meeting. No answers. The meeting asks Tusk to handle the preparations. A few days later he calls Vimont.

Vimont's job is to invite around half of all African states to Malta for November 2015. Here they are expected to agree to slashing the numbers of refugees coming to Europe. What would they demand? And what could the EU offer them? Vimont, the unretired negotiator, gets only 20 weeks to find out – and the title 'Personal Envoy of the President of the European Council. A small team from Vimont's old agency, the EEAS, is set up: Vimont, one assistant and an advisor sent by the EU Council. Vimont's discretionary power is mostly determined by the Justice and Home Affairs Council (JHA).

'The officials in Brussels are skeptical,' says Vimont. The number of deaths in the Mediterranean drops a bit over the following months, but the Balkan route is about to escalate. Hungary factually suspends the Dublin Agreement, Greece's capacity for taking in refugees collapses. 'Everyone was looking at the Balkan route, while we were working on the Africa summit,' says Vimont. Many people in Brussels do not see the use. 'People take care of first things first,' says Vimont, 'and back then, that was the Balkan route.' In early summer he visits capitals of member states and meets senior officials. He wants to know what they are willing to offer the Africans. They do not think like their colleagues in Brussels: 'The advisors to the heads of government told us: 'You're right! Keep going! When the situation in the Balkans calms down, the African migration will continue.'

A limited group

The so-called Rabat Process, a loose group of EU states and 23 states from Western and Eastern Africa, started in 2006. They talk about migration policy. The platform is organized by the Viennese think tank International Centre for Migration Policy Development (ICMPD). The ICMPD also coordinates the East African equivalent, the Khartoum Process, which started in 2014 in Rome between the EU and Egypt, Ethiopia, Djibouti, Eritrea, Kenya, Somalia, South Sudan and Sudan.

These two processes have not yielded many results so far, but the talks have a certain structure, which Vimont uses as a basis for the new platform. He invites representatives of all EU states and the Rabat and Khartoum processes to a meeting in Brussels in July. Other invitees are the AU, the UNHCR, the International Organisation for Migration (IOM) and the ICMPD. African states who are not part of the Rabat or Khartoum processes want to take part in the talks. 'But these other states were represented by the AU. We wanted to start with a limited group first,' says Vimont.

The invited African states send diplomats. 'I asked them: "What do you think should be the outcome of this summit?"' says Vimont. They sense that there is something in it for them and demand concrete favors in return. In September, EU Commission President Jean-Claude Juncker announces the endowment of a fund worth €1.8 billion for 'addressing root causes of irregular migration in Africa'.[4]

'The African states were pleasantly surprised,' says Vimont. The negotiators meet three more times in the following months: the day after Juncker's announcement in late September in the Egyptian coastal town of Sharm El Sheikh, in Rabat in October and finally in Malta in November.

The talks have one problem from the start: the 31 states of the Rabat and Khartoum processes include open dictatorships and authoritarian regimes. Eritrea and Sudan, but also Ethiopia, South Sudan and Egypt – military rulers, war criminals and civil war regimes. Vimont begins negotiating outside of public view, but this soon changes. The media, NGOs and members of parliament soon start asking whether working with these states is the right thing to do.

Brussels ponders this very early and the answer is yes. 'The interior ministers were mostly looking for effectiveness,' says

Vimont. 'The question was: How do we get results?' Hence the EU interior ministers work to get representatives of dictators to join the discussion, as long as they might be useful. Vimont uses a very diplomatic expression: 'It required some accommodation with our principles and values.' The ministers use the deaths in the Mediterranean as an argument: 'There were many Eritreans among them. Shouldn't we be trying to save their lives?' asks Vimont. 'But it's not easy, we all agree.'

Europe's interior ministers have various requests for Vimont to negotiate. They all have in common that they lead to fewer people reaching Europe and more people becoming deportable. The ministers draft an EU Action Plan on Return, which is published on 9 September, around two months before the Valletta Summit. Vimont's job briefing states: 'One of the most effective ways to address irregular migration is the systematic return, either voluntary or forced, of those who do not or no longer have the right to remain in Europe.'[5]

One way to achieve this is a new type of deportation papers, which the African states are meant to recognize, so-called EU laissez-passers. What makes them special is that EU member states can issue them. This is exceedingly practical if deportees have no passport and their embassy will not issue one. In December 2015, the Commission proposes a bill for an EU travel document for illegal third-country nationals. The problem: No non-EU state will recognize them, because this would mean giving up the sovereignty to decide who is allowed to enter. The AU even considers them a breach of international law. 'That was the hardest part,' says Vimont. The Africans let him know that they will not agree.

Neither are they overjoyed by Europe's call for more border controls in Africa. A high-ranking Brussels official describes it thus: 'In many African states, the government doesn't control [the borders]. The member states [of the EU] want more. Building new walls? Doesn't work. That's much too big. It's just about doing sporadic controls. Those without papers will then be sent back.' He admits this to be 'problematic from a development policy angle' and 'a not very traditional type of development cooperation.' African states are supposed to introduce controls where there used to be none. But sending back 'only those without papers' does not reflect the reality and is not nearly as harmless as it sounds.

African leaders even admit the need for more border controls – not least due to the Islamist terrorist groups active in the Sahel zone, Boko Haram and al-Qaeda in the Islamic Maghreb (AQIM). 'The Africans recognized existing dysfunctions,' says Vimont. He says this is also why so many states later accepted border control training missions from the Europeans.

Ramping up border controls between their own countries, just because Europe said so – sounds like the Europeans meddling in their internal affairs. It injures their national, their anti-colonial pride. 'It was a matter of principle,' says Vimont. Spain, for example, understood this early on. 'Spain demanded these border controls and readmissions from West African states and got them, too,' says Vimont. 'But this happened very quietly, without many statements, no public declarations, that was the secret of their success.' This time, the European states acted differently: 'They wanted to have it loud and clear in the communiqué for Valletta.'

Not even 30 percent leave

Readmission agreements are a curiosity of international law. They should not even exist – international law already requires every state to readmit its own citizens. In an agreement from the year 2000, signed in Benin's capital Cotonou, the EU once more required all states of the African, Caribbean and Pacific group (ACP) to guarantee that they would take back all of their citizens illegally staying in the EU.

It just never happened.

In the Action Plan on Return of 2015, Vimont's job briefing for the talks, the EU interior ministers write: 'The return rates to African countries are under 30 percent – well below the general rate of return from the EU, which, at 40 percent, is already insufficient.' Their hopes are on the upcoming Valletta Summit, which 'offered a chance for a renewed commitment towards readmission,' says Vimont.

The agreements are intended to ensure that African states cooperate in deportations by issuing passports and confirming people's identities. Among the 17 states who have closed readmission agreements with the EU as a whole so far, there is only a single African state, the tiny island nation of Cape Verde. This has to change now. To avoid meddling from the EU Parliament, which is more sensitive to human rights issues, the Commission prefers informal agreements that do not require the Parliament's approval.

The member states have done it before. Of the 60 agreements on deportation issues closed just by Germany, the UK, Italy, France and Spain with African states, only eight are formal readmission agreements. The rest are murky arrangements, often between police authorities.

The EU has been talking to African states about this issue since long before Vimont's mission, albeit with little success. The EU demanded that the African states take back not just their own citizens, but also foreign citizens who crossed their territory in transit. 'A very difficult issue,' says Martijn Pluim of the ICMPD think tank, which has co-organized many of the talks. 'Negotiations would be much easier without a third-country provision. As soon as it's in, the African states have much more room to negotiate, their demands get bigger.'[6] Yet, many EU states insist on including third country nationals. Benefits to the EU states are clear – deportations to North African transit countries become much easier, faster and cheaper to organize.

The EU Council and the European External Action Service (EEAS) also insist on including the clause. Questions of prestige also drive the EU – if it succeeds in the readmission negotiations, where individual member states have failed, it could establish itself as a major foreign policy player. Many EU members remain critical of the growing influence of the group surrounding Federica Mogherini, High Representative of the Union for Foreign Affairs and Security Policy.

Many African states are also wary of this issue, though. They reject readmission agreements while demanding visas for their own citizens, even though this is not a good time. In recent weeks, hundreds of thousands of refugees have been taking the Balkan route to Central Europe. The governments there are alarmed. Nobody wants to hear any demands that could lead to more immigration. 'In the EU they're saying the boat is full. From the partner countries' point of view, however, any refugee who is readmitted is a bad deal,' says a high-ranking official from the office of EU Development Commissioner Neven Mimica.

Negotiator Vimont's words fall on deaf ears in the EU. No country wants to offer refugee quotas, even though EU Commission VP Frans Timmermans encourages member states to show signs of goodwill. 'Nobody promised any visas to the Africans,' says Vimont. The Commission's efforts fail.

Pluim of the ICMPD considers this a fatal signal: 'If the African countries see that the EU is only interested in negotiating with [them] about readmission and does not want a positive message for more immigration, this creates new reservations.'

The talks extend for months. Vimont tries to negotiate between the European interior ministers and the AU but has little to offer. Friction occurs between the EEAS and the Commission. Many states think the Commission is not going far enough, while the Commission foresees that the ministers will not get everything they want from the Africans. 'To Africa, migration is an asset. To the EU, it's more of a challenge, if not a security risk. That's the problem,' says Vimont.

On the evening of 10 November 2015, the heads of state of 62 countries from Europe and Africa meet at the Auberge de la Castille, a Renaissance palace just outside Valletta's historical center. Sudan's President Bashir, who has an outstanding international arrest warrant, has to send a representative. Vimont and the envoys sit together all night until the early morning to negotiate the paper upon which the heads of state will agree the next day. Although it is their fourth meeting, many points are still open. Too many.

The highest policy level takes over the next day. Frans Timmermans, Commission VP, leads the discussion during the actual summit. The day before, he was in Ankara to wrest a promise from the government to keep the roughly two million Syrian refugees in Turkey. It transpires that apparently the EU was now ready to grant the €3 million and visa-free travel demanded by Erdoğan. Now Timmermans is sitting behind the massive walls of the centuries-old Maltese fortress in Valletta and has to explain to the 33 visiting African leaders why there are only €1.8 billion for all of them and a couple of student visas – in exchange for keeping back migrants and refugees from all over their continent. The Africans feel that the Europeans are in distress.

It is a quarter past noon on Thursday, 12 November 2015, the second day of the summit, when Hungarian-born translator Eva Szilva types the last paragraph of the final declaration into her computer.

The leaders promise joint efforts to 'fight against irregular migration' in a 17-page 'Action Plan,' that bears neither the EU nor the AU logo.[7] It does not say much else. Readmission agreements? Subject to further talks. Laissez-passers? Not mentioned. Visas for Africans? Covered by existing legislation. Stronger border controls inside Africa? The EU offers to support 'national capabilities.' All in all, this document says a whole lot of nothing. Neither Africans nor Europeans ceded any ground on their most decisive issues. The loudly heralded EU Emergency Trust Fund for Africa is already considered a scam by most of the Africans. Most of the money had already been allocated to development aid in the EU budget. Going out of their way to accommodate the Europeans is not an option for the African leaders: deportations are hugely unpopular among their own citizens, and remittances from Africans in Europe are too important.

All-inclusive collaboration packages

Vimont's job is done, but the EU realizes that its attempt to make a deal with half of a continent to solve its refugee problem will not work out.

Now what?

The EU picks five states in Valletta for more intensive negotiations in the future – individually, unlike Vimont's approach: Mali, Nigeria, Niger, Senegal and Ethiopia. The EU wants to close so-called migration compacts with them. These 'all-inclusive collaboration packages' cover investments, readmissions, deportation, counter-terrorism.

But differences remain. In bilateral talks with the five Compact states over the next few months, the EEAS is unable to win any major concessions. Niger is the only exception. All in all, the number of people returning to Africa does not increase – and neither does the number of those crossing the Mediterranean decrease.

Germany's government tries going solo: In February 2016, Foreign Minister Steinmeier and Interior Minister Thomas de Maizière (Christian Democratic Union (CDU)) both pen a letter to the governments of Algeria, Benin, Senegal, Guinea-Bissau, Niger, Nigeria, Morocco and Sudan. They declare their intention to use EU laissez-passer documents to repatriate all irregular immigrants, who have no prospects of staying in Germany.[8][9] Germany tries to woo the governments with the promise of entering a 'new phase,' which could also 'positively affect other areas of [their] cooperation.' It is no use – no country wants to work with these deportation papers 'made in Germany.'

A few weeks later, the Turkey deal takes effect. 'That was a turning point,' says Vimont. 'It reinforced the idea of readmission. Because everyone saw: This works.' Turkey proves that transit countries 'can find common ground with the EU,' says Vimont. Commission VP Timmermans now wants to copy the deal for the Central Mediterranean. Many EU states support for the initiative. 'The slightly harder narrative that followed had a lot to do with this,' says Vimont.

The 'slightly harder narrative' begins after 7 June 2016, half a year after the Valletta Summit. Now the EU's African partners have the gun to their heads. Its new, so-called partnership agreements with Africa openly threaten to use 'all policies and instruments at the EU's disposal to achieve concrete results' in migration management.[10] The same day, Timmermans explains the new Africa policy in Brussels, calling it 'a mix of positive and negative incentives'[11] and demanding that third countries who cooperate 'efficiently' with the EU should be 'rewarded' while the others should have to face 'consequences.'[12]

Vimont's approach was to emphasize shared interests with Africa to win over the AU as a whole. '[We need] real partnerships [that are] economic, social and cultural in nature,' claimed President of the European Parliament Martin Schulz (Social Democrats (SPD)).

But this is not the truth, and the Africans know. Their interests and Europe's interests in the migration question do not overlap. While the Valletta Process will continue as a dialog round, the political efforts shift towards the carrot and stick approach. Timmermans promises €8 billion through the end of the decade to those countries who help increase deportations and decrease new arrivals – a multiple of the sum initially intended for the EU Emergency Trust Fund (EUTF). The goal is to bring 'order' into the migration flows.

The Council reiterates this goal from mid-2016 to mid-2017. At its meetings of 28 June and 21 October 2016, the Council demands concrete and measurable results for the fast deportation of irregular migrants. If the African states fail to comply, involvement and aid will be adjusted.[13] In December 2016 it demands the systematic inclusion of other instruments and policy areas,[14] which include possible trade sanctions. Almost one year after Timmerman introduced the migration framework based mostly on political pressure at the Council meeting in June 2017, the EU finally announces the use of 'all possible levers.'[15] In EU lingo, this likely means cuts in development assistance.

Two years after Vimont the diplomat was unretired from his office at the Rue de Congrès, the EU has hardly made a step forward. No African country has signed a readmission agreement or officially accepted the laissez-passer papers. In June 2017, the Commission announces that still only 26 percent of the Nigerians without a valid visa are leaving the EU. Among the Senegalese, this figure has dropped from 12.5 to 9 percent. Ethiopian returnees make up only 9.8 percent and Malians 4.8 percent – a disastrous result for the EU measured by its own targets.

Now a realization is dawning on Brussels and Berlin: they need a new strategy based on economic policy.

Notes

1. Personal interview, Brussels, 16 June 2017

2. *UNHCR* (2016) 'Survivors report massive loss of life in latest Mediterranean Sea', 20 April | http://bit.ly/2hiBN9Z

3. Personal interview, Brussels, 16 June 2017

4. *EU Commission* (2015) 'Refugee Crisis: European Commission takes decisive action', 9 September | http://bit.ly/1OxXQiN

5. *EUR Lex* (2015) 'EU Action Plan on return', 9 September | https://bit.ly/2RJLqzK

6. Jakob, Christian (2017) 'Eine Brutstätte für Extremisten', *tageszeitung*, 11 February | http://bit.ly/2vcXEp4

7. '2015 Valletta Summit on Migration: 'Action Plan'", November 2015 | https://bit.ly/2Tftc7d

8. Personal interview, Brussels, 7 December 2016

9. *Die Welt* (2016) 'Diese 17 Staaten behindern Abschiebungen aus Deutschland', 23 February | http://bit.ly/2vZUowv

10. *EU Commission* (2016) 'Commission announces New Migration Partnership Framework: reinforced cooperation with third countries to better manage migration', 7 June | https://bit.ly/28hEsSG

11. *Ibid.*

12. *Zeit* (2016) 'Migration auf Zuckerbrot und Peitsche', 7 June | http://bit.ly/2uefxzy

13. *European Council conclusions, 20-21 October 2016* | http://bit.ly/2QMQheM

14. *European Council conclusions, 15 December 2016* | http://bit.ly/2AKEZCN

15. *European Council conclusions, 22-23/06/2017* | http://bit.ly/2AJqmQe

The blueprints

The €6 billion deal with Turkey

On Sunday, 7 March 2016, the Turkish Prime Minister Ahmet Davutoğlu, Dutch Prime Minister Mark Rutte – President of the European Council at the time – and German Chancellor Angela Merkel meet in Brussels. *Die Welt* editor Robin Alexander reconstructed their one-night sit-together at the office of the Turkish ambassador to the EU, Selim Yenel, in Brussels,[1] just hours before the decisive EU summit on the refugee crisis. These were 'the most important hours of Merkel's chancellorship,' says Alexander.[2]

It was only on the plane to Brussels that Davutoğlu, who was soon to be sidelined by Erdoğan, set out the final conditions for the 'EU-Turkey statement'. His country would 'take any necessary measures to prevent [...] illegal migration [...] from Turkey to the EU,' states point three.[3] Greece may, at the expense of the EU, return to Turkey all migrants who arrive on the Greek islands after 20 March 2016 and do not apply for asylum or whose applications are rejected. For each of these refugees, another refugee may leave Turkey and enter EU.

What appears to be an absurd cycle is the strategic centerpiece of the agreement: on one hand, the EU can claim to be keeping its doors open to refugees from Turkey. At the same time – just like Turkey – the EU is speculating that news will spread among the refugees that crossing the Aegean is not worth the risk. If you cross by boat, you gain nothing, but someone else will.

Officially, the paper is just a statement, not an international treaty – which is why a February 2017 appeal to the European Court of Human Rights by two Pakistanis and one Afghan was rejected stating that it lacked the jurisdiction to hear and determine the actions.[4]

The EU-Turkey statement continues: 'Once irregular crossings between Turkey and the EU are ending or at least have been substantially and sustainably reduced, a Voluntary Humanitarian Admission Scheme will be activated. EU Member States will contribute on a voluntary basis to this scheme.' A figure for this 'voluntary' admission scheme is not stated. Alexander's research showed that Merkel and Rutte promised to Davutoğlu orally, but with binding effect, to accept between 150,000 and 250,000 people annually.[5] Alexander claims that people attending the negotiations had confirmed this to him in person. Were this figure correct, it would exceed the number of people the UN refugee agency UNHCR is allowed to resettle annually from all crisis regions worldwide. For years, the UNHCR's 'resettlement program' has aimed to permit refugees in special emergencies to leave for a safe country.

In 2016, for example, the UNHCR asked for 162,500 places but only got 125,600[6] worldwide. The EU-Turkey deal is subject to different standards than all other crises around the world. However, in the end the EU admitted far fewer people from Turkey. In the first two years after the agreement, i.e. from March 2016 to April 2010, only 12,476 Syrians were allowed to leave Turkey for the EU.[7] Another unfulfilled promise was visa-free travel for Turkish citizens, which the EU undertook to achieve until June 2016[8] and which was obviously not realistic within a four-month period. Unlike point six of the 'Facility for Refugees' in Turkey: two billion euros from Brussels, and one billion from the member states, were to be spent by the end of 2017, and perhaps the same amount again from 2018. This money is Europe's commitment to refugees in Erdoğan's empire.

The importance of the agreement is hard to overestimate. Alexander and many others believe that it saved Merkel's job as chancellor.[9] Some, such as Slovenian Prime Minister Miro Cerar even think this applies to the EU as a whole, which would otherwise have disintegrated around the migration issue.[10] Critics such as Claudia Roth, *Bundestag* Vice-President for the Green Party, say that Europe has 'lost its soul and sold out its values' in this agreement.[11]

Many others think that the EU should also make similar deals with other countries to solve its refugee problem in the long run. As soon as the ink under the agreement with Erdoğan was dry, European politicians began echoing the idea. One of them being Merkel, who called for a similar agreement with Egypt at a meeting of the Balkan border states in Vienna in September 2016.[12] Germany's Interior Minister de Maizière[13] and Italy's Prime Minister Matteo Renzi[14] expressed similar views. In May 2017, Austria's Federal Chancellor Christian Kern (SPÖ) traveled to Cairo to speak to military ruler Abd al-Fattah al-Sisi in this matter.[15]

Billions in aid to transit states for stopping and taking back refugees seems to be the future of Europe's border policy. But is it really possible to replicate the EU-Turkey Statement? And what would be the consequences for refugees?

She lied to the Islamic State

The EU presents people like Sabha al-Mustafa from Raqqa as cases of Syrian refugees benefitting from EU payments. It is 4:49pm on 1 February 2017 when her golden smartphone gets a text message. 'Your application was processed. You were classified as eligible,' it says in Arabic. The next day, Ms. al-Mustafa picks up a red debit card at a branch of the state-owned Turkish Halkbank on Atatürk Street in downtown Urfa, southern Turkey. Soon she will be able to withdraw money – for the first time since reaching Turkey six months earlier.

Al-Mustafa talks about this in her apartment on the first floor of a house on the outskirts of Urfa. The ochre mountain range that separates war and peace looms in the background. Heading for the border, bombers of the Turkish army leave contrails in the ice-blue sky on their way to the Islamic State (IS).[16]

Al-Mustafa wears a turquoise coat and a black headscarf, her features are hardened. She is 42 years old. Her children are six, seven and eight. This age difference is unusual for a mother in a region where many women have children before reaching the legal age. But al-Mustafa studied and married late – to a carpenter who worked mostly in Saudi Arabia. Her apartment in Urfa has no furniture; there is a large cast-iron stove in the corner, but al-Mustafa has no fuel. Next to it there is a sewing machine. On top, a large cone of black yarn defies the icy air, underneath it hides one of the daughters.

On the other side of Urfa, the Turkish Red Crescent has rented a building. 400,000 Syrian refugees live here; more than in any other Turkish city besides Istanbul. Since December 2016, 240 different families have come here every day, strictly sorted by the districts in which they live. They apply for benefits from the EU's Emergency Social Safety Net (ESSN) program, which is funded with money from the EU-Turkey deal.

In early January 2017, al-Mustafa went to the Red Crescent office. She sat down on a blue metal bench, and when the digital display showed her number, she received a 17-page questionnaire. Everyone here has to complete it. Those who cannot read have to ask their neighbors. Then al-Mustafa stepped to one of the counters in the neon-lit inner room. She showed the Syrian identity cards for herself and her children and handed in the questionnaire.

Al-Mustafa used a lie to get out of IS-controlled Raqqa in mid-2016. Her daughter needed glasses, she told the jihadis. Her daughter's eyes are perfectly fine, but 'we were looking for something that couldn't be treated in Raqqa,' says al Mustafa.

When she left, there were no more opticians in Raqqa and no more schools. Just Quran lessons at the mosque. 'Brainwashing,' says al-Mustafa, so she homeschooled her children. They never went to school in Syria. The food in Raqqa was running out under the siege. Before the IS, a loaf of bread cost 30 Syrian liras; in the end it was more than 100. There was no shortage of public executions, though. 'I was able to keep my girls at home, but the boy had to watch them,' says al-Mustafa.

On 20 June 2016, the IS let her take her two daughters and son to Damascus. Here they have opticians – and an agency that issues passports. Al-Mustafa had to promise the IS to come back. When she saw her husband for the last time, they fixed an old mosque in a village outside the city as a meeting point. In a week, once she would have the passports. He planned to leave the town in secret.

'I worked for 23 years,' says al-Mustafa. When she left Raqqa in 2016, Turkey closed most of the border. The smugglers asked around $2,000 to get her and the three children out of Syria. 'All my savings and the jewelry I sold were just enough to pay this.' Her group had eleven people; they were shot at twice. Only ten of them reached Turkey on 3 July 2016, after four days and three nights. 'We didn't even have luggage left,' says al-Mustafa. When they arrived, in the sixth year of the war, Turkey's refugee camps were beyond crowded. Those who did not get in had to find their own shelter.

Whenever refugees from Raqqa arrive in Urfa, al-Mustafa asks them about her husband. She hopes the IS did not kill him. But there is hardly anyone left to ask; the IS executed smugglers. Al-Mustafa feels she will never see her husband again. In December, al Mustafa says, she was about to give up. Her strength had run out. 'I wanted to go back to Raqqa,' she says, 'at least there I have a house.'

A diplomatic insult

Sabha al-Mustafa's story shows how refugees live in Turkey. There were 3.64 million Syrians registered in Turkey in January 2019.[17] There are several hundred thousand more from Iran, Iraq, Afghanistan, Pakistan and Africa. No state in the world has taken in so many people. But their situation is dire.

Turkey has officially opened its labor market to the Syrians under pressure from the EU. In 2016 and 2017, the Ministry of Labour issued around 56,000 work permits to Syrians who found formal employment[18] – around 1.5 percent of Syrians living in the country. And not even one in ten Syrians (211,000)[19] has found shelter in one of the two dozen or so camps. Those who get in will be taken care of. The rest usually will not. Many face food insecurity,[20] only about two thirds of school-age children attended school in 2017.[21] The others usually go begging or work.

Aid organizations lack resources in all areas. For a long time, Europe did not feel responsible. This was also the main reason why so many Syrians came to Europe in 2015[22] – not because they felt 'invited' by Merkel. In October 2016, editors of the German weekly *Zeit* proved this by evaluating Google search queries.[23]

The crisis along the Balkan Route is what caused politicians to rethink. Europe paid Erdoğan to handle the refugees and got border security in return. Funds from Brussels have been flowing since late 2016. Erdoğan would prefer to see these funds on government accounts. After the attempted coup in July 2016, the lira lost almost half of its value against the euro.[24] Turkey's creditworthiness fell from 'stable' to 'negative,'[25] and by 2017, the foreign trade deficit stood at €77 billion.[26] The Turkish state needs foreign currency, but the Europeans are bypassing the government and decide where they spend their money. Turkey only has observer status in the council that decides about the allocation of funds from the Facility for Refugees in Turkey (FRT).

This is a diplomatic ploy to show Erdoğan he cannot get everything he wants. Hence, he repeatedly claimed the EU had not paid anything,[27] although this is not true. Under the deal with Erdoğan, the EU spent more money on emergency aid in Turkey in 2017/18 than in the rest of the world combined. A large part flowed into the ESSN. It is the largest program of its kind in the world. The key to it is an ordinary bank card issued by the state-owned Halkbank. The card bears the logo of the Red Crescent, which is implementing the project. In March 2017, Halkbank gave its ATMs an Arabic menu so that people like al-Mustafa could use it.

So far, only a few refugees have received 'conditional cash' cards for food or coal. Now the refugees are to receive cash payouts for two years. 1.6 million people received benefits in January 2019 – only about 44 percent of all Syrian refugees.[28] They are selected using computer questionnaires. An algorithm calculates their 'vulnerability.' The exact criteria are confidential. They payout is 120 Turkish liras per person, per month – about $22 – in a country where prices are only one third lower than in Germany.[29] However, there are special payouts, for example for clothing and heating costs or school supplies.

The EU's budget would probably have permitted a little more, but the Turkish government had objections. Jane Lewis, office manager of the EU Directorate-General for European Civil Protection and Humanitarian Aid Operations (DG-ECHO) in Turkey, said in February 2017 that more money for the Syrians could provoke protests from poor Turks feeling left behind. As it is, their payouts are not enough to live off of.

The card system clearly brings more independence for refugees. Unlike in other countries, they are not tied to distribution points at camps and can move freely within Turkey, since the card works at any ATM. They do not get bags of rice and flour, but they can decide what to buy and compare prices. The ESSN's administrative overhead is reportedly 15 percent of the budget – a historically low figure for such aid programs. The money is paid out and managed centrally. Were other donors to join, the aid payments could easily be increased.

However, the computer-aided system also works the other way around – to refuse benefits to refugees. The ESSN automatically compares data with Turkish government agencies. Should a refugee get a social security number after finding a job, all benefit payments stop immediately. Data from the Ministry of Education is also used: If schools report that children of a refugee family attend less than 80 percent of classes, any extra payments are cancelled automatically. The autonomy offered by the bank card comes at the price of a technological regime over which the benefactors have no influence. Text messages notify the refugees of any changes. Those feeling wronged by the vulnerability algorithm or the databases can call 168 free of charge, the Turkish Red Crescent's special Arabic hotline.

Almost two million Syrian refugees get nothing at all. This is the social reality of the EU-Turkey Deal.

In early February 2017, after receiving the text message on her smartphone, al-Mustafa picked up the red card at a Halkbank branch on Atatürk Street in downtown Urfa. Another message informed her the first payout would arrive towards the end of the month: 400 liras, around $75. What would she buy? 'Nothing,' says al-Mustafa, adding she would be glad to cover the rent.

Most don't speak Turkish

The ESSN is not enough. Syrian children are entitled to schooling, and Turkey would have to provide about 1.2 million additional places.[30] Syrians can be treated in state hospitals, so the Turkish health system has to cope with 3.6 million additional patients. Turkey's ministries of health and education receive more than €600 million from the EU for this – a smaller share of the European money also goes directly to the Turkish state.

One of the biggest problems is that most Syrian patients do not speak Turkish. Millions more therefore flow into the retraining of Syrian doctors. The World Health Organization (WHO) has counted around 1,000 of them among the refugees. Rules for foreign doctors seeking a license in Turkey are strict. The Syrians have a 'simplified procedure,'[31] says Mustafa Bahadır Sukacı of the WHO.

On a morning in February 2017, around 20 of these Syrian doctors are sitting in the ballroom of the Dedeman Hotel in Urfa. Weddings are usually celebrated here; today, a WHO lecturer stands in front of a screen. The organization has rented the hotel for a seminar. Doctors and nurses sit between golden columns at tables decked in white and listen to her talking about kidney stones, like a school class. The lecturer's laser pointer jumps back and forth between the words for 'bladder' and 'urethra.' Everyone in the room knows what kidney stones are, but they have to learn the Turkish terms. The training measure lasts six weeks. One of the participants is Majid al-Muhammad, a stocky pediatrician with a wool sweater and a crew cut. The 42-year-old Syrian left his hometown of Homs in 2012. Together with his family he has since been living in Kökenli, a container city for 16,000 people in the Harran district, right next to the Syrian border. He keeps in touch with Homs via Facebook. 'Language is the hardest thing to learn when you want to work as a doctor here,' says al-Muhammad. His training ends in February, after which he wants to work at the new health centers for his fellow Syrians. The government pays $750 to the Syrian doctors there. 'We will not forget Syria, but if we can, we will stay here,'[32] he says.

So the EU-Turkey deal helped people like Sabha al-Mustafa to survive and people like Majid al-Muhammad to find a job. But for millions more, the deal closed off their escape route from the war. Just when Turkey signed the pact with the EU, it began closing off the 566-mile-long border to Syria which al-Mustafa crossed. Construction was completed in March 2017. Today, the border is fortified.[33] The cost is estimated at €2 billion. The fortifications consist of fences and mobile concrete blocks weighing seven tons, topped off with NATO wire, ten feet high, over six feet wide, with radar and drone surveillance. Private security contractors guard the fence. In May 2016, the Turkish Ministry of National Defence announced that the Turkish armaments company Aselsan had won the contract to erect 'smart watchtowers that warn and fire automatically' to 'prevent illegal crossing.'[34] In other words, booby traps. There were no independent sources to confirm this until May 2017, since journalists are not allowed to enter the zone.

Human Rights Watch has documented that Turkish security forces have intercepted thousands of asylum seekers at the Turkish-Syrian border on several occasions since December 2017 and deported them to the war-ravaged Idlib Governorate.[35] Turkish border patrols have fired on asylum seekers trying to enter Turkey on smuggling routes and killed or injured them. Furthermore, HRW reports that Syrians who had arrived in the Turkish city of Antakya, 19 miles from the Syrian border, were deported to Idlib.

It was not the open borders

The deal also affected the refugees who went to Greece nevertheless. The EU likes to mention that after the deal, the number of deaths in the Aegean Sea and arrivals in Greece fell sharply. It is true that 1,082 people drowned in the Eastern Mediterranean in the seven months preceding the deal's starting date and 58 in the seven months thereafter.[36] The numbers of arrivals developed similarly: 154,000 people reached Greece in the first quarter of 2016, before the EU-Turkey deal. After that, the number dropped to around 10,000 per quarter. But most of this decline took place long before the agreement. In the last quarter of 2015 – with the deal not yet in sight – 483,000 refugees had arrived in Greece. Hence, the lion's share of the drop must have other causes than the bargain between Merkel, Rutte and Davutoğlu.

In fact, most of the refugees who wanted to leave Turkey had already done so by 2015. They did not come to Europe then because the borders were open – they were not – but because the aid system in Turkey collapsed. Aid organizations had only $0.50 per day for food rations. Those who stayed had reasons: a job, old age, illness, children, no money for smugglers, no contacts in Europe, needing to stay close to Syria. The Turkish army's crackdown on migrant smugglers after the EU-Turkey deal was one factor that reduced arrivals in Greece, but by no means the only one.

After the deal, from March 2016 throught at least the end of 2018, an average of about 30,000 people came to Greece by sea.[37] They are stuck under mostly miserable conditions on the Aegean islands. Greece denies most of them entry to the mainland, so they have to stay in overcrowded camps. The EU has set up registration centers called 'hotspots,' which are not accessible to the media. Amnesty International criticizes human rights violations there.[38] In March

2017, photos appear from inside the hotspot on the island of Chios. They show cages fit for animals.[39] After inmate protests in September 2016, a fire breaks out at the Moria internment camp on Lesbos. In April 2017, Kurdish Syrians go on hunger strike after being stuck there for eight months. Thousands spend the winters in tents, enduring snow and icy rain; some freeze to death.[40] 'They pay the price for Europe's cynicism and the disgraceful deal with Turkey,'[41] says Clement Perrin of Doctors Without Borders. The EU accuses Greece of producing these terrible images on purpose, for example, by not claiming over €100 million in disposable aid. Behind closed doors, people say that Greece still felt abandoned and wanted to build pressure.

In 2018 about 14,500 people waited on the Aegean islands, but the five hotspots only have room for 6,483. UNHCR members saw snakes and rats in Moria. 'Sewage and feces flow openly through the camp,' states their report.[42] Kumi Naidoo, General Secretary of Amnesty International, reported after a visit to Moria: 'What I witnessed was quite simply shocking.' He recalled the 'hardship and horror experienced on a daily basis by people who are already traumatized.' What particularly alarmed him was the fear of sexual harassment and violence expressed by many women in the camp.[43]

'To Europe by bus'

As is well known, Turkey's citizens never got visa-free entry into in the EU. Yet, despite the diplomatic alienation after the coup, despite all rhetorical extortion – Erdoğan threatened to send the refugees 'to Europe by bus,'[44] – Turkey honored its part of the deal. The police and the military cracked down on smugglers; migrant smuggling might be punishable as 'terrorism' in the future.[45] Frontex sent a liaison officer to Ankara; a law was drafted so Frontex can operate on Turkish territory. [46] Whether this will happen is still open, however.

In Dikili and other cities, closed deportation camps called 'pre-removal centers' were set up for deportees from Greece – with EU funding under the so-called Instrument for Pre-accession Assistance (IPA) for countries wishing to join the EU. Today there are 19 deportation camps with 6,810 places in Turkey. By the end of 2017, the internment centers are supposed to hold 17,130 inmates.[47]

However, the Greek asylum authority had doubts about Turkey being a 'safe third country' and thereby crossed the EU's plans. Nevertheless, 1,766 people were sent back to Turkey under the EU-Turkey Statement, including 337 Syrians.[48]

The deal also affects many people in Turkey who are not even refugees. The attempted coup of July 2016 accelerated the President's transformation of Turkey into a theocratic state. First, he waged war against the Kurds in the southeast of his own country, then from 2018, he engaged them in Northern Syria. Nobody knows how many people the Turkish army and its collaborating Islamist militias are killing. Kurdish organizations face severe repression. By the end of May 2017, the pro-Kurdish HDP (*Halkların Demokratik Partisi*) states, around 5,000 of its members, including 11 members of parliament, 218 local politicians and 750 municipal officials, were in prison, 18 of them facing life sentences.[49] After the July coup, over 150 journalists were arrested, 150 media outlets closed and more than 700 press passes revoked.[50] The West's criticism was half-hearted, unlike its supply of arms to Turkey.

This is the status quo of the EU-Turkey deal. Can it be copied in other countries, as European interior ministers would like to do? Or does it result from a unique mix of interests that cannot be reproduced?

The Merkel Plan

The general opinion is that the EU-Turkey deal is the brainchild of a small, private think tank – the European Stability Initiative (ESI). Its director, Austrian Gerald Knaus, is seen as the father of the agreement. Knaus posted a paper titled 'Why people don't need to drown in the Agean'[51] on the ESI website on 17 September 2015, just a few days after the opening of the Balkan route. It suggested that Germany should allow in 500,000 Syrian migrants directly from Turkey. In return, Greece should send all refugees coming across the Aegean back to Turkey. Then, Knaus imagined, no one would risk the dangerous crossing any more. It was the basic premise of the EU-Turkey deal. Two weeks later, Knaus published a revised version titled: 'The Merkel Plan – A proposal for the Syrian refugee crisis.'[52]

In the following months, Knaus became one of the prime political advisors to the EU, even though it was Turkish Prime Minister Davutoğlu who ultimately devised the details of the deal. One year later, in June 2017, Knaus is in high demand once more. For weeks, he commutes between European capitals, visits high-ranking member state and EU officials, even the campaign team of French presidential candidate Emmanuel Macron. He is hard to get hold of. 'I spent the whole last week in Italy,' he says. Or Brussels. Or Malta. Or Estonia. Knaus wants to use every chance to promote his idea. He published another paper proposing a solution to the EU's refugee problem. And Knaus is not surprised that the EU negotiated over a year in vain with the countries south of the Mediterranean.

His latest proposal is called the Rome Plan. It states what Knaus thinks the EU should do in order to replicate the Turkey deal with African states. 'Those politicians who want to translate the so-called Turkey Statement to other countries often have not understood its core meaning,' he says. Knaus sees two things at its center. On one hand, everyone who arrives must get an asylum procedure. 'A person may not be sent back until a decision has been made that they need no protection in the EU.' However, he adds, this would comply with the Refugee Convention only if it is possible to check what happens to the person after deportation. 'So it is clear that no one can be sent back to Libya.'

The EU, of course, sees things differently. And Greece, in turn, was not convinced that Turkey was 'safe' – and still was supposed to send refugees back there.

80 people a month, at most

Knaus' second principle is that it must be in the self-interest of the readmitting countries to take back those needing no protection in the EU. just like Turkey. 'In March 2016, Turkish politicians found it was in their own interest to stop the dying along the coast and on top receive six billion euros to support Syrian refugees in their country.' The money alone did not convince Davutoğlu's advisors, says Knaus. Another decisive factor was the expectation that declaring a cut-off date – 20 March 2016 – after which Turkey would take back people immediately, would 'dramatically' reduce the number of boats. Hence Turkey would actually have to take back fewer people than expected.

'Davutoğlu and his negotiators assumed that only a few people would be sent back in the end – in fact, from March 2016 until today, it has been fewer than 80 people a month. In return, no more corpses would wash up on the Turkish coast, and Turkey would cease to serve as a transit country for hundreds of thousands from Central Asia,' says Knaus in June 2017. However, the number increases from autumn onwards. 'This gives Ankara a vested interest in having the agreement stay in force. And that's what happened.'

For him, the deal's functional core is to deter migrants by making them risk being sent back to Turkey after crossing the Aegean. This reduced their incentive to step on a boat and also guaranteed that the number of readmissions to Turkey would stay manageable. Knaus sees the dramatic drop in crossings – less than 50 a day in the first half of 2017, the lowest number in years – as proof of his thesis. However, this number also rose again in autumn 2017.

He ignores other factors: the blockade of the Aegean Sea by the Turkish army and NATO, for example. Or that the number of crossings had started falling sharply earlier. And that, on average, 1,500 people still crossed the Aegean Sea every month, and there were only 80 deportations a month, only because the Greeks were unwilling to send anyone back to increasingly dictatorial Turkey.

Arrogance

Although the EU-Turkey Statement is a partnership with a transit country, Knaus is against repeating the deal with North African states. 'Libya is not Turkey. There are good reasons why sending people back to Turkey is difficult. With Libya, it's impossible. No Nigerian rescued from Libya can be sent back. And no other country in North Africa has an interest in taking back rejected asylum seekers from Europe. The idea of running reception centers and asylum procedures in Libya is also absurd. Right now, European countries don't even dare open embassies in Tripoli.' Therefore, he pleads against agreements with transit countries like Libya and Niger and for making deals with the major West African source countries.

They should have to immediately take back all their citizens who arrive in Europe after a fixed cut-off date and whose asylum claims are denied. 'This requires the realism to admit that most of those who came before the cut-off date can't be sent back,' says Knaus. This is difficult to concede for EU governments. 'But it's obvious that no EU country is in a position to send back thousands of citizens against the will of their source countries. As far as Africa is concerned, France sent back the most people to Algeria in 2016: exactly 1,105. Italy sent the most to Tunisia: 1,110. But last year, 38,000 people came to Italy from Nigeria alone, and only 165 went back. 'If you try to get Nigeria to suddenly take back 10,000 people, you won't get anything in the end. No source country will play along,' says Knaus.

For readmissions to work, the EU should 'offer something truly attractive' to countries of origin like Nigeria, especially options for safe and legal migration. The promise of 'mobility partnerships' appears in many EU declarations on Africa, but never materializes. Knaus imagines 'several thousand work visas and several thousand scholarships per year' for each partner country. Were Nigeria to take back all its rejected citizens after a cut-off date, Knaus believes this would 'save lives, take away the smugglers' business model and reduce the number of illegal arrivals.' It would give countries a vested interest in cooperating. Here he sees the precise failure of the EU's current diplomacy. 'We offer nothing concrete to the countries of origin, and hope that they'll cooperate anyway. That seems arrogant, as if you were trying to cheat them,' says Knaus. Instead, the EU relied almost exclusively on Libya, making itself dependent on a country in civil war without functioning institutions.

Notes

1. Alexander, R. (2017) *Die Getriebenen. Merkel und die Flüchtlingspolitik: Report aus dem Inneren der Macht*, Munich, 2017

2. Ibid.

3. EU Council (2016) *EU-Turkey statement*, 18 March | http://bit.ly/1VjZvOD

4. *General Court of the European Union (2017)* 'Press Release No. 19/17', 28 February | http://bit.ly/2E4ofIM

5. Alexander, R. (2017) *Die Getriebenen. Merkel und die Flüchtlingspolitik: Report aus dem Inneren der Macht*, Munich, 2017

6. *UNHCR* 'Resettlement' | http://bit.ly/2izX65W

7. *European Commission (2019)* 'European Agenda on Migration – Factsheets', 11 February | https://bit.ly/2p7dtd5

8. EU Council (2016) *EU-Turkey statement*, 18 March | http://bit.ly/1VjZvOD

9. *Die Welt* (2016) 'Vizekanzler Erdogan', 17 April | http://bit.ly/2uR0LjX

10. *Die Welt* (2016) 'Beim nächsten Flüchtlingsstrom bricht ein Konflikt aus', 6 September | http://bit.ly/2tXeFE5

11. *Die Welt* (2016) 'Europa hat seine Werte verschachert', 29 March | http://bit.ly/2uRovS9

12. *Die Zeit* (2016) 'EU lehnt weitere Verträge nach Vorbild des Türkei-Deals ab', 8 October | http://bit.ly/2dUwGM5

13. *Die Zeit* (2016) 'De Maizière will Türkei-Deal in Nordafrika kopieren', 5 April | http://bit.ly/1So2lc8

14. *Spiegel Online* (2016) 'Renzi schlägt Flüchtlingsdeal mit Afrika vor', 18 April | http://bit.ly/2vfGZB4

15. *Kurier* (2017) 'Kern lotet in Ägypten Flüchtlingsdeal aus', 24 May | http://bit.ly/2weKkxq

16. Personal interview with Sabha al Mustafa, Urfa, 16 March 2017

17. *UNHCR Operational Portal* (2019) 12 February | https://bit.ly/2Br8P1R

18. Cagaptay, S. and Yalkin, M. (2018) *Syrian Refugees in Turkey*, The Washington Institute, 22 August | https://bit.ly/2NusKhT

19. UNHCR Syria Regional Refugee Response | http://bit.ly/1z0szMq

20. Ibid.

21. World Food Programme (2016) *Off-Camp Syrian Refugees in Turkey. A Food Security Report*, April 2016 | http://bit.ly/23AXDn4

22. Asylum Information Database (AIDA) (2019) *Access to education*, 14 February 2019 | http://bit.ly/2X2sL1S

23. *Zeit* (2016) 'Merkel war es wirklich nicht', 11 October | http://bit.ly/2dTzszE

24. XE exchange rates| http://bit.ly/2f2Ahs7

25. *Trading Economics* 'Turkey. Credit Rating' | http://bit.ly/2tStTWL

26. *Statista* (2019) 'Türkei: Handelsbilanzsaldo von 2007 bis 2017', 14 February | https://bit.ly/2GIQzSw

27. *Bayrischer Rundfunk* (2016) 'Erdoğan: "EU hat ihr Wort gebrochen"', 25 July | http://bit.ly/2uP28So

28. *UNHCR Operational Portal* (2019) 'ESSN Task Force Turkey', 14 February | https://bit.ly/2TQcAm6

29. *Trading Economics* (2019) 'Turkey. Inflation', 14 February | http://bit.ly/2ue5s5u

30. Asylum Information Database (AIDA) (2019) *Access to education*, 14 February | http://bit.ly/2X2sL1S

31. Personal interview, Urfa, 15 February 2017

32. Asylum Information Database (AIDA) (2019) *Access to education*, 14 February | http://bit.ly/2X2sL1S

33. Migration Control Database, 'Turkey Country Report', *tageszeitung* | https://bit.ly/2G5bY8a

34. *Yeni Şafak* (2016) 'Turkey to establish smart towers on Syrian border', 5 April | https://bit.ly/2Gq5eCK

35. *Human Rights Watch* (2018) 'Turkey: Mass Deportations of Syrians', 22 March | https://bit.ly/2IFZjr8

36. *International Organization for Migration* 'Missing Migrants Project' | http://bit.ly/2fQfnJ1

37. *UNHCR* (2019) 'Sea arrivals by day', 14 February | https://bit.ly/2roctD6

38. *Amnesty International* (2016) 'Hotspot Italy – How EU's flagship approach leads to violations of refugee and migrants rights', October 2016 | http://bit.ly/2eCgnTE

39. *Vice Denmark* (2017) 'Er det her seriøst et bur fyldt med flygtninge?', 22 March | http://bit.ly/2f28yYu

40. *SWR Aktuell* (2017) 'Flüchtling in Griechenland erfroren', 16 January | http://bit.ly/2vZBWT4

41. 'Doctors Without Borders: "Von Europa ausgeschlossen"', Press release, 9 January 2017 | http://bit.ly/2hiky8L

42. Höhler, Gerd (2019) 'Flüchtlinge in der Hölle von Moria', 2 January | https://bit.ly/2SDpAPt

43. 'Open Letter Following Visit of Kumi Naidoo, Secretary General of Amnesty International to Lesvos Island and Moria Refugee Camp,' Amnesty International, 22 November 2018 | http://bit.ly/2Ewvo56

44. *Der Westen* (2016) 'Präsident Erdoğan droht Europa mit einer Flüchtlingswelle', 25 November | http://bit.ly/2vclAc4

45. *Süddeutsche Zeitung* (2016) 'Türkei will Schlepper als Terroristen verfolgen', 2 February | http://bit.ly/1PRW9BS

46. Migration Control Database, 'Turkey Country Report', *tageszeitung* | https://bit.ly/2G5bY8a

47. Ibid.

48. *EU Commission* (2017) 'Operational implementation of the EU-Turkey Statement', 26 May | http://bit.ly/2jjPFQr

49. Ibid.

50. Demir, Hayri (2017) 'Zeit, sich für den Frieden einzusetzen', *tageszeitung*, 22 May 2017 | http://bit.ly/2vcwFdm

51. *Reporter ohne Grenzen* 'Türkei' | http://bit.ly/1A5T8Cf

52. *European Stability Initiative* (2015) 'The Merkel Plan – A proposal for the Syrian refugee crisis', 4 October | http://bit.ly/1Wl4rnD

Israel's dealings:
Human commodities

In Uganda's capital Kampala, there is a sign in Eritrean script pointing towards an alley: A small hotel with few rooms, mostly empty. In room number 8, an old man sits on a worn-out couch. His pants and shirt are stained, and he wears flip-flops. Deep scars run across his arms. His fingers fidget with his sleeve. He wants to stay anonymous; his lawyer would prefer the same for security reasons. "He has been through a lot," says the lawyer about his client and speaks with him in Tigrinya, one of their home country Eritrea's main languages.[1]

The lawyer has been living in Ugandan exile for many years. In Kampala, he specializes in asylum procedures for his compatriots. Offering one of the world's most liberal immigration policies, Uganda has welcomed refugees from Congo, Burundi, South Sudan or Eritrea for decades. They used to come voluntarily, but for three years the lawyer has been hearing incredible stories about deportations from Israel. Many of his clients can really show documents in Hebrew and identity cards issued by Israel's Prison Service. Most, like the old man, even speak Hebrew.

The lawyer translates his story. Once a high-ranking officer in Eritrea's military, he was forced to flee in 2008 after refusing an order by President Afewerki. He reports that the dangerous journey saw him taken to the Sinai Peninsula via Sudan by smugglers, where he was taken captive by criminals for three months, until his family transferred $25,000. Otherwise, they would have cut out his kidney. This happens to many captives, he reports. After receiving the ransom, the kidnappers let him go near the Israeli border.

The migration route from Africa via Sinai to the Middle East is one of the world's oldest. It was taken by the Africans who left their continent around 55,000 years ago to settle in Europe and Asia.[2] The route was notorious for its slave trade during the Colonial Era. Until a few years ago, most migrants heading for Europe came across the Egyptian peninsula, with horrible outcomes. The flow ebbed in 2010 and 2011, when more and more Eritreans reported being kidnapped and tortured. Some fell victim to organ traders and lost a kidney, because their families did not wire the ransom money.[3]

At the same time, in November 2010, Israel began building a fortified fence along the border with Egypt. Today, it is seen as a model for an effective barrier against terrorists and migrants, especially by the USA. The US Department of Homeland Security reports that the number of illegal border crossings from Egypt to Israel was 16,000 in 2011 – five years after completion of the fence, it fell to 20.[4] So the border is practically impenetrable.

Back in 2008, the old Eritrean is lucky. When he is set free, there is no barrier yet. There are heavily armed special forces though, who detain him and later set him free. He spends six years in Tel Aviv, learns Hebrew and cleans houses to stay above water. Every three months, he stands in line at the Population Immigration and Borders Authority to extend his visa for another three months. Then in 2014 the government decides to clear the streets of refugees. This was when his life changed, says the old man in Kampala.[5]

Refugees: 'infiltrators' and 'a cancer'

Almost 2,200 miles north of Uganda stands the Holot migrant detention center in the flickering heat of the Negev, just south of the desert town of Be'er Sheva. At the entrance, armed guards check the ID cards of the Prison Service, which runs the facility. The people locked up here are those who might one day seek the lawyer's service in Kampala. Most are Eritreans, some from Sudan or even from Côte d'Ivoire. High fences with barbed wire, watchtowers and guards with heavy machine guns – Holot looks like a jail for dangerous criminals. Yet this is still the soft version, since inmates can move freely during the day and even leave the premises. Once a day, they all have to stand still for roll call.

Next to Holot towers the Saharonim supermax prison. It was built in 2007 in the military zone along the Egyptian border as a prison for so-called infiltrators. After amendments to the Prevention of Infiltration Law in 2012 and 2013, this includes all 'infiltrators' living in the country illegally,[6] which includes refugees who cross the border illegally like the old Eritrean.

Israel's Ministry of Interior counts around 45,000 refugees staying in Israel.[7] Most are Eritreans. In Israel, their legal situation is especially tricky. Although Israel recognizes that Eritrea is run by a criminal regime, which prevents Eritreans from being deported, it does not grant them full asylum, merely status as a 'temporary protection group' without full legal rights. They get only a limited visa which they must renew every three months.[8]

The Knesset has tightened Israel's laws against 'infiltration' several times in recent years. The 2012 amendment provided for the arrest of all 'infiltrators' for up to three years without trial. Saharonim Prison was built because regular jails were overcrowded. The law states that refugees would have the opportunity to demand asylum from prison. A group of Israeli human rights organizations went to court against the amendment – with initial success: In September 2013, Israel's Supreme Court rejected the amendment, calling the prison terms 'disproportionate'. But the government immediately submitted a new draft, which only mentioned 'open' detention for refugees until the situation in their home country changed or they were willing to return voluntarily.[9]

This is the reason why the Holot open detention center was built. But the NGOs sued again and won. In September 2014, the Supreme Court declared the law unconstitutional for its 'disproportionate' violation of refugees' basic rights. The judgment ordered Holot to be closed within 90 days, but again the government submitted a softer draft. This draft limited detention at Holot to 20 months, which was reduced to 12 months after the NGOs sued once more.[10]

Since the 2013 amendment, the Ministry of Interior 'invites' asylum seekers to Holot. From now on, they can only submit asylum claims from Holot, and are no longer allowed to work while waiting for their decision. If their claim is rejected, they have one choice: leave the country voluntarily or get sent next door – to Saharonim, for an unlimited time.[11] Israel is doing pretty much all it can to make life miserable for refugees and get rid of them as fast as possible.

Israeli politicians also have extreme words for the refugees. The current Minister of Culture, Miri Regev, called African migrants 'a cancer', while former Minister of Interior Eli Yishai promised to make sure every last one of them would leave the country.[12]

State-sponsored human trafficking

When the old Eritrean's temporary visa runs out in July 2014, he is still subject to the tighter law from 2013. 'At the office, the authorities took my papers and locked me up in Holot,' recalls the old man in Kampala. Here they gave him a paper in Hebrew to sign – to confirm his 'voluntary' return. 'We had no real choice,' he says. After 18 days in Holot, uniformed security contractors and two plainclothes officers drive him and five other Eritreans to Tel Aviv's airport. He found the procedure very strange – they passed through no official entrances or security checks and his passport did not get an exit stamp. Instead, he received $3,500 in cash, for which he had to sign a receipt. Nobody told him where the plane would go.

According to a 2015 report by the International Refugees Rights Initiative (IRRI), 1,500 Africans left Israel under 'massive pressure' from early 2014 to September 2015.[13] The IRRI estimates that this figure could have increased to 3,000 by May 2017.[14] The Africans land in so-called safe third countries – which Israel refuses to identify. In a statement by the Israeli government, the Prime Minister explains that naming these states which admit the 'infiltrators' [sic!] would harm Israel's relations with these countries.[15]

However, there is increasing evidence for the deportation destinations. Two Eritrean refugees went to court alongside Israeli NGOs to dispute the secret agreements. Their petition was denied in November 2015, but the judgment mentions the states 'R' and 'U'[16] – which likely refers to Rwanda and Uganda.

'It was a small airplane,' remembers the old man. He did not know which national flag was on it; he assumes it was a diplomat's plane. The long flight followed the Nile into Africa. He recalls African and Israeli diplomats sitting beside him, wearing passports around their necks. 'It wasn't until I saw the airport building that I knew: now we're in Rwanda.' He remembers being gripped by fear: 'I thought Eritrean spies were already waiting for me.' From his military service he knows the two states have close ties.

On the runway, the officials entered limousines with blue beacons. 'The other deportees and I were led away by Rwandan agents.' Again, no security check, no passport control – instead they took away his Eritrean passport and Hebrew papers. He got to keep only the ID card of the Israeli Prison Service. He and the other five Eritreans were driven to a house, a two-story, multi-bedroom mansion behind a high wall. He doesn't know details. 'The guy who placed us in the house said his name was John.'

Other deported Eritreans tell the same story. They all describe the same house in Kigali, the same 'John,' the same procedure. John explained that Israel's government paid the room for three nights. On the second day, John showed up again and said a car would be waiting in the morning to take them to Uganda. The old man had to pay John $250 for the transfer.

The car dropped off the refugees high up in the mountains, a short distance from the checkpoint. They crossed the border illegally on foot – their passports were gone anyway. A hired shepherd boy guided them along a rough trail, reports the old man. On the Ugandan side, a minibus was waiting on a field path and drove them to Kampala for another $250. Halfway along the route, they switched to an off-road vehicle driven by an Eritrean. This time the refugees had to pay $400. Their countryman brought them to this back-alley hotel in Kampala.

The old man's story matches the ones told by many other interviewed Eritrean deportees.[17] Some were brought to Rwanda by official carriers like Turkish Airlines, but all of them arrived in the same house in Kigali, met the same 'John' and had to hand over their passports.

While in principle, it is not illegal to move refugees back and forth internationally, the UN refugee agency UNHCR has set up guidelines for transfers to third countries. 'It is the duty of the state handing them over to make sure that they will not be subjected to any risk in their destination country,' says Andie Lambe of the IRRI in Kampala. 'But all their documents and passports are taken away upon arrival in Uganda or Rwanda. They receive no legal status of any sort, because they are coming to Uganda from a safe third country like Israel, so their legal situation is precarious.' The Eritrean lawyer confirms this – none of his clients received asylum in Uganda.

Uganda can refuse to grant them asylum, because they come from a safe country. They have broken the law by crossing the border without valid papers. Uganda can jail and try them as criminals. According to the Geneva Refugee Convention, the State of Israel is responsible. It must guarantee that the safety and rights of refugees are ensured in the destination countries. Uganda in turn has the right to deport them back to Israel, if their asylum claims are rejected. 'This is a vicious cycle,' says Lambe of the IRRI. Many have no choice but to leave Uganda again – illegally, with the help of smugglers. 'Most of the deportees we interviewed end up trying to use the remaining money to get to Europe and escape their lawless situation,' Lambe says. Hence, Israel is indirectly funding the trafficking business: 'The money they get from Israel makes them vulnerable to exploitation, because the agents know about it by now.'

Despite repeated requests, a response from Israel's Ministry of Interior was not obtainable.[18] However, Minister of Interior Gilad Erdan confirmed the practice in an interview with Israel News in March 2015: 'We give them a package that includes a flight and $3,500 – no small sum in these countries.'[19] Uganda's State Minister for Foreign Affairs, Henry Okello Oryem, speaking to the local Daily Monitor in April 2016 stated that there was no formal arrangement 'whatsoever' between Uganda and Israel.[20] Yet, more than 150 deported Eritreans seized without passports were imprisoned in Uganda in 2016, confirmed a Ugandan lawyer working for the immigration office. Uganda's State Minister for Relief and Disaster Preparedness, Musa Ecweru, clarified in an interview that his government would investigate the cases: 'Refugees should never be the subjects of bilateral government agreements,' he warned, 'This would make a mockery of all international conventions.'[21]

'Israel has looked around for ways to get rid of the refugees,' Rwanda's Foreign Minister Louise Mushikiwabo said in an interview with the German *tageszeitung* in January 2016.[22] 'This has been debated in our bilateral relations with Israel.' Yet she remained vague on whether the agreement was finally sealed and under which conditions. She recalls long discussions with her immigration office: 'I'm not sure where we stand right now.' Discussion topics she mentions include the freedom to travel within the East African Community (EAC), and also between Rwanda and Uganda. 'How can we ensure that people will stay? It's easy to travel back and forth in East Africa.'

Although more and more cases are coming to light and the evidence at the court in Tel Aviv is overwhelming, no country wants to take responsibility for the fate of the deportees. Deportations to Rwanda and Uganda continue, albeit to a lesser extent. In early 2018, Israel's immigration service in Holot began issuing deportation notices to young Sudanese and Eritrean males. These clearly state that the recipient must voluntarily leave the country within 60 days – either to Rwanda or to his home country.[23] In early 2019, Israel's Attorney General instructed the immigration service to examine whether fleeing Eritrea's national service was really legitimate grounds for asylum. If the service revises this previous regulation, Israel can directly reject and deport about 25,000 Eritrean asylum seekers – even to their home country if necessary.[24]

Those deported to Rwanda and Uganda, like the old Eritrean, are stranded in Kampala. Some are lucky, because the lawyer helps them finally get a residence permit, but it remains limited to three months, similar to the procedure in Israel. The lawyer's conclusion: 'It is tragic that we Eritreans are now treated like commodities and no longer like people.'

Deportations in full swing

Renowned regional newspaper *The East African* speaks of a multi-million-dollar deal between Rwanda, Uganda and Israel, in which all sides make a profit.[25] Israel repays the generous readmission of deportees by offering its services as a partner in the fight against terrorism.

More than 50 Israeli business people joined Avigdor Lieberman on his trip to Rwanda's capital Kigali in June 2014, only a few weeks before the first deportations started. Israel's foreign minister signed a deal for a closer partnership between the two states.[26] Rwanda announced it would open an embassy in Tel Aviv. In March 2015, Colonel Joseph Rutabana, previously secretary of state at Rwanda's Ministry of Defence and responsible for the procurement of new weapons technologies, was sent as a diplomat. According to information from military personnel in both armies, Rwanda and Uganda have since been able to train their special forces with drones and high-resolution cameras from Israel. At the time, deportations of asylum seekers were already in full swing. The same plane that brought trainees of the security forces to Tel Aviv took refugees back to Africa.

In November 2014, two Israelis were arrested at Uganda's Entebbe International Airport in connection with arms shipments for Uganda's special forces. President Yoweri Museveni personally campaigned for their release. Investigations by local journalists uncovered that agents of the Israeli arms exporter association Israel Weapon Industries (IWI) are active in Uganda. They usually run private security companies, as did the two arrested Israelis.[27] A UN expert report published in August 2016 on the war in South Sudan, which is being waged with the help of Uganda's special forces, also mentions arms deliveries from Israel.[28] In May 2015, Israel's Ministry of Defense declared that arms exports to Africa had increased by 40 percent in 2014. More and more African delegations were seen at the weapons industry trade shows in Tel Aviv. Even back in 2011, the Stockholm International Peace Research Institute (SIPRI) ranked Rwanda and Uganda among the 'top ten' state recipients of Israeli defense and security technology in Africa.[29]

To seal this new partnership, Benjamin Netanyahu became the first Israeli Prime Minister in 30 years to travel to East Africa in July 2016. In Kenya, he assured his support for building a fence along the border to neighboring Somalia to ward off terrorists and refugees. In Uganda, he was received by President Museveni on the tarmac of the international airport in the small town of Entebbe. Netanyahu was deeply moved: On this runway on the shore of Lake Victoria, his brother had been killed 40 years earlier as Israeli special forces stormed an Air France plane in which Palestinian terrorists were holding Israeli passengers hostage. Netanyahu's visit was to usher in a new era of friendship. He then visited the genocide memorial in Rwanda's capital Kigali. At the mass grave of the Tutsi murdered in 1994, he laid down a wreath – a symbolic gesture between two countries whose populations had suffered genocide. The last official act was the signing of a partnership agreement on business, agriculture as well as security and defense.[30]

When Ugandan journalists in an interview asked Netanyahu about the deported refugees, he did not deny the deportations, but said that the people coming to Israel in large numbers were migrants seeking work – healthy young men, mostly in their early twenties – and not refugees.[31]

Notes

1. This quote and following ones from interviews with Eritrean deportees from Israel and their lawyer, Kampala, 24 June 2015

2. *Daily Mail* (2015) 'The Egyptian in all of us: First modern humans spread out of Africa into Europe and Asia from the Sinai Peninsula', 28 May 2015 | http://dailym.ai/2uR346v

3. Van Reisen, M., Estefanos, M. and Rijken, C. (2012) 'Human Trafficking in the Sinai: Refugees between Life and Death', Brussels, October 2012 | http://bit.ly/2vbE9x9

4. 'Chairman Johnson Releases Report on Israeli Homeland Security and Applicable Lessons for the United States', Press release by Dept. of Homeland Security, Washington, D.C., 1 February 2017 | http://bit.ly/2kqKbVn

5. *Human Rights Watch* (2014) 'Make Their Lives Miserable – Israel's Coercion of Eritrean and Sudanese Asylum Seekers to Leave Israel', September 2014 | http://bit.ly/2tRIamr

6. *Ibid.*

7. Overview by Israeli Ministry of Interior about the number of infiltrators as of 2016 | http://bit.ly/2uR9Joy

8. *Human Rights Watch* (2014) 'Make Their Lives Miserable – Israel's Coercion of Eritrean and Sudanese Asylum Seekers to Leave Israel', September 2014 | http://bit.ly/2tRIamr

9. Background report about the development of the Israeli Prevention of Infiltration Law from 2012 to 2016 on the website of Israeli refugee

organization 'Hotline' | http://bit.ly/2vmhgrs Judgement in English | http://bit.ly/2vm4cT2

10. Ibid.

11. *Human Rights Watch* (2014) 'Make Their Lives Miserable – Israel's Coercion of Eritrean and Sudanese Asylum Seekers to Leave Israel', September 2014 | http://bit.ly/2tRIamr

12. *tageszeitung* (2016) Quotes from Knaul, Susanne and Schlindwein, Simone: 'Die Währung Mensch', 26 January | https://bit.ly/2tgYvCP

13. *IRRI* report (2015) 'I was left with nothing: "Voluntary" departures of asylum seekers from Israel to Rwanda and Uganda', September 2015 | http://bit.ly/2ucZEZZ

14. Background talk with Andie Lambe of IRRI, Kampala, 24 May 2017

15. Answer of the Office of the Prime Minister of Israel to an inquiry from the Supreme Court, Jerusalem, 30 March 2014

16. Bob, Yonah Jeremy (2015) 'Court upholds policy of "voluntary" departure or jail for illegal migrants', *Jerusalem Post*, 10 November | http://bit.ly/2weGLHk

17. Interviews led by IRRI in 2014 and 2015, Kampala, June 2015

18. Quotes from Knaul, Susanne and Schlindwein, Simone (2016) 'Die Währung Mensch', *tageszeitung*, 26 January | http://bit.ly/2wDyeX

19. *Israel News* (2015) 'Israel and Rwanda confirm "multimillion dollar" cash-for-refugees deal', 4 March | https://bit.ly/2RfDulw

20. *Daily Monitor* (2016) 'Government protests dumping of immigrants into country', 3 May | http://bit.ly/2f2844y

21. Interview with refugee minister Musa Ecweru, Kampala, 1 June 2017

22. These and other quotes from interview led by *tageszeitung* editor Dominic Johnson with Rwanda's Minister of Foreign Affairs, Louise Mushikiwabo, Berlin, 29 October 2015

23. *Haaretz* (2018) 'Israel Starts Issuing Deportation Notices to African Asylum Seekers', 4 February | http://bit.ly/2s6DU6g

24. *Haaretz* (2019) 'Israel Examines Whether Desertion From Eritrean Army Is Grounds for Asylum', 2 January | http://bit.ly/2F9q5sR

25. *The East African* (2015) 'President Paul Kagame confirms Rwanda-Israel deal to host African immigrants', 2 April | http://bit.ly/2uOn2AD

26. Karuhanga, James and Musoni, Edwin (2014) 'Rwanda, Israel sign deal for stronger ties', *The New Times*, 11 June | http://bit.ly/2vg1bCI

27. Matsiko, Haggai (2015) 'Museveni intervenes in Israeli arms dealer case.' *The Independent*, 15 February | http://bit.ly/2uU2IzB

28. Oduha, Joseph (2016) 'Israeli arms fuelling South Sudan conflict-Report', *The East African*, 24 October | http://bit.ly/2vYxfsR

29. Wezeman, Siemon T. (2011) 'Israeli arms transfers to Subsahara Africa', *SIPRI Background Paper*, October 2011 | http://bit.ly/2hhcCEN

30. *The New Times* (2016) 'Israel Premier makes historic visit to Rwanda, pledges stronger ties', 7 July | http://bit.ly/2ucJfVr

31. *The East African* (2016) 'Q & A with Israeli PM Benjamin Netanyahu', *The East African*, 6 July | http://bit.ly/2uOzmkp

Deportation dominoes

The example of Israel shows how states can get rid of refugees whom they cannot send back to their countries of origin. Israel does this by offering poor African countries expensive training and security technologies almost free of charge. Refugees become the currency of payment.

The EU also offers 'deportation for training' deals to its African partners. Country-specific packages and numerous framework agreements on border security propagate this barter trade. Just as Israel offers its African partners training assistance to sell its border security and surveillance technology, the EU also bribes third countries to get rid of its migrants. In return, it trains African border patrol units and security authorities. The equipment is just a bonus.

The EU-Turkey deal has put Turkey under pressure to push for more bilateral readmission agreements with other countries to deport more of its own refugees.[1] Outside of Europe, Turkey already has readmission agreements with Syria (2001), Kyrgyzstan (2003), Pakistan (2010), Russia (2011), Nigeria (2011) and Yemen (2011). The 1951 Geneva Refugee Convention does not permit Turkey to repatriate Syrians due to the civil war. Nevertheless, Turkey has already sent Syrians back home while calling it 'voluntary return'.[2] Israel's example has shown how to make people 'volunteer'.

A spokesman for the Ministry of Foreign Affairs in Ankara said in March 2016 that Turkey wanted to return refugees to their home countries faster by closing treaties with 14 other states. He does not name these countries.[3] 'It should stand undisputed that these are crisis countries and by no means safe countries of origin, where the situation has forced people to flee,' criticizes the NGO Pro Asyl in its legal report on the Turkey Deal in March 2016.[4]

Similar to Israel, Turkey also offers its partnership to African governments, mostly for infrastructure projects, but also in the military and refugee aid sectors. In recent years, Turkey has opened almost 40 embassies in Africa; only France has more on the continent. Turkey, which still receives financial aid from the EU, is now the fourth-largest donor in Africa.[5] The recently expanded route network of semi-public Turkish Airlines offers low-cost flights between Europe and Asia and almost all the capitals of Africa via Istanbul, including war zones.

Since the end of 2016, the seat pockets of Turkish Airlines planes feature a magazine in which the government and the airline boast about helping Somali refugees rebuild their destroyed country and return home. Turkey was already involved in the Dadaab refugee camp in Kenya, where Somalis found shelter for 20 years, and even built a mosque. Out of gratitude, the refugees named the district around the prayer house 'Istanbul'. When Kenya's and Somalia's heads of state decided at the UN Refugee Summit in Istanbul in May 2016 to close Dadaab, then the world's largest refugee camp, and to send the Somalis home, Turkey again offered to help. Since 2012, Turkish Airlines has been the only international airline to serve Somalia's capital Mogadishu – a risky move, since landing airplanes regularly serve as shooting targets.

In March 2017, Turkish Airlines launched a social media campaign, which spread the word that their flights were not booked out, so they were now transporting relief supplies for returnees to Mogadishu. Celebrities around the world sent donations for the humanitarian transports. Over €2 million were collected.[6]

Hence the refugee crisis allowed Turkish Airlines to win new customer segments, also in Israel: Some of the deported Eritreans claim that the carrier took them via Istanbul to Rwanda. By connecting African capitals such as Mogadishu to international flight routes, Turkish Airlines is laying the groundwork for deportations from Europe.[7]

Like Israel, Turkey is also rapidly expanding its involvement in Africa, both economic and military. Turkey is the largest foreign investor in Somalia. Not even a year after offering aid to Somalia, in April 2017, Turkey stations troops on a 1.5mi2 high-security base near the airport of Mogadishu. Here, Turkish officers train Somali soldiers in counter-terrorism tactics and provide equipment to the coast guard. The up-and-coming Turkish defense corporation Aselsan is also active in Somalia. Another Turkish company, Favori, secured the contract for managing the airport for the next 20 years, including security services.[8]

Numerous African generals were invited to the International Defence Industry Fair (IDEF) in Istanbul in May 2017. After the gun show, the Turkish Minister of Defence signed an agreement for a close military partnership with his Sudanese colleague Abdel Rahim Mohammed Hussein.[9] Less than six weeks later, President Erdoğan flew to Khartoum to sign an economic partnership agreement.[10] As in Israel, the deportation wave makes it likely that Turkey will use refugees and migrants as pawns in the negotiations with its new African partners. By showing how to do it, Israel has set off a domino effect.

Egypt on the tipping point

Since the Sinai route to Israel was closed and militias in Libya are detaining more people, refugees from Sudan now head for the Mediterranean via Egypt, states the 2017 Africa-Frontex-Intelligence Community Joint Report.[11] In September 2016 a smuggling vessel with over 600 people, mostly Africans, capsized off the coastal city of Alexandria – over 100 drowned. Nearly 10 percent of the African migrants arriving in Italy by boat are now passing through Egypt, according to a message from Italy's Ministry of the Interior to the German government in late 2016.[12]

The EU is trying to close this door, too. 'Agreements similar to those we now have with Turkey must be negotiated with Egypt, first of all, but also with other African states,' Chancellor Merkel said in Vienna in September 2016.[13] However, Merkel's statements raised concerns that African countries will expect the same generosity from Europe that Turkey is receiving. 'Then Merkel will have to see how she gets the Bundestag to approve these funds,' an EU diplomat told the German Spiegel.[14]

In November 2016, Germany's Foreign Office stated that deportations to Egypt violated German asylum law and that Berlin was 'concerned' about the human rights situation. There were 'credible reports of torture and abuse in police custody' The general conditions in Egyptian prisons were alarming, 'which is likely to affect detained migrants in the same way as other detainees.'[15]

The Egyptian government seems to be consistently violating the Geneva Convention on Refugees, which it has ratified. Although the right to asylum is guaranteed in the constitution, Egypt does not carry out any kind of asylum recognition procedure.[16] On the contrary: Egypt's Anti-Terrorism Law defines a 'terrorist act' as 'any use of force, violence, threat, or intimidation domestically or abroad for the purpose of disturbing public order, or endangering the safety, interests, or security of the community.'[17] This can mean not just opposition members, journalists or soccer fans, but also migrants and refugees. In March 2016, hundreds of Ethiopians of the Oromo ethnic group gathered outside the UNHCR office in Cairo to protest the long waiting times and the drop in recognition rates for Ethiopian applicants. The revolt culminated in the self-immolation of two women, who succumbed to their injuries in July 2016.[18]

Even though a deal between the EU and Egypt is not yet ready to be signed, most provisions were already part of the 2004 Euro-Mediterranean Association Agreements between the EU and seven Mediterranean countries. Working together to curb and control illegal migration was already part of the package, as was the mutual readmission of deported citizens. Egyptians are rarely granted asylum in the EU. Italy pioneered a bilateral agreement in 2007 and is very satisfied with it, according to a report by the European Migration Network (EMN).[19] When Chancellor Merkel met her colleague al-Sisi in Cairo in March 2017, they discussed the deportation of around 1,000 Egyptians from Germany.[20]

This tips over the next piece in the domino chain: While Egypt readily takes back its expelled nationals, the authorities in Cairo are in turn busy deporting African migrants back to their countries. Egyptian prisons are full of migrants detained by immigration authorities on their way to Europe.[21] By 31 August 2016, Egypt had deported 1,100 people not registered with the UNHCR, most of them to Sudan.[22] Sudan also repatriated refugees to Eritrea and Ethiopia in 2017.[23]

As in the Israel-Rwanda-Uganda deal, Egypt receives training and equipment from Europe for its security services to close the borders. Bilateral agreements are already in place: Great Britain and France extend military assistance, Germany and Italy support the police. Italian truck maker Iveco supplied the Egyptian police with armored personnel carriers. Egypt also receives ammunition and firearms. Back in 2007, when Italy and Egypt signed their own deportation agreement, Italy handed over two patrol boats to the Egyptian coast guard.

After al-Sisi's June 2015 visit to the Chancellor in Berlin, Germany also started supporting Egypt's anti-migration efforts. 'Considering the current migration situation, the Federal Police intends to intensify cooperation with Egyptian (border) police authorities by offering training and equipment for border protection,' stated the German government in May 2016, emphasizing that Egypt's police would get extra lessons on the principles of democracy, rule of law and human rights.[24]

During a visit to Cairo in April 2016, Federal Minister for Economic Affairs Sigmar Gabriel (Social Democrats) not only talked about the planned sale of two submarines, but also offered help for sealing off the Libyan-Egyptian border and for monitoring the Sinai Peninsula. Two months later, Federal Interior Minister de Maizière and his Egyptian colleague Magdy Abdel Ghaffar signed a memorandum outlining a security agreement on organized crime, terrorism and emergency management.[25] A corresponding draft was proposed to the German parliament in March 2017.[26] Gabriel had generously announced on a trip to Cairo in April 2016 that Germany was 'prepared to help' the country control its border with Libya.[27] A few weeks later, the German government confirmed that nothing stood in the way of providing 'equipment aid' to the Egyptian border authorities.[28]

The German Federal Police (*Bundespolizei*) has since trained Egyptian colleagues on border protection, document security as well as aviation and airport security. The Federal Criminal Police Office (BKΛ) sent a liaison officer to Cairo and trained an employee of the Egyptian National Security Service (NSS) in Wiesbaden.[29] Andrej Hunko, member of parliament for the Left Party, describes it as 'aiding and abetting repression.' After all, the NSS is accused of systematic torture.[30]

Egypt is regarded as Africa's largest military power. The military academy near Alexandria has long been a favorite destination for training Africa's senior officers. Egyptian soldiers are present in several war zones on the continent. Like Turkey, the Sahara state aims not just to stall the ambitions of Saudi Arabia or the United Arab Emirates, but also to enforce its interests in water disputes with southern neighboring states along the Nile. Hence, Egypt is also involved in South Sudan's civil war. In April 2017, Egyptian opposition members published information in the alternative media that the military would soon be building a base in Eritrea.[31] Egypt also just launched a close military cooperation with Kenya; the continent's two major military powers want to establish an African arms industry.[32]

Next piece: Sudan

Egypt is not the only country that continues to deport refugees to Sudan. Jordan has also flown hundreds of Sudanese refugees, most from the Darfur region, back to Khartoum since early 2017.[33] Even from Europe people are deported to Khartoum – from the refugee encampment in Calais, France, known as 'the Jungle.' Rome closed an agreement with Sudan's Ministry of Interior in August 2016. Italy was to fund a training course for Sudanese border troops; in return it deported 48 rejected asylum seekers. So the EU is starting to follow Israel's example.

Like yet another domino piece, Sudan began to systematically deport Eritreans to their neighboring home country in May 2016.

Gerry Simpson of Human Rights Watch (HRW) spoke of at least 442 people: 'Sudan has arrested the Eritreans and handed them over to a repressive government using force.'[34] The Eritreans had been caught by Sudan's border guards, imprisoned and charged with crossing the border illegally. Refugees must stay inside the camps and are only registered there by the authorities and the UNHCR. Those who enter illegally and are caught outside of the camps face up to two years' imprisonment.[35] The prisons and camps in Sudan are full of migrants and refugees, and the prison conditions are inhumane. General Awad al-Neel Dahiya, responsible for migration affairs at Sudan's Ministry of Interior, confirmed the systematic arrest of migrants and refugees along Sudan's borders in a January 2018 interview: 'If they are refugees, we bring them back to the camps,' said Dahiya, "If they are irregular migrants, they are issued travel documents in cooperation with their embassies and then we take them back to their home country.'[36]

The current UNHCR press spokesman Stefan Telöken had already warned in 1993: 'There is now a latent danger of a deportation chain – in breach of international law – at the end of which refugees will find themselves dumped back into the country from which they fled.' He further noted that the concept of safe third countries served primarily as a justification for denying asylum claims.[37] Considering the EU-Turkey Deal, this danger is as topical as ever.

Notes

1. Implementation of EU-Turkey readmission agreement, 8 May 2016 | http://bit.ly/2ihHLZi

2. Celikkan, Ali (2016) Country info on Turkey: 'Bouncer at the Bosphorus', Migration Control Database, *tageszeitung*, 15 December 2016 | https://bit.ly/2G5bY8a

3. *DW* (2016) 'Türkei vereinbart Rücknahmeabkommen', 2 March | http://bit.ly/2vbJqoB

4. Legal expertise by *PRO ASYL* (2016) 'Türkei ist kein sicherer Staat für Flüchtlinge!', Frankfurt, 4 March | http://bit.ly/2vbrqKQ

5. Lepeska, David (2014) 'Turkey's rise from aid recipient to mega-donor', *Al-Jazeera*, 25 April | http://bit.ly/1hHLoe3

6. *Blick am Abend* (2017) 'Turkish Airlines fliegt gratis Lebensmittel nach Somalia', 20 March | http://bit.ly/2tRODxV

7. 'Bundestags-Drucksache 18/11112', 9 February 2017 | http://bit.ly/2p28gSc

8. Sucuoğlu, Gizem; Stearns, Jaso (2016) 'Turkey in Somalia – Shifting Paradigms of Aid', *South African Institute of International Affairs*, Research Report, 24 November | http://bit.ly/2uRaNll

9. *Sudan Tribune* (2017) 'Sudan, Turkey discuss military cooperation in Istanbul', 10 May | http://bit.ly/2puFs3n

10. *Memo* (2017) 'Erdogan to visit Sudan to conclude investment talks', 19 June | http://bit.ly/2ucJBLL

11. *Africa-Frontex Intelligence Community Joint Report*, Warsaw, April 2017

12. *Bundestags-Drucksache 18/10121*, 23 November 2016 | http://bit.ly/2vbjXeI

13. *ZEIT Online* (2016) 'EU lehnt weitere Verträge nach Vorbild des Türkei-Deals ab', 8 October | http://bit.ly/2dUwGM5

14. *Spiegel* (2016) 'Dann muss Merkel schauen, wie sie das Geld zusammenbekommt', 8 October | http://bit.ly/2dAGZ80

15. *Bundestags-Drucksache 18/11112*, 9 February 2017 | http://bit.ly/2p28gSc ; http://bit.ly/2vbjXeI

16. Naceur, Philipp Sofian (2016) 'Racism, Violence, Despotism', Country info on Turkey, Migration Control Database, *tageszeitung*, 15 December | http://bit.ly/2CMZNtA

17. Egypt's Anti-Terrorism Law translated to English, *Official Gazette* No. 33, Cairo, 15 August 2015 | http://bit.ly/2vYAcJL

18. *The New Arab* (2016) 'Ethiopian refugee 'burns to death' outside Cairo's UNHCR office', 29 July | http://bit.ly/2ue6FKh

19. European Migration Network (2011) *ITALY – Annual Policy Report 2010*, Rome, 1 January | http://tinyurl.com/yd8Ksdaj

20. *Daily News* (2017) 'Germany will deport Egyptians who entered illegally: Merkel', 3 March | http://bit.ly/2vbwuPF

21. *Bundestags-Drucksache 18/1111*, 9 February 2017 | http://bit.ly/2p28gSc

22. *Ibid.*

23. *Africa Monitors* (2017) 'Egypt: deportation of migrants to Eritrea', 25 February | http://bit.ly/2f1oZnW

24. *Bundestags-Drucksache 18/8449*, Berlin, 31 May 2016 | http://bit.ly/2tRjY3T

25. *Ibid.*

26. *Bundestags-Drucksache 18/11508*, Berlin, 13 March 2017 | http://bit.ly/2fVCnKL

27. *Handelsblatt* (2016) 'Gabriel lobt umstrittenen al-Sisi in höchsten Tönen', 17 April | http://bit.ly/2tXgeSr

28. *Bundestags-Drucksache 18/8449*, Berlin, 31 May 2016 | http://bit.ly/

2fVCnKL

29. *Ibid.*

30. 'Beihilfe zur Repression in Ägypten', Press release by Andrej Hunko, Berlin, 25 May 2016 | http://bit.ly/2weppdL

31. *Middle East Observer* (2017) 'Egypt to establish military base in Eritrea: Opposition "RSADO"', 18 April | http://bit.ly/2f18Nmv

32. *The Intelligence Brief* (2017) 'Kenya To Engage Egypt in Military Production Cooperation', 7 May | http://bit.ly/2tSeyWe

33. Hayden, Sally (2017) 'Forced back to Syria? Jordan's unregistered refugees fear deportation', *Reuters*, 21 February | http://reut.rs/2l6KOAk

34. *Human Rights Watch (2016)* 'Sudan: Hundreds Deported to Likely Abuse', Nairobi, 30 May | http://bit.ly/2weHRmK

35. Wagner, Lea (2016) Country report on Sudan: Troublemaker or economic addon?' Migration Control Database, *tageszeitung*, 15 December | https://bit.ly/2sHk7WQ

36. Interview with Awad al-Neel Dahiya, responsible for cooperation with EU at the Ministry of Interior, Khartoum, 31 January 2018

37. Telöken, Stefan (1993) 'The Domino-Effect' *Refugees* vol. 94, p. 40; Hathaway, James (2005) *The Rights of Refugees under International Law*, p. 293, Cambridge

A continent in motion

Migrant smugglers:
Mafia states in action

Europe's secret services thought they were cracking down on human trafficking and people smuggling when, at 3pm on 24 May 2016, a Tuesday afternoon, Sudanese police forces stormed the 'Corner Café' in Aldiem, a neighborhood in Sudan's capital Khartoum where many Eritrean and Ethiopian refugees live. Here they arrested an Eritrean man sipping espresso and talking on his mobile.[1]

This had been a large-scale operation, with British, Italian and Canadian secret services working in the background. After the arrested Ethiopian had been put on a chartered plane by the Sudanese authorities and flown to Rome, it was celebrated as a decisive blow against human trafficking.

Wanted for years by secret services, 34-year-old Mered Medhanie called himself 'the General', like his great role model, Libya's dictator Gaddafi. The Eritrean is seen as the kingpin of a worldwide network of migrant smugglers and human traffickers, headquartered in Eritrea and active in Sudan, Libya, Italy, Great Britain and across the Atlantic in Canada. Once a resident of Sicily, Medhanie fell under observation of the Italian state prosecution in Palermo as part of investigations against the Italian Mafia.

In 2015, Italy issues an international arrest warrant against him, causing him to go underground, across the Mediterranean to crisis-plagued Libya, where he settles with his wife and children in Tripoli. When the investigators start closing in, he sends his family into exile in Sweden and goes on alone to Khartoum. Sudan's capital is a known hub for migrant smuggling gangs.[2]

Italian and Canadian investigators have transcripts of tapped phone conversations from his time in Tripoli in 2017, at the height of the refugee crisis in Europe. In these phone calls with a confidant, the General complains about being 'stressed' because he has so much to do and ponders expanding his business to 'America or Canada'.[3] The state prosecutors also found that he invested the millions earned from smuggling humans into IS-linked terrorist groups in Libya and the Sahel zone.[4]

Sicily's public prosecutors are also searching for one of Medhanie's close partners, an Ethiopian named Ermias Ghermay. Both men are considered responsible for the disastrous sinking of a ship with over 950 people on board off the Libyan coast in April 2015.[5] At least 800 people drowned in what is seen as one of the worst disasters in the Mediterranean's recent history, so European investigators started to search for the masterminds.

But in mid-June 2016, when Italian police officers drag a man in Sudanese prison garb from the plane on the runway of Rome-Fiumicino International Airport, it turns out to be the wrong guy. The arrested Ethiopian later tells his Italian lawyer his name is Medhanie Tesfamariam Berhe, a 29-year-old dairy farmer and refugee. The British *Guardian* publishes Facebook posts by the General commenting on the false arrest: 'They made a mistake with his name – but everyone knows he's not a smuggler.'[6]

The embarrassment was hard to beat. British intelligence officers assured journalists that they had tapped phone calls made by the General from this café. A voice recognition program had confirmed his identity without a doubt.[7] The European investigators must have wondered who exactly was fooling them. Nevertheless, the wrong arrest made public both the investigations against the transnational migrant smuggling rings and the close cooperation between secret services across continents.

European authorities depend on their African colleagues in the fight against migrant smuggling networks.[8] Sudan has had a National Committee to Combat Human Trafficking (NCCHT) for such investigations since 2014. Its steering committee includes police and army representatives as well as agents of the secret service NISS.[9] Under pressure from the EU, nearly all states of North Africa and the Sahel zone have created institutions to fight human smuggling networks in recent years. Sudan's NCCHT is an inter-ministerial workgroup headed by the Ministry of Justice. The German development agency GIZ offers workshops to advise the committee as part of its Better Migration Management project (BMM).

The Sicilian state prosecution has found that many migrant smuggling kingpins are living safely in Sudan's capital. Researchers of the Sahan Foundation, founded by Somalian intellectuals, and the Intergovernmental Authority on Development (IGAD), a regional organization for the Horn of Africa headquartered in Djibouti, published a report in 2016 that gathers all the records on these migrant smuggling kingpins living in Ethiopia, Italy, Sudan and Germany. The researchers looked into phone contacts, recorded conversations between smugglers, and bank transfer excerpts – from Sweden to Dubai to the Horn of Africa. Smartphone snapshots show the Eritrean and Somali kingpins posing, dressed up in gold chains and hip hop fashion – gangster style.

In two large-scale operations between 2013 and 2015, Palermo's public prosecution had more than two dozen suspected smugglers arrested, most of them in Italy, one in Germany.[10] Many of those arrested came from Eritrea, a former Italian colony, and are part of Mafia-like structures active worldwide that smuggle not just people but also arms and drugs.

Traces keep leading to Khartoum, where kingpins like the General use the Islamic *hawala* system to brazenly push large amounts of cash back and forth. 'The ringleaders are also the financial overlords of the trade, coordinating the transport and storage of human cargo by generating the principal revenue for paying off transporters and corrupting law enforcement agents in Ethiopia and Sudan, for renting out armed militia convoys and vast warehouses for the storage of human cargo in transit hubs – notably Ajdabiya, Libya – and for procuring passenger and support boats for the final sea journey launched from coastal locations near Tripoli,' states the report.[11]

The researchers name examples, such as the *hawala* money transfer office of a Somali businessman in Khartoum where huge amounts are transacted between Libya's Mediterranean coast, where most smuggling vessels embark, and Somalia's capital Mogadishu, where many refugees come from. One Eritrean even offers "first class" packages. Migrants who can afford $30,000 are flown to Singapore or even the Philippines, from where they head to Europe on a Schengen visa. Khartoum's airport is the hub for these operations.[12]

In a country as closely watched by the secret service as Sudan, it is hard to believe that the authorities know nothing of these criminal activities. The investigators found evidence that influential state officials in all countries along the Horn of Africa smuggling routes – Eritrea, Ethiopia and Sudan – are bribed by the kingpins. In the chaos of the Libyan civil war, they are working closely with militias whose income derives from smuggling migrants. Germans are still not sure about the extent of collaboration with officials in Sudan: 'A big problem are the many smuggling networks,' reads an internal paper of the German Foreign Office on Sudan dated June 2016, just after Medhanie's arrest. The Sahan report states that it cannot be ruled out that Sudanese border officials are being bribed to support the human traffickers.[13]

The billion-dollar human trade

Migrant smuggling and human trafficking have turned into a huge industry in recent years. During the investigations against the 'General,' Sicily's state prosecution spoke of millions of euros being earned from migrant smuggling. Medhanie's latest rate for a passage from Tripoli to Lampedusa was €5,000 per person. 'Given the scale of the human smuggling business in Libya, there can be little doubt that migrants and refugees have become a commodity fueling the war economy in the region,' write the Sahan researchers.[14]

Meron Estefanos, Eritrean journalist and director of the refugee organization EIRR, is running a hotline for distressed migrants from her exile in Stockholm, Sweden. Her standard questions include how much they had to pay the smugglers for which route. So far, she has found, the easiest but most expensive way was to be driven by a corrupt army officer from Eritrea's capital Asmara to Khartoum in neighboring Sudan, because government license plates are not checked at the border. This can cost up to €6,000 per person. In Sudan's capital, the refugees are handed to the next smugglers, who are also Eritreans. The trip across the Libyan border reportedly costs around €1,800. Here, various militias are in on the business. As in earlier cases on the Egyptian Sinai Peninsula, they kidnap the refugees and demand ransom money from their families back home. These pay up to €15,000, sometimes more, through various money transfer systems.[15] 'Those who are allowed to pay a ransom are still lucky,' says Estefanos. Some victims just disappear without a trace, in which case their families in Eritrea do not get any ransom demands. The Eritrean refugee organization director is alarmed by this tendency: 'This means the Islamic State is either abducting them as fighters and slave laborers or killing them.'

In April 2015, IS propaganda videos show up online. Several dozen Ethiopian and Eritrean refugees – Christians – are kneeling in the sand somewhere along the Mediterranean coast. They are wearing orange overalls, like the Guantánamo prisoners. Behind them stand masked henchmen with Kalashnikovs and sabers. The IS flag is flying in the wind. The IS fighter who is praying to Allah in Arabic has an English accent. He gives orders. Then they behead the refugees.[16] Later it turns out that three of the decapitated

Ethiopians had been deported from the Holot detention center in Israel.[17]

Mafia business: prostitution and drug trade

The videos of the brutal beheadings in the Libyan desert went across the world and slashed the number of Horn of Africa refugees risking the journey through civil war-torn Libya. Instead, they opted for Egypt to reach the Mediterranean. Even though smuggling boats embarking from Alexandria need around 13 days to reach Italy and the route is still dangerous, this is better than getting caught by the IS. Those migrants who still come to Libya are usually from Western or Central Africa. 90 percent reach Libya via Niger.

Mounting evidence shows that the Nigerian mafia is heavily involved in the people smuggling routes from Western Africa to Europe. Its extensive network is also involved in the drug trade and prostitution in Italy.[18] These branches usually intertwine: Nigerian women are forced into prostitution upon arrival in Italy to pay off their debts to the smugglers. The women also smuggle cocaine to Europe for these networks, usually on or inside their bodies.[19] Nigerian mafia gangs are known to run such operations from Colombia to Africa and Europe, all the way to Malaysia. The business is booming: The UN migration agency IOM estimates that 80 percent of the roughly 11,000 Nigerian women who arrived in Sicily in 2016 were human trafficking victims forced into prostitution. The number of women from Nigeria registered by the IOM nearly doubled over the previous year.[20]

Targeted efforts against criminal networks by the EU and its partners in North Africa have caused these intercontinental structures to shift southwards to escape Europe's growing influence in Africa.

A mere two years after the 'successful' arrest of the 'General' in Khartoum and his extradition to Italy, the wrong Mered Medhanie, the refugee arrested in his place, is still sitting in prison in Palermo. Eritrean witnesses were flown in from around the world to confirm that this is not the feared human trafficker. Genetic tests with family members were attempted. The case turned into a justice scandal.

Meanwhile, the real 'General' Medhanie has found a new home to run his smuggling business risk-free. In summer 2018, he is spotted in the Muyenga neighborhood of Uganda's capital Kampala, at the Eritrean-owned TNT supermarket, buying cigarettes. A Mercedes SUV with tinted windows and an Eritrean chauffeur is standing outside. Wealthy Eritreans have set up shop along Muyenga's main road in the last two years. They open hotels, restaurants, saunas, drive big cars and buy property. Their businesses are typical African money laundering enterprises. The Eritrean exile organization Africa Monitors, which researches Eritrea's smuggling networks, estimates that more than five major Eritrean migrant smuggling rings have settled in Uganda. Most were previously headquartered in Libya or Sudan. Uganda's corrupt government gives shelter to many criminal networks in Africa. Clients are plentiful. The country houses over a million refugees, among them many Eritreans. Most Eritreans settle as urban refugees in Kampala, often earning money here to rejoin relatives in other parts of the world. Those who have saved enough can book a hotel room, for example, at the Eritrean-owned Savana, and ask for the price of a ticket and a passport. Nowadays, you can even fly from Kampala via Turkey or Eastern Europe to Venezuela or Bolivia to join the South American refugee caravan headed for the USA. The price is $14,000.

Notes

1. *Reuters* (2016) 'Whisked to Rome from Khartoum: people-smuggling kingpin or wrong man?', 13 June | http://read.bi/2tWUnux

2. 'Human Trafficking and Smuggling on the Horn of Africa-Central Mediterranean Route' (2016) *Sahan Foundation and IGAD Security Sector Program (ISSP)*, February 2016

3. Nadeau, Latza Barbie (2015) 'Italy Is Finally Cracking Down on Slave Trade', *Daily Beast*, 20 April | https://bit.ly/2FyLVH4

4. Hughes, Chris (2015) 'ISIS paid millions by billionaire godfather of people smuggling ring named the 'General'', *The Mirror*, 14 June | http://bit.ly/2uQIgw5

5. Nadeau, Latza Barbie(2015) 'Italy Is Finally Cracking Down on Slave Trade', *Daily Beast*, 20 April | https://bit.ly/2FyLVH4

6. Tondo, Lorenzo and Kingsley, Patrick (2016) 'They got the wrong man,' says people-smuggling suspect. *The Guardian*, 22 November | http://bit.ly/2fXGcdI

7. *Reuters* (2016) 'Whisked to Rome from Khartoum: people-smuggling kingpin or wrong man?' 13 June | http://read.bi/2tWUnux

8. *Home Office* (2016) 'Country Information and Guidance Sudan: 'Sur place' activity in the UK', August 2016 | http://bit.ly/2wsEE6f

9. '*Bundestags-Drucksache 18/11841*', 4 May 2017 | http://bit.ly/2f109aH

10. 'Human Trafficking and Smuggling on the Horn of Africa-Central

Mediterranean Route' (2016) *Sahan Foundation and IGAD Security Sector Program (ISSP)*, February 2016, p. 18-19 | http://bit.ly/1KPxpIs

11. *Ibid.*

12. *Ibid.*

13. Internal paper of the German Foreign Office (2016) 'Lage von Flüchtlingen in Sudan', June 2016

14. 'Human Trafficking and Smuggling on the Horn of Africa-Central Mediterranean Route' (2016) *Sahan Foundation and IGAD Security Sector Program (ISSP)*, February 2016, p. 18-19 | http://bit.ly/1KPxpIs

15. Phone interview with Meron Estefanos, director of the Eritrean exile organization EIRR (Eritrean Initiative for Refugee Rights), Oslo, 1 October 2016

16. *The Telegraph* (2015) 'Islamic State murders 30 Ethiopian Christians in Libya', 20 April | http://bit.ly/2tXc1Ow

17. *The Times of Israel*, (2015) 'NGO: 3 killed by IS in Libya had sought asylum in Israel', *The Times of Israel*, 21 April | http://bit.ly/1QkVZAs

18. Gaffey, Conor (2017) 'The Mafia is Teaming up with Nigeria's "Viking" Gangsters to Run Sex Rings in Sicily', *Newsweek*, 28 June | http://bit.ly/2uNOtub

19. *Nigerian Documentary* (2017) 'From Benin City to the Shores of Italy: A New Hub of Human Trafficking', April 2017 | http://bit.ly/2vm1Z9V

20. *The Guardian* (2017) 'Number of Nigerian women trafficked to Italy for sex almost doubled in 2016', 12 January | http://bit.ly/2vfXL2R

Migration 'Karibu sana': Welcome culture

They don't come over the Mediterranean on boats, rather crossing the borders on foot or on the backs of battered trucks with all their belongings: a bundle of cookware and clothes, half a sack of millet flour, a mattress, a blanket, a water canister. Most cannot carry more or had too little time to pack up when they had to flee the fighting.

Family father Pierre Karimumujango also had nothing but the clothes on his back, when he, his wife and their three children fled their village in Burundi in late 2015. The farmer braved the over 600 miles to Uganda on foot and by bus to seek protection. A few months later, he is the proud owner of a new hut and hoes his cassava field with loving care. Soon he will harvest his first crop. 'We got asylum and a piece of land; I'm happy we found peace in Uganda,' says the 39-year-old.[1]

Like Karimumujango, hundreds, sometimes thousands of desperate people enter Uganda every day. The small East African nation has one of the world's most liberal refugee policies. Around 1.3 million people are currently seeking protection in Uganda. This exceeds the number of those who came to Germany along the Balkan route in the record year of 2015.[2] Nowadays, the small country of only 39 million hosts the world's largest refugee camp.

Uganda likes to present itself as a stable island at the heart of a crisis-plagued continent. Neighboring Congo has been wracked by civil war for over 20 years. In the northern neighbor state, South Sudan, a conflict broke out two years ago; fights have been raging since 2015. 1.8 million South Sudanese have since left their country, most for Uganda.[3] Burundi's state has been terrorizing the population since 2015, after President Pierre Nkurunziza had himself elected for a third term despite the constitutional limit of two. The government cracked down on protests and had opposition members murdered. More than 400,000 people fled, most to Rwanda and Tanzania initially, but camps there soon filled up, so the Burundians moved on to Uganda, since it offers chances of long-term settlement.[4] No other African nation has been providing for so many refugees for decades.

Uganda's oldest refugee camp, Nakivale, is 20 years old. With over 100,000 residents, it seems like a small city. The sprawling settlement among the green hills of Uganda's uninhabited Southwest is also where farmer Karimumujango has built his house. Refugees of various nationalities have formed neighborhoods named after their hometowns in Rwanda, Somalia or Eritrea: 'Little Kigali,' 'Little Mogadishu' or 'Little Asmara' is written on the signs leading through the camp. Each war in the region has left traces here. Now, Burundian refugees like Karimumujango are erecting Little Bujumbara atop one of the hills – straw-thatched huts made of wood and clay donated by Uganda's government. The UN refugee agency UNHCR has drilled a well in a central location and set up huge water tanks, where dozens of children holding canisters are standing in line. The circular settlement grows all around this well into the hillscape.

The government assigns a plot for growing food to each family. The unpopulated pastureland along Uganda's southwestern border to Tanzania belongs to the state. Usually, only cattle herds come here to graze and search for waterholes during the dry season. To bridge the time until Karimumujango's freshly plowed field yields a crop, the UN's World Food Programme (WFP) hands out rice, beans, oil, salt and milk powder for the children.

'Although we pursue a very open-hearted policy, providing for the refugees arriving in great numbers is an enormous challenge,' says Uganda's State Minister for Relief and Disaster Preparedness, Musa Ecweru.[5] One such challenge came up in July 2016, when heavy fighting broke out in South Sudan and thousands of people fled across the border within a few days. Ecweru explains that there is more to it than just registering them at the reception camps along the border. There is much to do: police officers must search the luggage for weapons; children from the war zones who have never seen a doctor in their lives must be vaccinated against polio and measles. Neighboring Congo suffered an Ebola breakout in April 2017. Now nurses from the health department need to take every Congolese refugee's temperature to prevent the deadly disease from spreading. A government that can hardly provide for its own citizens simply cannot afford all these services.

The Minister stresses that Uganda's government needs international aid to offer primary care at all the reception centers along the borders. The money is going elsewhere, though, since Europe has its own refugee stream to handle. The UNHCR estimates it will need $550 million for Uganda in 2017, yet only $150 million have been provided so far.[6] The UNHCR calls it 'the largest refugee crisis since the end of World War II' and praises Uganda's efforts, while adding that traditional donors, including Germany and the EU, are scaling down their contributions.[7] Hence, the small nation is nearly alone with all the refugees.

Uganda's liberal refugee policy has a long history; it took in Polish Jews back in World War II. In the 1970s and 1980s, when dictator Idi Amin and his successor Milton Obote spread terror, many Ugandans became refugees themselves. The Minister recalls: 'We were treated well then, so we now want to treat our neighbors well if they are having problems at home.' Uganda's current president, Museveni, started his guerrilla movement in Tanzanian exile and recruited his young fighters from the refugee camps. In 1986, they conquered and have since ruled the country. Refugee minister Ecweru estimates that three quarters of his colleagues are former refugees, just like himself. Hence, he says, Ugandans see refugees not as a burden, but recognizing their potential to become tomorrow's presidents. One well-known example is Paul Kagame, president of neighboring Rwanda, who grew up and went to school in Uganda's refugee camps.

Uganda: victim of EU anti-migration policy

The center of Nakivale, where the refugee camp's management is headquartered and goods and food are handed out, is a busy place crowded with small alleys full of carpenters, tailors, workshops, pharmacies and shops, all run by refugees. Many bring their sewing machines, workbenches, tools or even grain mills to Nakivale. One Internet café owner fled with all his computers and set them up again at the camp. Teenagers are staring at the screens and chatting online with their former schoolmates from back home, who live in the region's other camps.

A small distance from the huts, young men are playing soccer on a field with a rickety goal: Congolese against Somalis. Exercise is a good way to stay busy, overcome trauma and solve conflicts peacefully. Nakivale's soccer champions are the Eritreans. In late 2012, Eritrea's national team had stormed Minister Ecweru's office after losing a cup match in Uganda; he issued them asylum papers. Now some of them are training the youth in Nakivale.

Uganda's example disproves the notion that all Africans are fleeing to Europe across the Mediterranean. Those who arrive in Italy, Spain or Greece are just a fraction of the millions fleeing war or seeking work within Africa. The real refugee drama is happening in Africa's countless refugee camps in civil war zones and in tent cities across Uganda and other host countries. While sub-Saharan Africa shelters 30% of all refugees worldwide and another 40% are seeking shelter in North Africa and the Middle East, Europe hosts only around 6% of all refugees worldwide according to UNHCR figures.

'U are most welcome,' reads a poster at the counter for asylum applications at the immigration office in Uganda's capital Kampala, over 300 miles from Nakivale. Underneath stands the same greeting in the regional language Kiswahili: 'Karibu Sana.' Next to the greeting hangs a poster warning against human traffickers who promise jobs in Dubai or Qatar. Around the corner lies the Department of Refugees on the seventh floor of the Office of the Prime Minister. Minister Ecweru is signing residence permits non-stop. These papers allow refugees to work and start their own businesses – Uganda cannot feed them, but it profits from their labor.

Refugees from the crisis countries include entrepreneurs, the middle class and small business owners. In Kampala, you see mid-size cars with Burundian or Sudanese license plates; the so-called urban refugees own enough capital to keep themselves afloat for a while. Most arrive with their life savings in the trunk to start over. They rent a house, open a business or restaurant or trade with their relatives back home. Ideally, they even pay taxes and hire a few Ugandans. The colorful Kabalagala neighborhood hosts Eritrean restaurants and hotels side by side with Somalian gas stations and Rwandan dairy shops selling cheese and yoghurt. African longhorns may be grazing outside, since many Rwandan refugees came here with their cattle herds.

'Uganda has a very open refugee policy, and its economy is profiting in the long run,' confirms Charly Yaxley of the UNHCR. The UN's World Food Programme (WFP) buys the food from local farmers at a fair price and sells it to the newly arrived refugees at the reception camps.[8] This helps Uganda's farming sector. A WFP study released in October 2016 states that each field granted to a refugee family returns €200 in annual profit. This is a lot of money in Uganda.[9]

Owing to this experience, Uganda admits not just refugees but labor migrants from all over Africa, India and China. The labor migrants need a work permit, one for which they've been able to apply online since early 2017. Most middle-class businesspeople in

Uganda are migrants. Entrepreneurs from Eritrea are emigrating to Uganda for business, because their own economy is in ruins. They send their income back home and pay taxes to the regime in Asmara. To better integrate the East African Community (EAC), Kenya, Uganda and Rwanda have formed a common labor market, just like the EU. While more and more Ugandans move to Nairobi for work, Rwandans and Burundians come to Kampala. The transition from refugee to labor migrant tends to be fluid.

Ugandan President Museveni is a major advocate of the AU's idea to abolish visas on the continent or even introduce a single AU passport. In May 2017, more than 100 delegates met to formulate a visa-free travel agreement, which is set to take effect in 2018.[10] This was followed by the third Pan-African Forum on Migration under President Museveni's chairmanship in Kampala. After 30 years in power, the 72-year-old likes to play the grandfather figure for the region, or even the entire continent. Hence, he also feels the call to represent Africa's position in the migration debate to the international community. In November 2016, the UN General Assembly in New York City decided to develop a Global Compact for Migration by 2018. The meeting in Kampala was intended to produce a common African position in advance, as Museveni emphasized in his opening speech. The EU's delegation leader in Uganda, Kristian Schmidt from Denmark, agreed: '[The] EU and Africa work together and have dialogues on migration at continental, regional and national levels.'[11]

However, they are not on the same page. Museveni is against the EU's preferred method of fending off migrants and closing the borders, and in his opening speech underlined that he did not wish his people to die in dangerous journeys across the Mediterranean looking for a better life.[12] He added that migration was known as the oldest remedy to poverty and a driver of positive development if managed well, especially since most current migrants and refugees were people of prime working age. Their labor could be put to good use in the EU as well. Uganda could serve as an example. Refugee Minister Ecweru is indignant and considers it a grave mistake by Europe to close its borders now. He considers refugees the victims of a failed international peacekeeping system, for which the European powers and the UN Security Council are very much responsible. 'These people are running for their lives, and if we don't open the door, they will die,' says Ecweru: 'We can't say "Sorry, go and die!" like they are now doing with the drowning migrants in the Mediterranean. This is not acceptable.' He adds that Europe is the cradle of human rights, since Europeans have not only written down these rights, but also exported them into the world. 'They have to respect these rights, otherwise they're hypocrites.'

In June 2017, Uganda convened the Uganda Solidarity Summit on Refugees in Kampala and invited UN General Secretary António Guterres. The summit demanded more support for Uganda and was intended as a wake-up call to the EU. Uganda's Refugee Minister Ecweru said the EU was acting deceptively and following a very bad policy, which is why Uganda was now trying to show alternatives by welcoming in the world.

Europe's anti-migration policy negatively affects this small country. Uganda plays only a minor role – also financially – in all the EU migration talks with African states. While the Europeans promise countries like Sudan, Niger or Eritrea aid packages worth hundreds of millions of euros, Uganda was granted only a fraction – around €7 million – in the first half of 2016.[13] Only when the refugee streams from South Sudan steadily increased in the second half of 2016, overwhelming Uganda's government, did the EU send another €13 million. For 2017, the EU then promised around €65 million.[14] But there still is not enough money. The UN aid agencies WFP and UNHCR as well as the international NGOs in Uganda are badly underfunded. Uganda's refugee minister estimates that $2 billion per annum over the next four years would be needed to take care of the refugees, totaling $8 billion over four years. In informal conversations about why the EU is not sending more aid, European actors mention Uganda's location – far away, along the equator. Europe's generosity instead targets the states north of the equator, which border directly on the EU and are crossed by refugees and migrants advancing towards the Mediterranean.

The two-day summit produced only $352.6 million of the estimated $2 billion. Speaking in Kampala, UN General Secretary Guterres said: 'International solidarity is not just a matter of solidarity. It is a matter of justice.'[15] The former High Commissioner of the UNHCR visited the overcrowded camps before the summit and tweeted: 'Don't stop the refugees; stop the wars that produce them.'[16]

In mid-August 2017, German Foreign Minister Sigmar Gabriel goes to Uganda and visits the refugee settlements along the northern border to South Sudan. Sporting a functional khaki outfit, he boards the helicopter. His first stop is a solar-powered well drilled by the German Catholic organization *Malteser Hilfsdienst,* followed by a school a short distance away, where refugee children are sitting in crowded classrooms. A South Sudanese woman tells the minister how a sewing machine donated by the German *Welthungerhilfe* organization allows her to make dresses and feed her kids. Gabriel listens attentively and asks questions in English. Then he presents soccer balls from Berlin bearing the *Bundesliga* logo to the children, and they sing well-rehearsed thank-you songs.

A retinue of journalists has come from Berlin. By now, the refugees are used to elaborately staged VIP visits. The NGOs want to raise awareness for Uganda. Just a week before, the UNHCR had hauled in some journalists to welcome the one-millionth refugee from South Sudan. Occasions for publicity events are quickly found. But ongoing fighting along the border caused the refugee flow to stop. The one million mark had to wait. When Gabriel arrives, the number is at 994,642.

Foreign Minister Gabriel was impressed nonetheless. After his 'field trip', he expressed 'great admiration' for Uganda's refugee policy to President Museveni at his palace next to the airport. Germany had promised Uganda €55 million in refugee aid, while contributing another €22 million via EU funding. 'I wish other states in Europe to would show the same openness to refugees,' said Gabriel at the later press conference. He also found the work permit policy could serve as an example to Germany: 'We keep being surprised over parallel societies and the lack of integration.'

Shortly thereafter, information emerges which takes Uganda's refugee problem to the tipping point. The model nation is committing a mortal sin – systematic embezzlement of refugee aid money. When UN High Commissioner for Refugees Filippo Grandi visits Uganda in late 2018, the relationship is visibly strained. After a helicopter stopover in the northern refugee camps, he meets Prime Minister Ruhakana Rugunda. When the journalists enter the conference hall after a two-hour delay, the air is thick. Grandi briefly praises Uganda as a model country for its refugee policy and calls for peace in the source countries South Sudan and Congo before taking questions. Asked by the German newspaper *tageszeitung* about the consequences, should Uganda's government really be embezzling the scarce refugee aid money, the UNHCR chief turns dead serious: 'We have a zero-tolerance policy toward corruption.' Should the claims be true, sanctions would have to follow, and Uganda would have to repay every missing cent.

That blow struck home. As soon as the conference was over, Uganda's Prime Minister and his delegation stormed out of the room. Grandi was left standing in the hallway alone. That same day, he demanded full disclosure from Uganda's authorities and initiated an internal investigation into UNHCR efforts in Uganda. The internal report published ten months later speaks of fraud, theft and corruption. It starts with Uganda's official refugee figures. The country claimed to be harboring 1.4 million refugees in summer 2018 – more than any other country in Africa. With this figure in hand, the government went out demanding solidarity and soliciting aid money. It worked – UNHCR spending in Uganda rose to over $200 million in 2017/18. The EU, Germany, Great Britain and the

USA paid the lion's share. But biometric verification proved that 300,000 refugees existed only in the database – either Ugandans were registered as refugees, or the figures were manipulated. The investigation alone cost $11 million.[17]

Hence, all the aid money was granted on the basis of inflated figures. But it goes on: The 41-page report criticizes a lack of oversight over the spending of project funds. In 2017, the UNHCR handed out more than $31 million to partners – international or local aid agencies, as well as contractors providing the camps with cookware, toilets or drinking water. In a breach of UNHCR policy, however, Uganda's Ministry of Disaster Preparedness and Refugees decided who would run the projects, which opened the doors wide to cronyism. It is an embarrassment for the UNHCR and for Uganda – this model country so desperately in need of more funding. Aid agencies are estimating that 60,000 Congolese citizens could come fleeing across the border during the December 2018 elections in neighboring DRC.

Global village: 'We're also part of it'

'Africa is often seen as a continent of mass migration and displacement caused by poverty, violent conflict and environmental stress. Yet such perceptions are based on stereotypes,' states a comparative study on migration in Africa from 2016.[18] According to this study, only 14 percent of all migration on the continent is caused by 'people in refugee-like situation[s]'. The overwhelming majority of Africans on the move (86%) are labor migrants. Most job seekers do not travel north to Europe. South Africa, for example, is attracting more migrants than the EU.

After all, those seeking their luck elsewhere are not the poorest Africans, but the well-educated, urban middle class, who can afford to migrate. According to Richard Danziger, IOM Regional Director for West Africa, 40% of all job-seeking migrants have completed secondary school. However, their qualifications do not earn them jobs due to prevailing cronyism. Hence, well-educated migrants hope their training will be appreciated elsewhere.[19] A GIZ study from June 2017 confirms that corruption is a decisive push factor for voluntary and involuntary migration.[20]

Nigeria is a good example. Africa's most populous nation of 182 million also ranks among the continent's most developed economies. Around 20 million Nigerians are working abroad. In 2015, this diaspora remitted $21 billion to relatives back home, states the Central Bank of Nigeria.[21] This far exceeds the aid from all EU member states put together. While remittances amount to $117 per capita, European development aid does not even amount to $3 per capita.[22]

The great majority of Nigerian labor migrants live in other African countries.[23] In comparison, the number of Nigerians who requested asylum in the EU in the last decades is small. In the entire 15 years from 2000-15, the total for all EU member states was 165,000. Nevertheless, Nigerians remain second only to Eritreans among all African asylum seekers in the EU. Only 25% of Nigerian applicants in 2015 were granted asylum – all others are marked for deportation. And deportation is exactly what the EU Commission and the member states consider to be the problem.

The 'Clearing Point' of the German Federal Office for Migration and Refugees (BAMF) maintains a list of 'problematic states'. These states readmit only small numbers of rejected asylum seekers. The country statistics read like cost calculations. Nigeria leads the list for 2014. From 2003-13, Germany registered exactly 9,415 'incoming' Nigerians but only 3,335 'outgoing' ones (due to deportation or voluntary return). The remaining 'balance' are 6,080 suspected Nigerians who cannot leave Germany because missing travel documents make their identity unverifiable, causing Nigeria to refuse their readmission. Nigeria is considered a passport forging hub. The stranded Nigerians seem to be very expensive – the list reports 'average costs' of over €10 million for all of them.[24]

The EU, led by Germany, wants to make Nigeria a 'partner'. A Joint Declaration on a Common Agenda on Migration and Mobility was signed back in 2015 – it explicitly excludes labor migration to Europe.[25]

Border demarcation: resettling whole villages

Many Africans cannot understand why the EU is closing its labor market, or they see it as pure racism. 'After all, many industries in Europe need labor migrants,' notes Mohamed Ibn Chambas in an interview.[26] He is the current head of the UN Office for West Africa (UNOWAS) and chairs the joint border committee for Cameroon and Nigeria, which was set up in 2002 to monitor the demarcation process between the two countries. Before, he was Secretary General of the Economic Community of West African States (ECOWAS). On his latest visit to Berlin, Paris and Brussels in October 2016, this Ghanaian diplomat denounced the EU's anti-migration policy and demanded legal routes for labor migration: 'We must realize these opportunities and allow Africans to generate income in Europe and take their savings back home after a while. I can guarantee that a good percentage of migrants are just seeking a chance to save start-up capital and open a business back home. They don't want to stay forever.'

Chambas sees migration as an 'elementary part of human nature,' especially now with globalization. 'The world is becoming a global village, and we Africans are also part of it,' he says. From his experience as ECOWAS Secretary General, he knows: 'The majority of Africans migrate from one African country to the other, especially in West Africa.' He says this is the reason why governments refuse to build border fences in the desert. Migration and cross-border trade are not just crucial to the regional economy and everyday life, but especially to the local communities along the borders.

The 1,300 mile-long line between Cameroon and Nigeria was drawn up by the colonial powers at the Berlin Conference from 1884 to 1885. Like many borders on the continent, its exact shape was disputed for over a century and caused frequent conflicts. In 2002, after a trial that lasted years, the International Court of Justice (ICJ) in The Hague passed a judgement fixing the border. Since then, Chambas' UN agency has been responsible for installing the demarcation on the ground using satellite data and maps. 198 concrete blocks were rammed into the barren desert at regular intervals to serve as border markers. 1,800 are still missing, so Chambas came to Berlin to ask for money.

He says the countries had explicitly decided not to build insurmountable fences or walls: 'Like in all African border regions, the local communities on both sides of the border have strong ties.' Some of the villagers have never been to the capital to have a passport or ID card issued, but they cross the border every day and hardly notice it. They are herders guiding their cattle and goats through the desert searching for watering holes; they are traders buying or selling goods in the neighboring country; they are families whose ties span the artificial borders, speak the same language, visit each other and intermarry. Chambas says:

'People here generally have a good notion of which river, which mountain or tree is on Nigerian or Cameroonian territory. But during our demarcations, some communities who thought they were living in Nigeria actually lived in Cameroon and vice versa. We resettled entire villages across the border. Those who wanted to stay were allowed to but had to take the other state's nationality. Most African borders are like this, and ethnic groups are related across borders and speak the same language. Therefore, we asked the two states not to separate these communities through a wall or a fence. We want to respect the free flow of people and goods to promote the principles of integration and free movement,' Chambas says. 'Although it is important to know the exact location of the border, we have to place the demarcations in a way that doesn't threaten mobility and trade.'

Notes

1. Interviews and description after visit to the camps, Nakivale, 23 March 2016

2. *Süddeutsche Zeitung* (2016) As stated by Federal Minister of the Interior de Maizière: 'In 2015, 890,000 asylum seekers came instead of 1.1 million', 30 September | http://bit.ly/2cQmTDU

3. *UNHCR* (2017) Fact sheet on South Sudan, 30 April | http://bit.ly/2uOotMk

4. *UNHCR* (2017) Uganda fact sheet, latest update, 31 March | http://bit.ly/2f1Oa9D

5. This quote and following ones from personal interview with Uganda's State Minister for Relief and Disaster Preparedness Musa Ecweru, Kampala, 1 June 2017

6. *UNHCR* (2017) Uganda fact sheet, latest update, 31 March | http://bit.ly/2f1Oa9D

7. Interview with Uganda's UNHCR spokesperson Charly Yaxley, 27 June 2015

8. Interview with Uganda WFP speaker Lydia Wamala, Kampala, 5 August 2014

9. USAID (2016) *Economic Impact of Refugees Settlements in Uganda*, Study by WFP and USAID

10. *The East African* (2017) 'Visa-free travel across Africa closer to reality', 27 May

11. Musisi, Frederick (2017) 'Uganda's Museveni Urges Countries to Open Borders to Migrants', *East African Business News*, 17 May | http://bit.ly/2ihbYYA

12. Speech read by Prime Minister Ruhakana Rugunda, Kampala, 15 May

2017

13. EU fact sheet on Uganda (2017) *'European Civil Protection and Humanitarian Aid Operations'*, 6 April | http://bit.ly/2vbRFkj

14. Ibid.

15. *UNHCR* (2017) 'UNHCR chief praises Uganda's commitment to refugees', 23 June | https://bit.ly/2FQVrVs

16. Gerres, António (2017) 'Don't stop the refugees; stop the wars that produce them', *Twitter*, 20 June | https://bit.ly/2FIxyzV

17. *Tageszeitung* (2018) 'So schummelt das Musterland Uganda', 4 December | http://www.taz.de/!5553354/

18. Flahaux, Marie-Laurence and De Haas, Hein (2016) 'African migration: trends, patterns, drivers', *Comparative Migration Studies* 22 January | http://bit.ly/2vbKSHz

19. Danziger, Richard (2017) 'Voting with their feet? Why young Africans are choosing migration over the ballot box', *World Economic Forum*, 11 July | http://bit.ly/2tXtMo6

20. GIZ (2017) *A Study on the Link between Corruption and the Causes of Migration and Forced Displacement*, 29 March | http://bit.ly/2weoNFh

21. Stäritz, Andrea (2016) 'Immer auf Augenhöhe',' Migration Control Database, *Tageszeitung*, 15 December | http://bit.ly/2ifJLBl

22. Migration Control Database, 'Statistics and charts under Thesis 3', *Tageszeitung* | http://bit.ly/2vTVjPq

23. Information by Nigerian Diaspora Organization | http://bit.ly/2uOv6Bl

24. Problematic states list for Nigeria, *BAMF*, 4 February 2014 in authors' archive

25. *Joint Declaration on a Common Agenda on Migration and Mobility between the Federal Republic of Nigeria and the European Union and its Member States*, 12 March 2015 | http://bit.ly/2hgVpeM

26. This quote and following ones from interview with Mohamed Ibn Chambas, Berlin, 24 October 2016

Europe's new borders in Africa

Freedom of movement: Schengen in Europe, fences in the Sahel

Issak Abdou strides across his barracks yard like a used car dealer at a clearance sale. White Toyota pickups are parked in long lines on the Agadez army base at the southern edge of the Sahara. Abdou paces between the rows, his hands behind his back, followed closely by his adjutant, who is cradling a Kalashnikov. 'This one's seven million francs,' Abdou says, nodding towards a pickup. 'That one's 10 million.'[1]

This would be equivalent to almost $17,000, but the pickup is not for sale. Abdou's barracks yard is a storage for evidence. Until recently, each of these vehicles was shuttling from Agadez in Niger to Libya, each truck bed filled with Nigerian, Senegalese, Cameroonian or Gambian nationals traveling 950 mi – three days' drive if everything went smoothly. Now, in November 2017, the desert dust buries the abandoned belongings of the former passengers like relics of a bygone civilization: old shoes, empty pill packets, water canisters decorated with bears for the children. And a Quran. A Quran? Abdou knocks off the dust and takes it with him. The Word of God must not lie in the dirt.

Fog and sand blend into a dusty grey haze. By Sahara standards it is cool this morning. To the side of the yard, a soldier in a tank top hoses off an armored vehicle like an animal keeper rinsing a dirty elephant. A few soldiers load their scout car with ammunition belts before setting off to patrol the desert.

Abdou became commander three years ago. Soon afterwards, the National Assembly of Niger passed Law No. 2015-36 against unlawful trafficking of migrants. Since then, Issak Abdou has had to arrest the drivers who take people across the desert. Their vehicles are impounded, 107 by now. Almost as many drivers are sitting in the prisons of the desert cities of Agadez and Bilma. Most of them are awaiting trial and could face up to 30 years in prison. 'What they did used to be legal,' says Abdou. 'Now it's considered human trafficking. Worse than dealing drugs or guns.'[2]

People smuggling? Human trafficking? The pickup drivers were actually running nothing more than a taxi service from Agadez through the Sahara. Since flights are expensive, Africans prefer to travel by bus, or in the taxi vans that are common on the continent. Until recently, the millennia-old city of Agadez was a tourist attraction. Much of the local population earned an income from international visitors, especially in the transportation sector. But since Islamist militias have become active in the Sahara, fewer tourists visit. Increasingly, local taxi and bus drivers transport migrants to make money. To the EU, however, they are smugglers. As stated in a 2015 Frontex report: 'Human traffickers in Agadez see themselves as service providers. Attempts to combat this growing industry could trigger local protests.'[3]

This is how the desert state became Europe's main partner in the fight against irregular migration in Africa, although the EU hardly cared about Niger until then. Screens at the Frontex headquarters in Warsaw show high-resolution satellite images. The EU border agency traces tire tracks in the sand of the central Sahara, over 2,500 mi to the south. From Agadez, trucks, buses or desert-proof pickups loaded with goods and migrants must travel thousands of miles through the desert to reach the Libyan border. Frontex officials in Warsaw analyze onscreen images of drivers stopping to fill up containers at the few water points on this route. A 2016 Frontex report states: 'It was observed that smugglers tend to move between Agadez and the Libyan border on Mondays, when the weekly military convoys usually leave to provide supplies to bases in northern Niger. The presence of the military offers additional protection to the smugglers.'[4]

The confiscated trucks are testament to what people go through to get closer to Europe. The back of a Toyota Hilux Single Cab, Series 7, the model used by almost all 'smugglers' here, is 7.6ft long and 5ft wide, slightly larger than a double bed. In this space, up to 25 people would ride through the desert. Abdou picks up a stick lying in the sand. He puts it between his legs, bends his knees slightly and grips the wood with both hands. 'That's how they held on. No one could stand it otherwise,' he says.[5]

The closer migrants get to Europe, the more crime-ridden, expensive and dangerous the journey becomes. Starting out, they can board buses for little money; in the end they pay a fortune for a life-threatening boat trip. Agadez is the turning point. Until here, the law is on their side. Beyond this place they can rely on nothing.

The village of Tourayet, population 100, lies a few hours by car east of Agadez. Along the way, the landscape varies between gravel, sand and bushland. A group of Touareg waters its camels at the single village well. Now and then, the outlines of trucks appear on the dusty horizon. They lumber along the dirt road, ludicrously overloaded with hundreds of bundles of cheap Libyan imports.

At the entrance to Tourayet, a limp rope crosses the road. Traders in a few huts sell firewood and grilled goat. This village is one of the many checkpoints on the route through the Sahara. Along the way there are some wells, small settlements and traffic, so accidents do not go unnoticed.

National Guardsman Hamdou stands next to his jeep chewing on a twig of *miswak* wood and watching a red truck roll up. About 30 men are sitting in the cargo area. They wear loose robes; turbans cover their heads and their faces. The driver gets out, a blue folder in his hand. The guardsmen slowly leaf through it, then pull the rope aside. The truck moves on.

'They're Nigeriens. They want to go to a mine nearby to look for gold,' says Hamdou. 'Nigeriens and Libyans. Nobody else can pass here anymore.'[6]

The rope controlled by the guardsmen is the barrier blocking the somewhat safe path through the desert for many. 'Every Monday when the convoys left Agadez, 200 cars came through here,' says Hamdou. According to a census by the International Organization for Migration (IOM), an average of 6,300 people per week left Agadez for Libya and Algeria in 2016. Now just a lonely donkey plods over the gravel; its legs are hobbled so that it can only take small steps. 'These days, nobody comes anymore,' says Hamdou. 'The drivers are going to jail.'[7]

Hamdou's uniform bears the badge of the G5 Sahel Joint Force, the new multinational squad against terrorism, drug smuggling and human trafficking in the Sahel. The EU is giving more than €100[8] million for the desert army. Hamdou's unit last found a group of migrants abandoned in the desert four months earlier. 60 people, three bodies. 'That also used to happen before the ban,' he says. But now the traffickers drive straight through the desert instead of taking the road. 'Sometimes they get lost, sometimes there are accidents and sometimes they just leave people behind when they think we're following them.'[9]

Hussein Chani is no longer driving through the desert. On a hot morning, the Tuareg man stands in an empty courtyard on the outskirts of Agadez. He wears jeans and sunglasses, his cell phone in his shirt pocket. The clay walls are too high for anyone to see inside, but the entire neighborhood knows what this house was: 'My ghetto,' says Chani. That was what everyone called the hostels in Agadez where the migrants slept before setting off through the desert. Chani knows his way around there, so he became a trafficker.[10]

He and three friends rented this house, now eerily empty, plus three Toyotas from Libyan businessmen. Every month, they brought 400 to 500 people through the desert, he says. He married a second wife and could have afforded a third, he says, had the business kept going as it was.

'This is where they slept,' Chani says, pointing to the sand floor. His customers were crowded together on woven mats; they sat in the blazing sun for days, waiting for their turn to set out. A small house stands in the middle of the courtyard. Families were allowed to sleep in the room on the left, women traveling alone on the right. Reminders of them are still scattered here: plastic cups, sheepskins, paper scraps with phone numbers, plastic slippers, pill packets.

'Anyone who arrived and had no money could just wait here for someone to send it,' Chani claims. He was generous and let the migrants pay later, he says. The waiting travelers all cooked together: rice on the fire in the courtyard. Where they washed and relieved themselves is anyone's guess.[11]

Chani ran the hostel most of the time. 'Ghetto boss,' Frontex calls this activity in a recent report on the Agadez human trafficking business.[12] Chani also drove sometimes: 75 times, he estimates, from 2009 until 2016, when everything suddenly ended. 'It took three days to prepare each trip.' Chani bought wood, water and gas, three 60-liter canisters per pickup truck.[13]

They took 28 people on every truck for 80,000 francs (€120) per passenger, Chani claims, except when people from the same country joined for a group discount.

They drove all day until dusk, despite the heat. 'At night there are too many bandits. We slept at 10pm, and at 4am we set off again.' On the evening of the third day they reached Sabha in Libya. 'Nothing ever went wrong,' he says. 'My partners called me from every station.' Chani and his partners each made around $2,000 at the end of the month, he says.

There were dozens of hostels like this in Agadez, all of them closed now. Chani's partners went to prison and their trucks are parked on Commander Abdou's military compound. He has nothing left, Chani says. 'I look for work every day.'[14]

The law prohibiting Chani's business is passed in May 2015,[15] but not enforced right away. In June 2016, Niger's President Mahamadou Issoufou travels to Berlin; in October 2016, German

Chancellor Angela Merkel comes to his country. She stays only five hours but makes her intentions clear: 'We will work together more closely on three new priorities,' says Merkel. 'The first of these priorities is the fight against illegal migration.'[16] Merkel promises €27 million in aid,[17] but President Issoufou knows there is a lot more to be made. He demands €1 billion – and ensures that Merkel gets what she wants: the consistent enforcement of Law No. 2015-36.

The law was passed under pressure from the EU, says Hassane Boukar of the Alternative Citizens' Space in Niger (AECN; *Alternative Espaces Citoyens du Niger*). Furthermore, the Nigerien government had 'made these bizarre decisions without any dialogue with civil society.'[18]

This paid off for Issoufou: EU Development Commissioner Neven Mimica meets Niger's Finance Minister Hassoumi Massoudou in Paris in December 2017. Mimica promises Massoudou €1 billion in development aid for the period from 2017 to 2020.[19] The annual share of this is more than 11 percent of Niger's national budget, and does not even include bilateral aid to Niger from Italy, France and Germany. On just one visit to Niamey in July 2017, German Defense Minister Ursula von der Leyen (CDU) presented 100 flatbed trucks, 115 motorcycles and 55 satellite telephones to the police and the army.[20] Germany also has three officials and two policemen involved in the EUCAP-Sahel mission in Niger, which views traffickers primarily as members of organized crime and Islamist terrorist groups, and trains the Nigerien authorities to fight them.[21]

'Drivers were turned into human traffickers and hotel keepers into criminals,'[22] says Ibrahim Manzo Diallo, editor-in-chief of Radio Sahara in Agadez. His office is next to the studio; the transmitter mast towers above the courtyard, editors pass along the small corridor. A map on the wall shows which areas of the desert can receive the signal. Radio Sahara also broadcasts an hourly Hausa language program from the German international broadcaster Deutsche Welle. Radio is the only mass medium in large parts of the country.

'The EU got Niger to block the way through the Sahara,' says Diallo. He considers this illegal: 'The migrants are citizens of the West African community,' he says. 'They have the right to move freely here. Instead, they are treated like criminals, detained and put in camps.'[23]

In December 2017, the IOM estimated that 5,700 migrants a month traveled from Niger to Libya that year, about one-fifth of the previous year's figure. The government says there have been 31 deaths so far this year. We believe there were actually hundreds.' In 2017, his station received four reports of corpses from local correspondents in the desert.[24]

Diallo has the photos on his laptop: mummified bodies, emaciated, thirsty, dried out, stiff. Some lie on the ground beside the vehicles, others still inside, their limbs folded. Some of the dead were children. Some have only their arms still sticking out of the sand.

'But most of the bodies are never found.' He finds the problem is that the new drivers lack routine. 'In the ghettos, people always knew exactly who was going where and when. Now everything runs undercover, in secret. The drivers take other routes that are longer and dangerous. They use GPS, but they don't know their way around because they're not from here.' Nobody knows the routes they take. 'The desert is bigger than the Mediterranean. Some still don't reach Libya after a month or two.' Nobody can survive this long. 'If Europe doesn't want any more migrants, why doesn't it stop them at its own borders?'[25]

In October 2016, the Regional Council of Agadez presented a study showing the new policy's impact on the region. They estimated that every migrant had spent around $330 in the city on accommodation, food, provisions, exit taxes and the desert trip. By IOM estimates, 330,000 people traveled through Agadez in 2016. According to the regional council, the new law would result in a loss of over $100 million per year.[26]

Hence, the new policy is so unpopular in Agadez that Niger's president Issoufu had to appoint an outsider as regional governor. Sadou Soloke comes from the West of Niger. His headquarters are within view of the offices of the United Nations, the IOM and the German Corporation for International Cooperation (GIZ). One evening he sits in in his office, watched over by the national guard, wearing the traditional flowing white robe known as *babban riga* and a red felt cap. He states: 'We aren't doing this just because the Europeans say so, as many people claim.'[27]

Fighting the traffickers is the right thing to do, says Soloke, 'because we believe they are inhuman and endanger our youth.' Traffickers manipulated young people into taking fatal risks. 'It's a dishonorable business. How can we tolerate it?' Soloke does not say why the authorities only awoke to this 'moral obligation' after the EU began shelling out millions to fulfill it.[28]

He admits that the law cost many people in Agadez their source of income. 'We were aware of this,' says Soloke. 'They need to find completely new activities. We're working on it,' he states. 'But the aid is coming slowly.' Former traffickers receive up to $1,700 to establish a new livelihood. So far, 3,000 of them have applied. The money comes from the EU, which is financing a whole series of other projects in Agadez to compensate for the destroyed businesses.[29]

He rejects the accusation of violating West Africa's free travel regime. 'Of course people are free to travel,' says Soloke. 'Just not if they want to go to Libya.' Moreover, the authorities were not targeting migrants. 'We don't touch them. We only punish the traffickers.' This made an impact: 'Numbers have declined dramatically.' The migrants still being picked up today are sent to an open camp in Agadez run by the UN migration agency IOM, which then organizes their trips back home.

He was aware that the new routes were more dangerous: 'We're watching this. And then we will close off these routes too. They always find other ways, so we can't stop working.'[30]

On Thursday, 1 June 2017, Lawal Taher, head of the Red Cross in northern Niger's Bilma region, made a sad announcement. The day before, a truck had broken down on the way from Agadez to Dirkou in the middle of the Sahara. Only six people managed to walk to the nearest water source. Two of the survivors then led rescuers to the scene of the accident, where 44 passengers' bodies were found, including 17 women and six children. The victims were migrants from the West African states of Ghana and Nigeria. That same day, the Nigerien army rescued 40 people abandoned by traffickers in the Sahara a little further east. Just weeks earlier, eight migrants, five of them children, had died of thirst in the Nigerien desert on their way to Algeria.[31]

Vincent Cochetel, the UN refugee agency's (UNHCR) Special Envoy for the Sahel region, says in February 2018 that more people probably die in the Sahara than drown in the Mediterranean.[32] Albert Chaibou, a journalist from Niger and the founder of a migrant emergency hotline, laments: 'By serving Europe, our country has degenerated into a cemetery.'[33]

Niger is a member of the Economic Community of West African States (ECOWAS), a union of 15 states at present. The founders of ECOWAS wanted freedom of movement to overcome the colonial borders. Visa-free stays of 90 days within the member states have been possible since 2005. The confederation resembles the EU: 'In my opinion, your greatest achievements include the Common External Tariff, freedom of movement and freedom of establishment,' praised German Federal President Joachim Gauck during a visit to Nigeria in February 2016.[34] 'The history of your family of nations sounds somewhat familiar to us in Europe,' said Gauck. 'What Europeans and West Africans also have in common is the experience that integration is always a gradual process.' Or not

– because Europe's policies undermine freedom of movement, the core element of the Schengen Area, in West Africa.

'Just a few years ago, all the borders here were open,' says Alassane Dicko of the NGO Afrique-Europe-Interact (AEI).[35] Today there are special border posts all along Mali's borders to Senegal and Mauritania, Ghana's borders to Burkina Faso, Togo's to Burkina Faso and Burkina Faso's to Niger. These new border posts no longer just collect bribes as usual; they bear the logo of the IOM, which cooperates with the EU. Some were constructed by the German Corporation for International Cooperation (GIZ), others equipped by the IOM with EU money. 'The border guards there ask people, "Where are you going? Why do you want to go there?" And if you don't have a good answer, it ends right there,' says Dicko. For travelers suspected of wanting to get to Europe, the journey is over.

The IOM points out that it was working with the ministries of the interior and defense on 'effective management of cross-border flows'. To this end, it was 'strengthening institutional capacity', for example, through the 'construction of border posts, training of immigration officers and provision of border control equipment'.[36]

'We have the tradition of free movement here in the region,' says Sanoh N'Faly, ECOWAS Director of Free Movement and Migration. 'Reinforcing borders to prevent young people from migrating is not a rational solution. It's an attempt to criminalize migration. If the borders are monitored in one place, they find another possibility somewhere else. It just gets more dangerous, and they die. That's the tragedy.'[37]

About 377 million[38] people now live in the ECOWAS region and around six million[39] are considered migrants from ECOWAS member states. Most migrate within the region; the migration corridor between Côte d'Ivoire and Burkina Faso is the busiest in Africa. Migration here is not a police and security issue, but a traditional social and economic practice. Nevertheless, since the fall of the Libyan dictator Gaddafi, ECOWAS has had to face fighters and weapons entering from Libya, enabling Islamist groups to advance in Mali and Nigeria. This has made migration a security issue.

'Border management is not only restrictive,' says Ralph Genetzke from the Brussels office of the think tank International Centre for Migration and Policy Development (ICMPD). 'It is also important for combatting corruption, for customs and security in the Sahel. This plays very strongly into the area of governance. Spending development aid on border management is the right thing to do.'[40]

In fact, many African governments consider more border controls necessary against terrorism. Better border management in Africa was one of the EU's major goals at the 2015 Valletta Summit.

West Africa's border controls are being intensified and upgraded – for example with the EU-funded West Africa Information System (WAPIS) database, into which West African authorities feed all collected fingerprints and match them with Interpol. The consequences are seen and felt in the Gao region in northeastern Mali, which borders on Niger, the major trans-Saharan transit country.

Vienna-based publicist, filmmaker and activist Hans-Georg Eberl[41] visited the region several times between October 2016 and March 2017. The following observations are based on his research.

Mutiple travelers reported being rejected at the Yassan border crossing and sent back to the Malian side by the 'Service de Migration', the immigration department of the Nigerian police. According to Eberl's research, this affected Malian citizens on one hand and, to a greater extent, people from other West African countries. To enter Niger, Malian travelers must provide ID cards valid for at least three more months and a contact person, preferably in the capital of Niamey. This person must be called immediately and then contact the border post from a police station to confirm that the person waiting at the border is actually expected.[42]

'Along with Agadez in Niger, Gao is one of the central hubs for people from various West African countries heading north,' says Éric Alain Kamden, who has been on the ground for the Catholic NGO Caritas since 2009. This was already true before the war started in 2012. By now, according to IOM statistics, about 150 migrants pass through Gao per day, many of whom travel on to Niger.[43]

Travelers from the south of Mali who come with only an ID card, regardless of how long it is still valid, may only pass if they have a contact on the Nigerian side. For persons from other West African states, such as Ghana, Sierra Leone, Côte d'Ivoire, Gambia, Senegal and Guinea who are believed to be on their way to the Mediterranean, Eberl quotes a border officer in Yassan as saying that there are instructions not to let them pass at all.[44]

There are several documented cases from 2016 of Senegalese travelers who were rejected even though they carried all the necessary documents: an ECOWAS passport, an ID card and a vaccination passport. In July, for example, four young people from Mali, Togo, Senegal and Burkina Faso who wanted to cross the border to set up Orange cellular towers for a Nigerien employer were stopped. Although they carried their tools with them and it was obvious that they were on the job, they were initially turned away at the border and could only travel on when Caritas employee Kamden vouched for them.[45] Kamden was even threatened with losing his visa for Niger if the four were to be picked up in Agadez traveling further north, Eberl reports.

Kamden knows such cases from his daily work with travelers stranded in Gao after being rejected at the border or returning from the desert. He is certain that the repressive practices at the Mali-Niger border are a direct outcome of the Valletta Process, especially since the Nigerien border guards only started being stricter around 2015.

Until then, says Kamden, it was quite normal to cross the border between Mali and Niger, even without valid papers. Persons who could not show a passport on inspection and still wanted to enter Niger only had to pay a fine of 1,500 FCFA, about $23, and were then issued a pass to enter Niger within the next 24 hours. This is impossible today.[46]

Just over a mile from the current Yassan border post, the IOM works with the authorities to set up a new border crossing. At the entrance to the city of Gao and in Kidal in northern Mali, the IOM also runs stations that register all travelers who are believed to be migrants.[47]

The new policy also affects Gao. Many destitute people are stranded here after robberies or other incidents force them to quit their northbound journey. They return from the north on the trucks of Libyan grocery merchants. Libyan products such as noodles, soap or cigarettes are customer favorites throughout Africa. The merchants transport goods from Libya to the south and take migrants northward on their way back. When the merchants lie down somewhere in Gao to sleep, soldiers often pick them up and take them to the police station. English speakers in particular are quickly suspected of being spies for the terrorist group Boko Haram. If the police cannot substantiate this suspicion, they accuse the merchants of 'nighttime loitering'. According to Kamden, there were no such charges and detentions in Gao before. These practices are a 'direct consequence of increased pressure from the European side', Eberl says.[48]

Malian police officers have also targeted travelers in recent years; the transition from routine inspection duties to 'small-scale police corruption' is smooth, says Eberl. They now frequently stop northbound buses and check passengers' papers. While travelers have always had to pay 'fees', Kamden says, security forces are now picking out those they suspect of being 'candidates for migration'.[49]

A similar approach was witnessed on the route between the Malian capital Bamako and Ouagadougou in Burkina Faso. Locals from Heremakono in southern Mali's Ségou region told Eberl that larger groups of travelers were regularly intercepted at the border after officials refused to accept their papers or they failed to pay up.[50]

It 'cannot be verified to what extent police harassment aimed at travelers directly relates to migration policy requirements,' Eberl writes. But unlike just a few years ago, it has become much harder to travel without ID in a part of the world where not everyone has a passport. Controls are more restrictive since the Valletta Summit. Interests overlap between police officers, who earn extra income from the fees, and the migration regime, which wants to block the way north.[51]

In April 2016, Mali introduced new biometric passports that were claimed to be forgery-proof, although the previous version already recorded biometric information. Mali also just issued a biometric ECOWAS identity card.

This makes Mali one of the biometric ID pioneers in West Africa. Agencies and governments at home and abroad applaud this measure to combat irregular migration and to improve national security. For a long time, fake Malian passports and ID cards were traded along the Sahel and Maghreb migration routes, because Malian citizens are officially allowed to enter Algeria without a visa and move freely. This greatly enhanced the safety of migrants temporarily seeking a livelihood in Algeria or wanting to cross the country on their way to other Maghreb states or to Europe, says Eberl. [52]

The Malian government would like to shut down this practice. Various voices in the Malian public also promote a nationalist discourse by claiming that other nationalities traveling with Malian passports posed a national security threat. This discourse links the passport question to the real threat from armed criminal groups, which exists regardless of migration. The new passports and ID cards are also advertised as travel facilitators and signs of a modern state, reports Eberl.[53]

However, many Malians complain about serious complications related to the new documents. For example, citizens must pay the fee for the new, 'top-security' passport to the private Ecobanc. This transaction, in turn, requires them to present a 'Carte NINA' (Numéro d'Identification Nationale), an ID card that was originally conceived as a voter registration document.[54]

In practice, this convoluted process has barred many Malians, including those living abroad, from obtaining a new passport. The stricter controls at the borders also domestically curtail free movement for everyone who, for various reasons, has no current travel documents. This affects not just migrants, but also threatens the livelihood of population groups whose everyday life and work depend on cross-border travel:[55] traveling merchants and migrant workers, but also nomadic or semi-nomadic herders, such as the Tuareg in the border regions of northern Mali. Their identity is not tied to citizenship, and for a long time they crossed different territories without presenting passports. Last but not least, Mali's biometric passport system is vulnerable, since the EU is trying to access Malian databases to identify and deport Malian nationals.[56]

At Bamako-Sénou International Airport it is now standard practice to scan the fingerprints and handprints of all incoming and outgoing travelers. Combined with the biometric features, this makes it more difficult to travel with a borrowed passport, which was one loophole for aspiring emigrants who had no chance of winning one of the rarely granted visas and did not wish to risk their lives in the desert and at sea.[57]

Burkina Faso also faces new restrictions. Since 2016, several terrorist attacks with dozens of victims have hit the country. As Burkina Faso had not experienced comparable attacks in decades, it brought the terrorist threat back onto the political agenda and created a climate in which large parts of the population welcome the increased presence of state security forces and tighter border surveillance.[58]

The incidents also justified measures targeting suspected or actual migrants, such as upgraded border posts. According to the Burkinabé press, a new IT system was installed at the border posts in Madouba (Burkina Faso – Mali), Yendéré (Burkina Faso – Côte d'Ivoire) and Dakola (Burkina Faso – Ghana) at the IOM's initiative, with funding from Japan. The official reason is 'managing the migration flow' ('gestion du flux migratoire') as well as protection against terrorism, gang crime, arms and drug trafficking.[59]

Police controls on the travel routes have also intensified. A dense network of permanent stations as well as mobile police and gendarmerie posts was set up along the highways. Buses are stopped frequently and all passenger papers checked – not only near the border. In November 2016, a total of six such checkpoints were counted on the Ouagadougou – Bobo-Dioulasso route and another five between Bobo – Dioulasso and the Burkina – Mali border crossing in Kologo., Officers regularly turn back travelers without valid ID, especially in border areas. In the country's interior, authorities impose additional fines if travelers lack certain extra documents such as vaccination passports or travel orders (ordre de mission). The experience of an artist-activist from the pan-African artist collective Faso Kele also shows how controls have tightened: in February 2016, he reports, Burkinabé border guards refused him entry from Mali, claiming his papers were not valid, although on previous trips he had crossed the border without incident.[60]

Travelers experience increasing restrictions on the northbound roads towards the Nigerien border. Here, too, the gendarmerie and the military have set up multiple checkpoints. It is also standard practice at many of these posts to fine travelers without valid documents. Some posts conduct additional searches. At posts closest to the border, people viewed as 'migration candidates' face stricter treatment than other travelers. The last post on Burkinabe territory in Kantchari is a notable example. All bus passengers are searched first, then their buses. All travelers who are not citizens of Burkina Faso are required to pay fees, even if they carry valid documents. If they fail to pay, the authorities confiscate their documents to coerce them. Travelers without valid ID are turned back. Alleged 'migration candidates' face special harassment, even if they carry valid documents and are technically allowed to travel freely from Burkina Faso to Niger. Those carrying no money are locked up by the police for a day and robbed of their belongings before being let go. Here, Eberl writes, conventional corruption borders on extortion and kidnapping.[61]

The authorities are trying to train the population to their supposed obligation to carry valid documents at all times, especially when traveling. The 'we need to know who's who and who crosses our borders' rationale is also popular in Burkina Faso, as terrorist attacks and assaults are acute issues, says Eberl.[62]

For Olawale Maiyegun, Secretary for Migration and Social Affairs at the AU, there is a fundamental conflict of interest between the EU's desires to see the movements of people in Africa channeled, documented and regulated, and the AU's ideas. 'In 2014 we decided to create freedom of movement throughout the continent by 2018,' says Maiyegun. 'Yet today, people with German passports can travel more easily throughout Africa than those with African passports.' If Europe wants to support Africa, it should help to 'build institutions that enable mobility within Africa.' This would be much more useful than traditional development projects. 'Is there any country that development aid has actually developed? I know of none,' says Maiyegun. 'Africa has enormous potential, especially its youth. Their abilities need development. This means they must be able to move freely within Africa and continue their education. If we succeed, then in 10 or 15 years, Europeans will be coming to us to recruit workers.'[63]

Tony Luka Elumelu, head of migration for ECOWAS, shares a similar view: 'By 2050 there will be about 600 million people living in the ECOWAS region, most of them young people. If you put people in a cage for too long, someday they won't take it anymore.'[64]

Notes

1. Jakob, Christian (2017) 'Endstation Agadez', *tageszeitung*, 18 December | https://taz.de/!5468121/

2. Ibid.

3. Africa-Frontex Intelligence Community Joint Report 2015, Warsaw, 21 January 2016, p. 6 | http://bit.ly/2ucN8tm

4. Africa-Frontex Intelligence Community Joint Report 2016, Warsaw, 6 April 2017, p. 12 | http://bit.ly/2tXcErm

5. Jakob (18 December 2017)

6. Ibid.

7. Ibid.

8. EU (2018) *The European Union's partnership with the G5 Sahel countries* | https://bit.ly/2TwZcaC

9. Jakob (18 December 2017)

10. Ibid.

11. Ibid.

12. Africa-Frontex Intelligence Community Joint Report (2017)

13. Jakob (18 December 2017)

14. Ibid.

15. Diallo, Ibrahim Manzo (2017) 'EU strategy stems migrant flow from Niger, but at what cost?' *IRIN*, Agadez, 2 February | http://bit.ly/2l8ywY2

16. 'Notes from press conference with German Chancellor Merkel and President of the Republic of the Niger, Mahamadou Issoufou, Niamey, 10 October 2016', *Bundesregierung*, 10 March 2019 | http://bit.ly/2CbSlq7

17. Leithäuser, Johannes (2016) 'Merkel sagt Niger Millionenhilfe zu', *Frankfurter Allgemeine Zeitung*, 10 October | http://bit.ly/2dEe8O7

18. Gänsler, Katrin (2017) 'Country report: Niger', Migration Control Database, *tageszeitung*, 5 March 2019 | https://bit.ly/2Txw8jm

19. EU will support Niger with assistance of €1 billion by 2020', European Commission press release database, Brussels, 13 December 2017 | http://bit.ly/2qfjlUc

20. Jakob (18 December 2017)

21. Ibid.

22. Ibid.

23. Ibid.

24. Ibid.

25. Ibid.

26. Ibid.

27. Ibid.

28. Ibid.

29. Chaibou, Albert (2017) 'Europas neue Grenze', *tageszeitung*, 28 June | http://www.taz.de/!5423916/

30. Jakob (18 December 2017)

31. *Niger News, Aljazeera* 'More than 40 migrants "die of thirst" in Niger' | https://bit.ly/2F8t4jk

32. Personal interview, for documentary 'Türsteher Europas', Geneva, January 2018, | https://bit.ly/2WmChM1

33. Public discussion with Albert Chaibou, Berlin, 28 June 2017

34. 'Speech by Federal President Joachim Gauck to the Commission of the Economic Community of West African States (ECOWAS) in Abuja/ Nigeria on 10 February 2016', *Bundespraesident*, 6 March 2019 | https://bit.ly/2NTrW7l

35. Personal interview with Alassane Dicko in Abidjan, November 2017

36. International Organization for Migration (IOM) Database (2019) 'Mali', *UN Migration*, West and Central Africa, 6 March | http://bit.ly/ 2e9Bucm

37. Stäritz, Andrea (2016) 'Man kriminalisiert Migration', *tageszeitung*, 12 December | http://bit.ly/2wfYT3I

38. DSW Subregion Report (2019) 'West Africa', *Deutsche Stiftung Weltbevölkerung (DSW)*, 6 March | http://bit.ly/2udaTSp

39. Dick, Eva and Schraven, Benjamin (2018) 'Regional Migration Governance in Africa and Beyond', Discussion paper, *Deutsches Institut für Entwicklungspolitik*, Bonn, 2018

40. Personal interview with Ralph Genetzke, Brussels, 7 December 2016,

41. Biographical reference, Hans-Georg Eberl | http://bit.ly/2wsMMEO

42. Eberl, Hans-Georg (2016) 'Corruption and control. Mali: Country Report', Migration Control Database, *tageszeitung*, December 2016 | https://bit.ly/2NS5Odr

43. Ibid.

44. Ibid.

45. Ibid.

46. Ibid.

47. Ibid.

48. Ibid.

49. Ibid.

50. Ibid.

51. Ibid.

52. Ibid.

53. Ibid.

54. Ibid.

55. Ibid.

56. Ibid.

57. Ibid.

58. Ibid.

59. Ibid.

60. Ibid.

61. Ibid.

62. Ibid.

63. Jakob, Christian (2017) 'Eine Brutstätte für Extremisten', *tageszeitung*, 11 February | http://bit.ly/2vcXEp4

64. Stäritz, Andrea (2016) 'Die große Vision: offene Grenzen', *tageszeitung*, 12 December | http://bit.ly/2uP5DrE

Deportations:
'Then make him a Nigerian'

They knocked on his door at 3am on a Tuesday in October 2013. The police had come with two vans to Joseph Koroma's apartment at Heilbronner Straße 2 in the town of Walheim, in Southern Germany. An officer told Koroma that he was being deported to Nigeria and should go pack his suitcase. Koroma has been living in Germany since 2006 and has never been to Nigeria.

He panics. 'I was beside myself,' he told US journalist Cooper Inveen at a meeting in December 2016 about that day. He remembers that the police told him to calm down and pack the things he would need most urgently. 'I can't go to Nigeria. I come from Sierra Leone,' he says. The officers reply that they have their orders. Koroma has to leave behind everything that does not fit into his backpack. The police officers take him to the Foreigners' Registration Office. They hold him there for three hours and confiscate his German ID. His lawyer does not answer the phone.

Koroma was one of about 33,000 people registered nationwide by the German Ministry of the Interior in 2012 as 'obliged to leave the country immediately.'[1] Yet only about one in six could actually be deported in that year. Such was the complaint of AG Rück, a work group of German federal and state-level officials dealing with deportations. The group listed roughly two dozen reasons why deportations were so difficult. At the top of the list: 'Procurement of passports (or replacement papers).' In second place: 'Cooperation behavior of the countries of origin.'[2] As in Joseph Koroma's case.

Koroma had arrived in Germany in May 2006. At the time, he was 42 years old. From 1991 to 2002, Sierra Leone was engulfed in civil war. As many as 300,000 people may have been killed and

2.6 million displaced. But when Koroma reaches Germany, the war is over. His asylum claim is denied after just five months. This decision takes effect in 2008. In 2011, the regional authority in Karlsruhe orders Koroma to present himself at his national embassy, which does not issue him passport.

It emerged back in 2006 that Foreign Minister Steinmeier had furiously complained to several diplomats, because 29 embassies (which his ministry had placed on a secret 'list of problem states') were making deportations difficult. Sierra Leone is also on the list. The work group AG Rück states reasons why embassies often cause deportations to fail. Some will only issue passports if the person involved consents. Koroma did not. The embassies wished to protect their citizens from the German authorities, writes AG Rück; it also lists corruption, arbitrariness and a lack of 'political interest in deportations';[3] some countries even wanted to extort concessions or money from Germany.

In order to get around the balking embassies, in previous years the Federal Police had come up with the scheme of flying in West African state officials. In 2008, officials from Freetown, Sierra Leone's capital, came to Hamburg for one of these special visits. The *Süddeutsche Zeitung* later found that they were paid €250 per deportation paper and a 'daily flat rate' of €200, plus a per diem allowance.[4] The Federal Police gave them tickets to a soccer game of Hamburg's team HSV; for a €63.50 fee, they even had a locksmith service make an official stamp for the Sierra Leonian officials, who had come without their national insignia. Unlike the embassy, this delegation issued deportation papers to two-thirds of all denied asylum applicants presented to them. A smashing success for the Foreigners' Registration Office and the Federal Police, who could now deport dozens of backlogged cases in one blow. The media and courts, however, were not too happy about this affair. It smelled too much of corruption. Some time later, the federal police halted the practice.

The regional authority in Karlsruhe cannot deport Joseph Koroma, although he is 'obliged to leave the country immediately', because they have no passport for him. However, the officials are not easily discouraged. Koroma comes from Africa, and Africa is a big continent. Sierra Leone is not the only country there. Early on 10 April 2012, they pick up Joseph at his apartment and take him to Karlsruhe, where a delegation of the Nigerian embassy in Berlin is waiting for him. The delegates are supposed to examine the possibility that Joseph Koroma might come from Nigeria rather than Sierra Leone. Koroma tells them he will sue if they make him a Nigerian, so the embassy people send him and the German officers away. But the Foreigners' Registration Office will not be deterred.

On 25 June 2013, they come for Koroma at his apartment and take him to Karlsruhe once more. The same Nigerian delegation from Berlin is there. This time, it decides that Koroma is Nigerian.

Hence, five months later, Koroma sits at the Federal Police office of Frankfurt Airport, waiting to board the deportation plane. He is allowed to keep his mobile phone. 'My lawyer said he would write letters to the court and the Foreigners' Registration Office,' Koroma says. 'That was the last time we spoke.' At 11:10am, Lufthansa flight LH 568 takes off for Lagos, Nigeria.

In Lagos, police officers take him to officials at the Nigeria Immigration Service (NIS). Koroma tells them that he is not Nigerian, knows nobody in the country and does not know where to go. A short time later, a man from Togo, who lives in a suburb of Lagos, presents himself to the officials. He wants to take Koroma with him. He is the brother of a friend of Koroma's from the German town of Kornwestheim, where they played table tennis together. The news had reached the club, so the friend asked his brother to take in Koroma.

Koroma stays with this man for one month, rarely leaving the apartment. He mostly sits at the computer, writes emails and makes phone calls to his family in Sierra Leone and his table tennis buddies in Kornwestheim. Freetown is over 1,550 mi from Lagos, and the bus passes through rebel territory. A flight would cost several hundred euros and Koroma has nothing. A month later, he receives a payment through Western Union. His friends in Kornwestheim collected it for him.

When Koroma gets off the plane in Freetown in November 2013, he is grateful to his friends in Germany for enabling him to see his family. But Sierra Leone is no longer the place he left seven years earlier. Back then, he worked at a small mine in the east of this mineral-rich country famous for its diamonds. Whatever he could save, the family invested in his journey to Europe. Now he looks for steady work but finds none. Soon afterwards, Ebola breaks out. His family is spared from the epidemic but not from the economic crisis that follows. The money his friends collected does not keep paying for his small apartment long.

His relationship to his relatives has 'changed completely' since he returned, says Koroma's wife Mariama. 'When you have been out in the world and get deported, it is a scandal. They despise you instead of offering a helping hand. People say: "That man did not try hard enough when he was in Europe." But they don't understand how things work there.'[5]

Koroma is jobless and his family is threatened with eviction. His son Emmanuel is 17 years old. 'It's a gift from God that he's smart enough to go to university next year,' Mariama hopes. But this is unlikely. The entrance examination costs almost $200, and the average wage in Sierra Leone is under $2 per day. There is nobody who would help the Koromas.

So the son passes the time just like his father: playing table tennis. Joseph earns a bit of money by training a youth team. Soon, together with his son, he wants to open a youth training center. Young people should have opportunities that he did not. 'If my friends in Germany taught me anything, it was that you should always help people whenever you can,' he says. 'The world works better that way.'

It reeked of corruption

A man deported by Germany to a country not his own: Joseph Koroma is not the only case. But he is one of the few to be documented. Rex Osa, an activist in Stuttgart who is originally from Nigeria, made sure of that. Shortly after Koroma's deportation, he followed him all the way to Sierra Leone and recorded his statement, as well as others from similar cases in which deportees suddenly became Nigerians.

The Nigerian embassy in Berlin had fixed fees, as Osa's research found: the Foreigners' Registration Offices had apparently been charged €250 per hearing since 2005.[6] Then, suspicion arose that the embassy was making money off deportation papers. Criticism mounted; this practice also reeked of corruption. In response, the embassy officially eliminated the fees in 2011. Activist Rex Osa is certain that embassy workers were taking bribes; in Koroma's case, they even pocketed a double fee. That was also why they had themselves invited to Karlsruhe twice. 'It is an absolutely corrupt system. They're dealing in deportations,' says Osa.[7]

In 2015, Berlin journalist Daniel Mützel asked the Federal Police officers responsible for Koroma's deportation if this could be true. Did the Federal Police offer 'incentives' to turn Koroma and others into Nigerians in order to deport them? The Federal Police headquarters in Potsdam near Berlin replied: 'No incentives are offered by the Federal Police. Regarding the embassy's motivation, no statement can be made from here.'

So is Koroma telling the truth? Does he really come from Sierra Leone? It certainly seems so. In any case, on 6 November 2013, shortly after his arrival, the authorities in Freetown issue him a passport numbered E0143344, which he has shown to the authors. According to this document, he was born on 7 December 1964 in Freetown, as he had told the authorities in Germany. When Osa visits him in 2014, they meet in Freetown at his family home. So does journalist Cooper Inveen in November 2016, on assignment for the German *tageszeitung*.[8]

The reason why Koroma and a succession of other deportees landed in Nigeria is that many consulates do not cooperate with the German Foreigners' Registration Office, but Nigeria's does. It is a dubious procedure: expensive, laborious, lengthy and, for those affected by it, torturous.

Yet it seems that the Foreigners' Registration Office may not need to rely on such cooperation for much longer. The future of deportations could be different. Soon, everyone could be doing it just like Arne Sahlstedt, a police inspector in Gävle, central Sweden, a city of 70,000, a two-hour drive from Stockholm. Sahlstedt was also supposed to deport a man without a passport in October 2016. The man's name is Fulani Camara, age 29, from Mali, an orphan.

The Migration Agency in Gävle had expelled Camara after his asylum claim was denied, the same as had happened in Germany to Joseph Koroma. Like him, Camara did not leave the country. The Malian Embassy in Stockholm would not issue him a passport either. When the German *tageszeitung* inquires why not, the Gävle police do not want to give a reason, citing only 'data protection'.[9] Mali is probably also listed as a 'problem state'.

For the past two years, Sweden has had a directive to tell people like Sahlstedt what to do in cases like this. 'RPSFS 2014:8 FAP 638-1' states that Sahlstedt can issue a travel document himself, if the embassy does not. It is a simple, standard letter-sized page with the EU flag printed at the top; Sahlstedt has to merely fill in a person's name, height, Swedish registration number, date of birth and 'presumed nationality'. In Camara's case, Sahlstedt wrote 'Mali'. On 24 October 2016, Sahlstedt stamped and signed the paper.[10] Three days later, Fulani Camara was on a plane.

On the day of Camara's flight, a mobile phone rang in Mali's capital Bamako for Ousmane Diarra,[11] an activist with the Malian Association for Deportees (AME) (*L'Association Malienne des Expulsés*). For years, he has been going to the airport to wait for the 7:55pm arrival of the one daily direct flight from Paris, whenever there are people on board who were taken by the police from their homes somewhere in Europe that same morning because they lost their right to remain. Most of these people have no idea where to go; very few have any money. The airport personnel are glad that the AME takes care of them, so they call Diarra whenever deportees get off the plane.

Diarra waits for them outside the airport police office and then takes them to the office of the AME. A place to sleep for the first night, a meal – Diarra has little more to offer. Each time, however, he asks about the circumstances of their deportation. Diarra has heard possibly thousands of these stories by now.

Camara's case was special, however, because of that paper with the EU flag, signed by Swedish police inspector Sahlstedt – the Malian authorities do not recognize it at all. Back in 1994, the EU had expressed its 'recommendation' for the use of such deportation papers. The problem of uncooperative embassies is an old one. Yet until now, all African states – with the exception of the island state of Cape Verde – have refused to officially accept these papers. If they did, their embassies would lose the possibility to examine whether a person is actually a citizen of their countries – and also the chance to earn bribes from this sideline. Unofficially, however, there have been cases where these so-called EU laissez-passers were used.

Diarra asked Camara to stay for a few days. On 5 November 2016, the AME celebrated its 20-year anniversary. It rented a room for the occasion in Bamako's National Museum, which lies between the soccer stadium and the city hall. It was a big day for the association. Mali's citizens traditionally go elsewhere for work. Most go to other West African states, some to Europe. For this reason, the country has a long-standing 'Ministry of Malians Abroad'. This department has been under pressure throughout its existence. Several countries, France especially, want to deport many Malians. Mali's government is not keen on this plan.

An internal strategy paper of the EU Commission from January 2016 in preparation for a readmission agreement with Mali describes the situation thus: Views on migration between the EU and Mali 'do not coincide'. In Mali, migration has a 'cultural dimension ... as a model of success'; 'the economic importance of remittances has to be taken into consideration.' The Malian government viewed even irregular migration as a 'resource'. Therefore, the paper says, Mali was opposed to readmission agreements with the EU.[12]

The AME had invited the 'Advisor to the Minister for Malians Abroad', Broulaye Keïta, to its anniversary celebration to speak about how the government would handle the growing pressure from Europe. The AME wanted to know the government's position on the current deportation agreement, in which the EU was offering states like Mali hundreds of millions of euros. The agreement also supposedly stated that Europe would be able to issue its own deportation papers from now on.

Filmmaker Hans-Georg Eberl of Vienna was present at the celebration. He reports that Keïta said the government would be staying the course: No deportation to Mali without a Malian passport. There would be no exceptions. Diarra had scanned Camara's paper just for this moment: In front of all the assembled guests, he projected the image of the EU laissez-passer from the Swedish authorities onto a big screen. Keïta claimed to know nothing about it. The 'Haut Conseil', the high council of his ministry, he promised, would open an investigation into the matter.

Keïta was probably lying. Just three days after the celebration, an EU delegation landed in Bamako: Italy's Foreign Minister and future head of government Gentiloni, secretary of state Domenico Manzione and EU Commission representative Franco Lucani were among them. They met with President Ibrahim Boubacar Keïta. As the EU described it, the exchange focused primarily on issues of migration.[13]

In 2008, 7,605 Malians were ordered to exit the EU, yet just 1,750 of them followed the orders or were deported in that year – a rate of 23.1 percent (Table 1). By the time of the AU-EU summit in November 2015 in the Maltese capital Valletta, this rate had sunk even lower, to 11.4 percent. The rates looked similar for deportation rates of citizens of other African states. Raising these rates was a top priority for the EU. To Mali alone, the Europeans offered €145 million immediately and even more in the following year – if it could give 'specific and measurable results in terms of fast and operational returns of irregular migrants',[14] as one Council paper states.

	2008	2009	2010	2011	2012	2013	2014	2015	2016	2017	Change 2010-2017
	920	790	775	860	955	865	1105	1475	1475	2560	
Ethiopia	235	225	210	210	295	300	175	180	210	360	
	25.5%	28.5%	27.1%	24.4%	31.6%	31.6%	15.8%	12.2%	14.2%	14.1%	-45.0%
	2225	2535	2130	2195	1965	1635	1.565	2650	2650	6560	
The Gambia	805	600	515	600	515	585	440	420	470	595	
	36.2%	23.7%	24.2%	27.3%	27.3%	35.78%.	23.6%	20.4%	17.7%	9.1%	-75.0%
	7605	6200	4060	3730	3720	4405	5495	3505	3695	4705	
Mali	1750	770	415	465	385	630	605	400	385	355	
	23.0%	12.4%	10.2%	12.5%	10.4%	14.3%	11.0%	11.4%	10.4%	7.6%	-67.0%
	10285	10260	8655	7035	6 555	5455	5510	4695	5445	5275	
Senegal	2175	1180	1105	1110	1245	1265	1255	1055	790	795	
	21.1.5%	11.5%	12.8%	15.8%	19.0%	23.2%	22.8%	22.5%	14.5%	15.1%	-29.0%
	15765	16195	16590	13765	12450	12490	13830	12915	11450	15660	
Nigeria	5820	5850	6140	6045	5700	6055	4590	4605	3945	3710	
	36.9%	36.1%	37.0%	43.9%	45.8%	48.5%	33.2%	35.7%	34.5%	23.7%	-36.0%
	5140	4695	4,56(0	4490	4245	4270	4285	3710	4155	5030	
Ghana	1940	1710	1720	1730	1860	1825	1340	1080	1085	1115	
	37.7%	36.4%	37.7%	38.5%	43.8%	42.7%	31.3%	29.1%	26.1%	22.2%	-41.0%

Yet this cooperation is highly controversial in Mali, as in many other African states. In these countries, migration is a promise for many who seek something better. It is also vital for many Malians with family members in the diaspora. And so, shortly after Camara's arrival, Mali backed out of the deal.

To Bamako and back

On 29 December 2016, two jets approached Mali's capital Bamako: Air France flight AF 914 and Aigle Azur flight ZI 521, both from Paris-Orly. Each flight had a man on board whom France wanted to deport to Mali. Neither man had a passport. This was a test run. The EU wanted to know whether Mali would officially give way; to see whether it would do what Brussels had been trying to wrest from the African states in the preceding year's marathon negotiations: the unlimited, unconditional readmission of African refugees and migrants. However, on the evening of 29 December, the Malian border police at the international airport in Bamako did not allow the two Malians into the country. The accompanying French police officers and representatives of both airlines protested this decision for hours. The Malian officials held firm. On the following morning, both Malians were back in Paris.

Within hours, the international media spread the news across the globe. Mali, the desperately poor desert state, a jihad-wracked ex-colony of France, had defied the EU on its most crucial current political issue. Newspapers wrote about the 'tension' and 'conflict' between Bamako and Brussels. The EU's boldest political offensive toward Africa thus far – on that day, it ended in a fiasco.

At the Valletta II summit in February 2017, Olawale Maiyegun, AU Department Director of Migration and Social Affairs, told the Europeans to their faces: 'At the start of the Valletta Process in late 2015 you said that it should be a partnership with no strings attached. But then, bit by bit, all the strings came back into play.' The laissez-passers, for example: he considers them to be flatly illegal. 'This is unacceptable to us, and it violates international law. So far, the EU has not gotten away with them, but it makes them into a condition for talks about paths to the legal migration of people from Africa to Europe.' He does not criticize the obstinacy of the often-corrupt embassies.

Yet the EU continues to negotiate with Mali, as well as with Senegal, Nigeria, Niger and others. Should they succeed, all of the AG Rück's problems would be solved. What happened to Fulani Camara or Joseph Koroma could become the fate of many other Africans. States like Germany or Sweden would no longer depend on the unpredictable, sometimes corrupt embassies. In principle, they could deport every denied asylum applicant to any country that accepts the EU papers – regardless of the person's actual country of origin. The European Commission's External Action Service (EEAS), which is responsible for the criteria for issuing this paper, will disclose nothing on the subject. The national authorities seem to have free rein.

As of early 2019, no African state has officially accepted the laissez-passers.

However, the EU finally wrested its first deportation agreement for expelled refugees from one country, Ethiopia. The agreement, signed in December 2017, states that Ethiopian embassies must issue deportation papers within three days of receiving a request from a European immigration office. If the deportee lacks a passport, European authorities are permitted to provide documents to the Ethiopian secret services – renamed in the agreement as 'the intelligence and security services' – from which a person's nationality can be inferred, such as a copy of an expired ID card. The Ethiopians must respond within two weeks.

If no such documents exist, the immigration offices can present the presumed Ethiopian to the embassy for questioning. The embassy must hold the interrogation within two weeks and decide whether the person is an Ethiopian.

The agreement further permits EU states to have officials flown in directly from Ethiopia by request for special missions. The EU presumably wants to keep this possibility open in case the embassies issue too few deportation papers. The officials are to interrogate the potential deportees in order to determine their nationalities. Such agreements are very controversial.

The EEAS praised Ethiopia in a September 2017 report for its progress in combatting human trafficking networks. This is why the number of irregular migrants to reach Europe from the Horn of Africa has fallen, the report claims. However, the report continues, cooperation for readmission from the EU – that is, for deportations – was unsatisfactory and the rate of readmission was one of the lowest in the region. The conclusion states that political involvement at the highest level must be transformed into operative cooperation.

Amnesty International is concerned about the planned cooperation with the Ethiopian secret service NISS to determine people's identity. Within the past year, Amnesty International has heard repeatedly of asylum procedures in which the German Federal Office for Migration and Refugees (BAMF) doubted asylum seekers' Eritrean nationality and presumed them to be Ethiopian nationals, says Franziska Ulm-Düsterhöft, Amnesty's specialist on Africa.

She says the EU document has no fixed criteria at all for how the NISS will establish a person's Ethiopian nationality. For Ulm-Düsterhöft, this raises the question how to ensure that Eritreans, some of whom speak the same language, will not be wrongly declared Ethiopian citizens and deported to Ethiopia. Further, she says, Amnesty was fundamentally opposed to bringing people to the direct attention of the NISS, which was known for repeatedly persecuting and jailing critics of the government and for human rights violations. This procedure required no assurance from Ethiopia to protect the human rights of readmitted individuals, she concludes.

Notes

1. *Bild* (2014) 'Mehr als 131 000 abgelehnte Asylbewerber immer noch da', *Bild*, 13 February | http://bit.ly/1kE1Wdi

2. *Vollzugsdefizite – Ein Bericht über die Probleme bei der praktischen Umsetzung von ausländerbehördlichen Ausreiseaufforderungen*, Report by AG Rück, Clearingstelle Trier, April 2011

3. Bewarder, Manuel (2015) 'Der gesetzestreue Ausländer ist der Dumme', *Die Welt*, 18 May | http://bit.ly/2uqQRUo

4. *Süddeutsche Zeitung*, (2011) 'Besonders Sierra Leone stellt bereitwillig Papiere aus', 7 November | http://bit.ly/2hi8CUM

5. Jakob, Christian (2016) 'Dann ist er halt Nigerianer', *tageszeitung*, 17 December | http://bit.ly/2vcvCu9

6. The Voice Refugee Forum (2011) *Nigeria Embassy In Germany Corruptly Collects € 500 On Each Deported Nigerian*, 15 August | http://bit.ly/2uS5cex

7. Personal interview, December 2016

8. Jakob (2016) | http://bit.ly/2vcvCu9

9. Ibid.

10. Document held by the authors

11. Personal interview, January 2017

12. EU Commission and European External Action Service (EEAS) (2016) 'Joint Commission-EEAS non-paper on enhancing cooperation on migration, mobility and readmission with Mali', 24 February | https://bit.ly/2TWCuoB

13. Jakob (2016) | http://bit.ly/2vcvCu9

14. EU Council (2016) 'General Secretary of the Council—Draft conclusions', 28–29 June | https://bit.ly/2DvLn1e

Development Aid:
'A mix of positive and
negative incentives'

Development aid once had many great aspirations. It wanted to combat global poverty, hunger, illiteracy and disease. It planned to distribute land fairly, ensure access to clean water and education, create infrastructure, help women and girls – and much more.

In Germany, the government-run *Gesellschaft für Internationale Zusammmenarbeit* (known as GIZ) was primarily responsible for these goals, along with church-owned and private NGOs. GIZ is a large organization; with a €2.6 million budget in 2017, it employed over 19,000 people in about 120 countries.[1] However, anyone attending one recent GIZ showcase event may wonder whether development aid still has these high aspirations.

On 6 July 2016, GIZ's Chair of the Management Board, Tanja Gönner, and the State Secretary at the German Ministry for Economic Cooperation and Development (BMZ), Friedrich Kitschelt, hosted the press in the wood-paneled room no. 1 of the Federal Press Conference building along Berlin's Spree river. They presented the GIZ annual report and a promotional film to about 20 journalists. For nearly an hour, Gönner and Kitschelt spoke on just one topic: how GIZ was handling the refugee situation. Gönner spoke about nothing else. Climate change, sustainability, clean water, nutrition, land, education, health – the speakers mentioned none of the GIZ's former core issues. That was no coincidence, because the so-called war on poverty, in the form of irregular migration, is the new paradigm of development aid.

For a while, policymakers have been selling migration control as part of a package labeled 'development aid'. Between the start of the millennium and the 2015 Valletta Summit, European states and the EU paid or granted about €2 billion to African governments to combat irregular migration.[2] Since then, the EU has also financed the Emergency Trust Fund for Africa (endowed with €4.1 billion as of January 2019) and sent up to €6 billion to Turkey since 2016. The External Investment Plan (EIP) gave Africa another €3.7 billion[3] for economic development through 2018. Here again, the purpose is to 'tackle the root causes of irregular migration'. Finally, during a trip to Tunis in November 2017, President of the European Parliament Antonio Tajani demanded that the EU pump a staggering €40 billion into Africa between 2020 and 2026, among other things, 'to counter migration.'[4]

The outcomes remain to be seen. What we do know is that in the past 15 years, the EU has granted at least €15 billion to keep refugees and irregular migrants where they are. The funded projects have one thing in common: they explicitly list 'border control exercises', 'better migration/border management' or 'tackling the root causes of migration.'

€15 billion is a small sum overall: in 2017, official development assistance (ODA) payments rose slightly to $146.6 billion worldwide; about €30 billion flowed from Europe to Africa.[5] However, aid is increasingly channeled towards 'tackling the causes of migration'. The goal is always the same: partner states should keep refugees and migrants in their countries or take them back.

Payment only for services rendered. 'The Europeans have had this idea since negotiations for the Valletta Process began,' says EU chief negotiator Pierre Vimont.[6] Many interior ministers tell him clearly that they will increase development aid to African countries only if more migrants return there and if their countries take them back. This mechanism is not yet mentioned in the Valletta Summit Action Plan. But the EU makes it an explicit condition for aid in its 2016 New Migration Partnership Framework: 'A mix of positive and negative incentives will be integrated into the EU's development and trade policies to reward those countries willing to cooperate effectively with the EU on migration management and ensure there are consequences for those who refuse.' Then-President of the European Parliament Martin Schulz amplified: 'The EU Commission proposes to *reward* those third countries willing to cooperate effectively with us ... When third countries refuse to cooperate on returns, we should be clear that this has consequences.'[7]

The EU thereby uses aid to put pressure on some of the world's poorest states. More openly than ever, Europe is linking assistance to far-reaching conditions to meet its own political priorities.

Countries who do not help to fend off undesirable migrants risk losing not just money, but market access as well. The EU Council's conclusions from June[8] and October[9] 2016 state: 'to create and apply the necessary leverage, by using all relevant EU policies, instruments and tools, including development and trade.'

In the past decade, states with external EU borders like Italy and Spain were the pioneers, for obvious reasons. They learned how to use traditional development aid projects to control migration. These projects might aim to modernize the administration, develop a port, expand education or healthcare infrastructure – goals completely unrelated to border protection. However, the donor countries found that they could tie their funding to the condition that the recipient countries would stop or take back refugees.

The major examples were the programs of the Spanish *Plan África* I & II. In the four years after their launch in 2004, Spain nearly quadrupled its aid to West Africa. Spanish ODA shot up by 529 percent in West Africa, a key region for transit migration.[10] 'We believe that it makes sense to link the increase in development aid to the drafting of readmission agreements,'[11] former justice minister and current Socialist MEP Juan Fernando López Aguilar said in 2006: 'Countries that receive European money have to recognize the challenges we are facing and assume joint responsibility for coping with migration flows,'[12] Spanish Foreign Minister Miguel Ángel Moratinos stated earlier that year.

Between 2005 and 2010, for example, Madrid gave Morocco a total of €430.2 million in development aid. In this period Spain increased its annual grants to Senegal from €14 to €48 million, to Guinea-Bissau from €1.4 to about €15 million and to Mauritania from €9 to €30 million.[13] All countries first had to commit to intensifying their border protection efforts. Overall, Spain signed 12 anti-migration agreements with West African states between 2006 and 2008.

In January 2007, Juan Carlos, King of Spain, invited Malian President Amadou Toumani Touré to his palace for lunch. Until then, Spain had ignored this West African core state and did not even run an embassy there. But more and more Africans were crossing Mali to reach Canary Island beaches. After lunch, Touré signed two agreements with Spanish Prime Minister José Luis Rodríguez Zapatero.[14]

In the first agreement, Spain bestowed a fairy-tale sum upon Mali: In 2006, the poverty-ridden country had received only €7.3 million, which soared to €13 million in 2007 and €40 million in 2008. In the second agreement, Touré promised 'effective cooperation' on border controls – and to cause no problems if Spain deported Malians.

'Reinforcements' as development aid

Using this tactic, Spain bought half of West Africa, so in the years following, African refugees rarely reached the Canaries. Italy tried a similar approach with the Mediterranean states of Tunisia and Libya.

Generous development aid on the condition that recipient countries stop or readmit refugees – that was one strategy. However, there are two other ways in which the EU's migration control tactics crept into the fight against poverty.

One was grants for expanding border infrastructure: a 'grey zone of development cooperation',[15] says Benjamin Schraven of the German Development Institute (GDI). In 2016, for example, the German Defense Ministry and the Foreign Office supplied about €100 million for 'reinforcements' in African states.[16] Tunisia got €20 million of this sum for electronic surveillance at the Libyan border and training the border police, among other things. Germany allocated further funds for 2017. Whether the 'upgrade initiatives' count as development aid is still open. In any case, the German Ministry of Economic Cooperation and Development lists them as one 'pillar' of its 'Marshall Plan with Africa'.[17] In April 2017, the German government announced that it would launch a similar initiative on the EU level, 'Capacity Building for Security and Development,' which would be classified as development cooperation.[18] The Trust Fund for Africa, which is largely paid for from the European Development Fund (EDF), also falls under this category.

The second overlap between development aid and migration control is the EU's payments to non-member states for holding back migrants. The best-known example is the €6 billion deal with Turkey. This money came from the budget of the European Commission's Directorate-General for Civil Protection and Humanitarian Aid Operations (DG ECHO). EU member states can record their contributions to this agency's budget as development aid, along with parts of the cost for supporting refugees within their borders.

Phenomenal leverage

Border management is becoming increasingly important for the mostly state-run development agencies as well as for NGOs. 'This does not mean that they shift all their activities to this area,' says Schraven. More often, they just relabel existing projects. '"Rural

development" is simply renamed to "tackling causes of migration."[19]

Researcher Schraven speaks of the 'absurdity of the "causes of migration" rationale.' A popular assumption expressed across a wide spectrum, from the far-right AfD party through the more moderate CDU, FDP and the European Commission, but also by many on the Left, is that Africa needs more aid so that people will stay there. This is a fallacy. 'The narrative goes that poverty and lack of perspectives cause migration. The relationship is actually the reverse: Higher income and socioeconomic status make people more likely to come.' Migrants are in fact coming not from the poorest countries, but from relatively better-off states such as Senegal, Ghana or Nigeria – the main partners of the new EU initiatives.

A study by the Kiel Institute for the World Economy[20] supports this finding. 'When aid primarily raises domestic incomes, migration can be expected to increase as more people can finance the costs of migration,' write the researchers. 'Only at much higher development levels do rising incomes provide an incentive to stay – when the potential income gains to be achieved abroad have become very low.' The causal relationships between development aid and migration appear to be much less clear-cut than many policymakers would wish. The study suggests that only if development cooperation were to consistently expand infrastructure and improve public services, would this aid mitigate the causes of migration to a certain extent. 'The primary objective of aid should be to foster development and reduce poverty in recipient countries – regardless of any indirect impact on migration,' the researchers state. For income-generating projects like supplying better seed to small farmers, which make sense from a development perspective, it would be 'problematic if such projects were not realized because a small fraction of beneficiaries might emigrate as a result'.[21]

However, the EU is strictly following the equation 'more aid = less migration'. For example, the Trust Fund for Africa, which now holds €4.1 billion, contains mostly unspent reserves from the EDF. The same is true of the EU's External Investment Plan (EIP), which is intended to boost the African economy in order to – what else? – 'tackle root causes of migration.'[22] The EU will provide €4.5 billion from the European Fund for Sustainable Development for the EIP. The plan intends for European companies to invest the phenomenal sum of €44 billion in Africa by 2020.[23] The hope is that this will create jobs to finally keep young people in Africa.

'That money didn't fall from the sky, it came from development cooperation funds,'[24] criticizes Inge Brees of the NGO CARE in

Brussels. When EU aid concentrates on countries along the migration routes, this funding goes missing elsewhere. This is exactly what happened in the EU-Turkey deal. The billions from the funds of emergency aid agency DG ECHO that the EU promised to Erdoğan 'would otherwise have been available for other crises'.

The transit country Niger, one of the world's poorest states, shows the power of these concentration effects. In 2015, Niger received $868 million in net development aid.[25] After the country caught the EU's attention as a transit point through the Western Sahara,[26] Development Commissioner Mimica approved an additional €1 billion in aid by 2020 – significantly more than the country previously received per year from all donor countries put together.[27] Hence, in 2017 Niger received €1.206 billion – nearly 40 percent more than just two years earlier – and clearly a political reward for gatekeeper services in the Sahara.

'There is a danger that development cooperation will focus on fewer states and that "less important" ones will get less,' says Schraven of the GDI. The goal of aid-funded projects increasingly appeared to be 'migration management, combating the causes of migration. And that usually means combating migration itself. This is becoming the *raison d'être* of development cooperation'. Schraven fears the shift will undermine standards achieved over the past 25 years in the development cooperation community: recipient needs, good governance and transparency.

Just when states located farther from Europe will feel these concentration effects remains to be seen. 'The trend towards migration control as a core issue is still fairly recent. In two, three, four years we may see a shift towards the more cooperative countries,' says Schraven.

'It was clearly not about Africa as a whole, but about migration,' says EU diplomat Vimont.[28] This was why the EU invited only the partner states from the Rabat and Khartoum Processes to the Valletta Summit on Migration. Other African states that asked for more involvement in the summit were rejected. Vimont says: 'We told them: "Not yet."'

'When 20 of 55 African states are excluded, that is not a legitimate procedure,' says the African Union's (AU) Director of Social Affairs Maiyegun.[29] 'Angola could say: "We're not part of the process. The Europeans just picked out the states that seemed important to them."' He adds, 'African states have no adequate participation in the Trust Fund for Africa. Decisions were made without African involvement.' Maiyegun describes how the EU had given contracts to European institutions and NGOs that claimed to know Africa. These claims were often wrong, so failure was guaranteed, he warns. Further, Maiyegun criticizes that the AU was not included when the EU distributed money from the Trust Fund for Africa. 'The AU Commission should sit on the Fund's governing bodies,' he argues. 'We represent the interests of the entire continent. We should have a say.'

'Whoever does not cooperate will be sanctioned'

Restricting aid to 'useful' African states is one approach. Another is targeted sanctions for unsatisfactory border protection and deportation efforts. The EU speaks of a 'mix of positive and negative incentives.' During his term as President of the European Parliament, Martin Schulz wanted to show uncooperative countries that their behavior 'has consequences.' He is not alone. After the terrorist attack on a Berlin Christmas market by Tunisian national Anis Amri, the legal affairs speaker of the SPD's parliamentary group, Burkhard Lischka, demanded to cut off EU funds to Tunisia if its government did not cooperate in deportations: 'There are ways to raise the pressure, and not all of them involve development aid.'[30] German Minister of Justice Heiko Maas (SPD) threatened: 'Whoever does not cooperate will be sanctioned.'[31] Similar expressions came from Minister of the Interior Thomas de Maizière and SPD parliamentary group chairman Thomas Oppermann.[32] His fellow party member, Hamburg's First Mayor Olaf Scholz, wanted to immediately slash funding to all states who did not sign readmission agreements: 'In negotiations with other countries, all issues are on the table.'[33] Of course this also applied to development aid, he said in January 2017. SPD leader Sigmar Gabriel accused Development Minister Gerd Müller of 'blocking' the appropriate measures.[34]

Too few deportations equal less development aid – Schraven of the GDI calls this idea 'not terribly smart'. Simply cutting off funding would hardly be feasible for the EU. He considers such statements to be 'largely empty threats' which could be applied selectively at best. 'This will definitely not become a mass phenomenon.'[35]

Uncooperative states will lose EU aid money, cooperative ones will get more – regardless of their political integrity. Migration control helps pariah states like Sudan or Eritrea benefit from Western aid once more.[36] 'Cooperating with some states, like those in East Africa, is questionable, to put it mildly, if you apply the usual criteria for development aid,' Schraven criticizes. The EU Commission points out that money for Eritrea flows only to 'NGOs' and 'civil society' actors. Nicole Hirt, Eritrea specialist at the

German Institute of Global and Area Studies (GIGA), calls this claim 'absurd.'[37]

However, official aid is not the only way to finance development. In 2006, Africa received almost $50 billion in development aid.[38] In the same period, emigrants remitted about €63 billion to their source countries.[39]

This money goes directly to families and small businesses. If the EU is buying readmission agreements with tailor-made aid packages, 'then the Europeans will not be able to avoid offering more options for regular migration to Europe,' says Schraven.[40] This seems unlikely. The Valletta Summit Action Plan still mentioned 'promoting regular channels for migration and mobility from and between European and African countries'.[41] But the latest progress report on the Partnership Framework for Migration dropped any mention.[42]

The EU has obviously chosen to make migration control the main condition for development aid. It also wants to officially subordinate aid for Africa and other poor regions to its foreign and security policy – and get rid of its separate budget for development aid.

On 1 March 2018, EU Commissioner Jean-Claude Juncker and Budget Commissioner Günther Oettinger (CDU) wrote a letter to the EU development ministers. It stated that the next EU budget for 2021-27 would require 'some difficult decisions' which they should represent externally with 'a high level of discipline'.[43]

The commissioners urged the ministers to assert the 'primacy of external policy'[44] and commit development aid to new and controversial goals. The Commission planned to combine 12 previously independent budget lines for development policy, democracy and human rights under a single new budget item.

This Foreign Policy Instrument' (FPI) would not only concentrate more on immediate neighbors (i.e., Ukraine or Georgia) – to the detriment of traditional aid recipients in Africa or Asia – it would also have a 'strong focus on migration', states an annex.[45]

Any unused funds would flow primarily to the EU's refugee policy – that is, reinforcing the EU's external borders and so-called migration partnerships with African countries.

The FPI would 'simplify and accelerate the misappropriation of EU development funds that has been observable for years', criticized Greens MEP Barbara Lochbihler. 'These plans are bad for our political credibility and for the transparency of our budget.' Throwing established financial instruments into one big foreign policy pot would bring far more than the alleged budget simplification, argued Lochbihler. It would also permit the EU to divert funds intended for civil conflict prevention to finance military aims, such as equipment and training for armies in Africa.[46]

Notes

1. Gesellschaft für Internationale Zusammenarbeit *Unternehmensberichte* | http://bit.ly/2udAFpA

2. Migration Control Database, *tageszeitung* | https://migration-control.taz.de/#de

3. European Commission (2019) *External Investment Plan – Progress so far*, 21 February | https://bit.ly/2SRJAy8

4. Ibid. and *Finanzen* (2017) 'EU-Parlamentspräsident will 40 Milliarden Euro für Afrika', Tunis, 31 October | https://bit.ly/2Y6sLOH

5. European Commission (2019) *Africa-EU continental cooperation*, 20 February | http://bit.ly/2vgNYJW

6. European Commission (2016) 'Commission announces New Migration Partnership Framework: reinforced cooperation with third countries to better manage migration', European Commission press release, Strasbourg, 7 June | https://bit.ly/28hEsSG | and Personal interview, Brussels, 16 June 2017

7. European Parliament (2016) President Martin Schulz, Speech at European Council session, 28 June | https://bit.ly/2NoCk6B

8. EU Council (2016) Conclusions, EU Council session, 28 June | https://bit.ly/2Vh1eIl

9. EU Council (2016) Conclusions, EU Council session 20-21 October 2016 | https://bit.ly/2EfUWlt

10. Azkona, Nerea (2011) 'Políticas de control migratorioy de cooperación al desarrollo entre España y África Occidental durantela ejecución del primer Plan África', *Alboan y Entreculturas*, Madrid, 2011 | http://bit.ly/2uOG75x

11. Migration Control Database, 'Spain Country Report', *tageszeitung*, 21 February 2019| http://bit.ly/2hih7yU

12. Machado, Decio (2016) 'Plan África: impedir las migraciones', *Diagonal*, 16 October | http://bit.ly/2f2mpoP

13. Azkona, Nerea (2011) | http://bit.ly/2uOG75x

14. Migration Policy Group (2007) 'Migration News Sheet', Brussels, February 2007, p. 10 | https://bit.ly/2SkqLyv

15. Telephone interview with Benjamin Schraven, July 2017

16. German Federal Ministry for Defense, *Fragen und Antworten zu Ertüchtigung* | http://bit.ly/2vncgTc

17. German Federal Ministry for Economic Cooperation and Development (BMZ) (2017) 'A Marshall Plan with Africa. Chapter 3, Pillar 2: Peace, Security and Stability', January 2017 | https://bit.ly/2Vlzen1

18. *Bundestags-Drucksache 18/11889* | http://bit.ly/2wfx5N8

19. Schraven (2017)

20. Thiele, Rainer (2019) 'Development aid alone will not reduce migration', Media information, *Kiel Institute for the World Economy*, Kiel, 15 January | https://bit.ly/2GIzWak

21. Ibid.

22. European Commission (2017) 'EU External Investment Plan. Factsheet', Brussels, 20 November | http://bit.ly/2vn5KMy

23. EU Parliament (2017) *Report on the proposal for a regulation of the European Parliament and of the Council on the European Fund for Sustainable Development (EFSD) and establishing the EFSD Guarantee and the EFSD Guarantee Fund*, EU Parliament, Brussels, 25 April | http://bit.ly/2vZQYsc

24. Personal interview with Inge Brees, 4 December 2016, Brussels

25. Trading Economics (2019) 'Niger – Net ODA received per capita', *Trading Economics* 22 February | http://bit.ly/2vn8TMl

26. Maier, Anja (2016) 'Kein Marshall-Plan für Afrika', *tageszeitung*, 10 October | http://bit.ly/2wfi6CG

27. European Commission (2017) 'EU will support Niger with assistance of €1 billion by 2020', European Commission press release, 13 December | http://bit.ly/2qfjlUc

28. Personal interview, Brussels, 16 June 2017

29. Personal interview, Malta, 8 February 2017

30. *Die Welt (2017)* 'SPD stellt Sicherheitshilfen für Tunesien infrage', 12 January | http://bit.ly/2jGaIht

31. *Frankfurter Allgemeine Zeitung (2017)* 'Merkel kündigt "nationale Kraftanstrengung" bei Abschiebungen an', 9 January | http://bit.ly/2eWUWO1

32. *Frankfurter Allgemeine Zeitung (2017)* 'Oppermann fordert Sanktionen gegen Herkunftsländer', 9 January | http://bit.ly/2tSTNcZ

33. *Die Zeit (2017)* 'Scholz fordert schnellere Abschiebungen', 11 January | http://bit.ly/2f2vdE7

34. *Frankfurter Allgemeine Zeitung* (2017) 'Gabriel: CSU blockiert Lösung bei Abschiebungen nach Nordafrika', 7 January | http://bit.ly/2i4qeBI

35. Schraven (2017)

36. Titz, Christoph (2016) 'Unser Partner, der Diktator', *Spiegel Online*, 10 June | http://bit.ly/2vcwSNM

37. Sagener, Nicole (2016) 'EU decried for seeking deal with "North Korea of Africa"', *Euractiv*, 6 July | https://bit.ly/2U3haxC

38. OECD Database (2019) *Aid (ODA) disbursements to countries and regions [DAC2a]*, 18 March | https://bit.ly/2Cl1IG3

39. 'Record high remittances to low- and middle-income countries in 2017', World Bank press release, Washington, 23 April 2018 | https://bit.ly/2CooSzl

40. Schraven (2017)

41. EU Council (2015) *Valletta Summit Action Plan, 11-12. November 2015*, 12 November | https://bit.ly/2Tftc7d

42. European Commission (2017) *Partnership Framework on Migration: Commission reports on results and lessons learnt one year one*, European Commission, Strasbourg, 13 June | http://bit.ly/2vcdekN

43. Bonse, Eric (2018) 'Abschottung geht vor Entwicklung', *tageszeitung*, Brussels, 19 March | https://bit.ly/2Xl4gwT

44. Ibid.

45. Ibid.

46. Ibid.

Europe's Guards:
Frontex has no borders

Pål Erik Teigen's ship has almost everything: a corpse freezer, a playroom with a movie screen and an enormous deck with sun protection that can hold over 1,100 people when Teigen's crew pulls them out of the water. But the deck is sunless today, on a bleak afternoon in mid-November 2016. Rain is falling at the port of Catania, Sicily, where the Siem Pilot, the giant, signal-red flagship of the EU border protection agency Frontex is docked at the quay, taking aboard new crewmembers who have just arrived on the Alitalia flight from Rome.[1]

Teigen, 50, has been an officer with Norway's criminal police Kripos for 30 years. To show what he does here, he runs a video on his laptop. A cheerful soundtrack jars with the images compiled by Norwegian navy members.

Usually the Siem Pilot traverses the North Sea supplying oil rigs. Since June 2015 however, it has been Norway's most important contribution to managing the EU's refugee crisis. The government in Oslo chartered the ship and paid for the 15-member crew, 11 Norwegian police officers, 10 marine soldiers and six coast guard officers.

Teigen is deployed as commander for the fourth time: 'This was harder than all my years with the police put together.' Tomorrow his last four-week assignment with Frontex will be over. 'It was a strange summer,' he sums up. 'Sometimes 2,000 come, then 7,000, then it's quiet for several weeks in between.' The Siem Pilot has taken on board exactly 28,598 living and 91 dead persons during its Frontex deployment. In some cases, it took aboard people from other ships and brought them to Italy. 'Why do I do it?' Teigen asks himself. 'For this,' he says, showing a picture of two laughing African girls in a red lifeboat.

The Siem Pilot rescues people, but that is not its main reason for being here. In mid-April 2017, an unprecedented series of emergencies at sea broke out, endangering thousands of refugees and volunteer sea rescuers. Yet, the Siem Pilot did not respond until 24 hours later, taking aboard 150 people from a shipwrecked dinghy off the Libyan coast. Had activists from the Alarm Phone initiative not exerted public pressure, these people would probably have died.[2]

Normally Teigen's boat navigates close to Italy, far away from Libya. It is no coincidence that the ship is commanded by a police officer. Refugee boats are 'crime scenes', his little film explains – crime scenes for people smuggling. Teigen's real assignment is not to rescue the shipwrecked, but to fight people smugglers – regular police work. Teigen's men and women are here to find those among the thousands of refugees and migrants who run sea crossings as a racket. While heading towards safe mainland ports, they observe the rescued migrants, photograph and question them, analyze mobile phones, examine corpses in a separate forensics department, take DNA samples. So far, they have located 300 'persons of interest', smuggling suspects, and handed them over to the Italian police.

Teigen says the people on board are those whom his staff members can first get hold of. Beyond the sea, where smugglers are actually based, Frontex has no access, he explains. 'We don't know what's in Libya. The closer we are to Libya, the riskier it is. Nothing works over there. When we get closer to Libya, we have to use binoculars to watch out for dangers.'

Border guards as diplomats

This is only partly true. In fact, Frontex has had its sights set on Africa for a long time. The agency, restructured in September 2016 as the European Border and Coast Guard Agency (EBCG) (the short name Frontex was retained), needs no binoculars to find out what happens over there, from where the refugees start out towards Europe.

'It is clear that cooperation with migrants' countries of origin and transit is one of the key elements of a successful migration management,' writes Frontex director Fabrice Leggeri in an April 2017 annual report. Frontex had thus been 'extending its reach beyond Europe'[3] for tasks ranging from information exchange to deportation cooperation.

The agency has closed formal 'Working Arrangements' with at least 19 states. The agreements allow Frontex to cooperate with national authorities, exchange officials and data and set common technical standards. The partners include mostly Eastern European states, but also the USA, Canada, Cape Verde and Nigeria. As Frontex is negotiating new arrangements with Libya, Morocco, Senegal, Mauritania, Egypt and Tunisia, its current focus is clearly Africa.

Frontex' plan for the future is to extend Europe's borders far beyond the Schengen Area to catch irregular migrants long before they enter. By 'reinforcing and extending cooperations' with so-called third states – those not belonging to the EU – the agency wants to fully exploit its mandate 'in the area of the EU's foreign and security policy', states an internal November 2017 planning document.[4] A core goal of the new mandate is 'operational cooperation with priority third countries'.[5] Frontex will send liaison officers[6] to prepare potential 'operations on the territory of neighbouring third countries'.[7]

The EU would like to speed things up. In February 2017, EU presidency holder Malta invited member state representatives to a breakfast meeting in Valletta to prepare for the upcoming EU summit. The priority on the agenda was how to stop arrivals of refugees from Libya in Italy.

Frontex, they determined, should join forces with neighbor states to watch the Mediterranean using the satellite communication network 'Seahorse Mediterranean', which was initially set up by Spain. Furthermore, the EU diplomats asked the agency to tap into its own European-African Intelligence network.[8] Frontex had established the Africa-Frontex-Intelligence Community (AFIC) as one of four 'Risk Analysis Networks' it operates with countries outside the EU. Two of these networks include Eastern European states and one is for the Balkans and Turkey. The AFIC however, is the largest.

Since the AFIC's founding in 2010, Frontex has invited African Intelligence heads to Warsaw dozens of times, every four months on average. 28 states are involved in the AFIC so far, including the dictatorships of Eritrea and Sudan. Frontex has also 'invited' Ethiopia, Algeria and Tunisia. Overall, more than half of the African continent participates in this 'framework for regular knowledge and intelligence sharing in the field of border security'[9] – which describes the AFIC in Frontex-speak.

Regimes responsible for some of the refugees are also brought to the table. In Africa, like anywhere else, the less a state cares about basic human rights, the more it needs intelligence services to prop up its power. According to the outcomes of a recent Democracy

Index, a measure of democracy in 167 countries published by *The Economist*, not a single one of the 28 AFIC states is a democracy, while 15 of them rank as 'authoritarian' and nine as 'hybrid'. Frontex systematically collects information from these partners and helps them access secret intelligence from other African states.[10]

Once the AFIC just held meetings, but today it also shares data through an online platform. It trained African Intelligence members on EU databases and gave them user accounts so that they can feed information into the AFIC system every three months. Since May 2016, Frontex has created monthly reports from this data. The goal is a comprehensive, current picture of migration throughout Africa.

In 2016 the AFIC became a growing priority for Frontex. Among the people getting onto boats in Libya, hardly any were still coming from the Middle East – 91 percent came from Africa.[11] In order to convey a sense of ownership to the partners in Africa, the AFIC held two meetings there in 2016 – in Ghana in March, and in Mauritania in June.[12] Frontex proudly notes that the Africans were allowed to lead discussions.[13]

A 2017 AFIC report lists typologies of smugglers ('ghetto boss,' 'fixer,' 'chasseur'), details on their car preferences ('Toyota Hilux') and the starting days for trips through the Sahara (at the time, 'most likely Sundays'). Put together, all these trifles form an increasingly precise image of migration within Africa. In any case, we can assume the Intelligence is unlikely to publish its most interesting information.

Not their money anyhow

Frontex calls the AFIC 'an unparalleled platform for information-sharing'.[14] In its seventh year of existence, the association had reached a new 'enhanced maturity' that 'captured further attention from the key policy makers in Europe and Africa'.[15]

Frontex used to shun 'further attention'. In its early years the agency was secretive, preferring to stay in the background. Not anymore. Today it responds to enquiries within hours; its director often makes public appearances and gives interviews. One reason could be Frontex' growing importance. The EU has 44 agencies for specific policy areas, but none has grown as fast and been as well-endowed as Frontex. At its founding in Warsaw in 2006, it had 45 staff members and an annual budget of €12 million.[16] In 2016, Frontex had a budget of €254 million;[17] this could reach €320 million by 2020.[18] Of this, the Schengen states pay less than 10 percent and the European Commission pays over 90 percent.

The EU Commission wants to expand Frontex even further – preferably into a full-fledged border police force. The agency's rebranding as EBCG in September 2016 was a major step, giving it a range of new powers in conducting deportations.

Frontex has organized joint deportation charter flights at the request – and expense – of EU member states for several years now. These transports carry deportees of the same nationality from all over Europe. In 2017, Frontex deported over 13,000 people, almost four times as many as in 2015.[19]

As the EBCG, Frontex can also conduct deportation flights at its own initiative and cost. The EU budget provides €63 million per year for this as of 2019.[20] To improve deportation efficiency, the agency can search Europe for matching deportees and make sure its planes fly at full capacity. The first months after the new arrangement show that national immigration authorities are happy to use the offer – after all, it's not their money.

On 6 January 2017, a chartered plane took two rejected asylum seekers from Mali, Amadou Ba and Mamadou Drame from Düsseldorf to the Malian capital Bamako, accompanied just by a few German police officers. The flight, carried out by the Federal Police (Bundespolizei) by request of the Saale district, cost €82,000 and was paid by Frontex. To explain the nearly empty airplane, a speaker for the Ministry of the Interior of Saxony-Anhalt said: 'No other German states currently had any need for repatriations to Mali.'[21] After all, Frontex paid for it. Why wait?

Ba and Drame had 'sabotaged' two previous deportations 'through passive and active resistance',[22] the speaker said. They had injured Federal Police officers, biting and kicking them. Another deportation via scheduled flight was therefore out of the question. Both men had spent the last three months in a German prison.

However, an online video shows one of the failed prior deportations on an Air France airliner in Paris on 27 October 2016.[23] It shows how Ba, visibly exhausted, is pushed into his seat by two much bulkier police officers while other passengers shout at them: 'No violence!' Ba is then taken off the plane.

Activists from the NGO Afrique-Europe-Interact (AEI) met with the two men after they reached Bamako. The men reported mistreatment during deportation. 'They were bound at the ankles, knees and hands – the hands even twice with handcuffs and cable ties,'[24] says Olaf Bernau of AEI. 'Their upper arms were also held tightly to their bodies with a wide chest strap, practically immobilizing them.' The two men were forced to wait in this position for two to three hours before takeoff; Drame was restrained for the entire flight, Ba's feet and knees were released after a few hours.

'Return support' is what Frontex calls this service for national immigration authorities. The chartered plane, accommodation for the escorts, meals on the ground and fees for medical personnel and interpreters are paid by Frontex. It can also finance the cost of obtaining passports for deportees and 'voluntary departures' from a country – all expenses that member states previously had to bear.

At the same time, Frontex is creating a pool of 690 'return experts'. These include police and border protection officers from the EU states initiating deportations; among them are also the so-called escorts. The EU's Fundamental Rights Agency (FRA) criticizes that Frontex escorts do not 'necessarily have sufficient experience' to ensure that deportees' rights are observed.[25] Further, Frontex plans to dispatch 'return specialists' to EU member states to arrange deportations in case national authorities have been too lax.

The UN refugee agency UNHCR believes that people who do not need international protection should be deported more quickly and efficiently. This would help to 'build trust in the integrity of the asylum system', states a December 2016 publication. The UNHCR also recommends that Frontex cooperate more closely with countries of origin on readmissions.[26]

This is already happening. For a while, Frontex has been holding seminars for police officers from non-EU states, for example, on how to better recognize fake passports. Since 2010, it has conducted over 500 such courses outside the EU, most in Eastern Europe, some in Morocco. More are to follow. In reconstituting Frontex, the EU gave it a mandate to help African states cooperate with Europe on deportations. In March 2017, the EU Commission demanded that the agency make 'more extensive use of this operation'.[27] By no later than October of that year, Frontex should start training officers from non-member states to accompany deportation flights from Europe – which would be far cheaper for the EU than continuing to send its member state police officers. The EU also set up a fund for this purpose.[28]

Frontex exists to protect borders. However, the agency itself knows no geographical boundaries. It continually develops activities in other states. By now, its ever-expanding new networks, platforms, dialogues and surveillance systems are beyond comprehension.

One focus for Frontex is Libya. About 650,000 people migrated irregularly from Libya to the EU between 2014 and 2018.[29]

Since November 2016, Frontex has been involved in training the Libyan coast guard through the EU military anti-smuggling 'Operation Sophia'.[30] The EU High Representative for Foreign Affairs and Security, Federica Mogherini, handed certificates to the first batch of officers on board the Italian battleship San Georgio in port at Valletta on 9 February 2017. The training mission is very controversial, and not just because it is unknown to which extent armed militant groups are involved with the Libyan coast guard. Yet the mission is one of the main elements of the EU's anti-smuggling policy. By November 2018, 305 Libyans had completed the training. The graduates bring refugees picked up in Libyan territorial waters back to Libya.[31] The Libyan coast guard gets the initial data from Frontex, then from the satellite surveillance system EUROSUR via an exchange platform called SMART.[32]

As for the AFIC network, the EU's plans go beyond tapping extensive information from the African Intelligences. African states are also to exchange information with each other so they can quickly react to new migration flows. The process will be tested in Libya. The European External Affairs Service (EEAS) describes its ideas in a January 2017 document; the paper states that the EU has built a border management network between Libya and its neighbor states to the south.[33] These states are to conduct dialogues on African border management within the AFIC, while Frontex could provide satellite images. These information exchanges would 'use the AFIC's full potential', writes the EEAS.[34]

By March 2017, the EU foresees that again over 100,000 people could cross the sea from Libya to Italy that year. Due to the security situation at the time, Europe sends no officials to Libya, so Frontex was to watch the boats' departure points via satellite and air surveillance. Using the new, satellite-based reconnaissance program EUROSUR, the agency was to identify refugee boats and notify the EU police authority Europol, stated leading EU officials.[35] It did not occur to them to share this data with sea rescue organizations even though the death toll from shipwrecks was higher than ever before.

The EU also worried about Libya's neighbor Egypt, the most populous Arab state, with nearly 98 million people. In October 2016, Frontex dispatched a negotiating team to Cairo to talk the Egyptian government into closing a working agreement with Frontex and joining the reconnaissance network 'Seahorse Mediterranean'.[36] However, Egypt refused.

Italian political scientist Paolo Cuttitta asked Egyptian officials about the reasons for their reluctance. Egypt was very 'skeptical regarding the European Union and prefers to maintain bilateral relations with individual countries, which guarantee a greater possibility of manoeuvre and negotiation', Cuttitta quotes one Egyptian official. The Frontex delegation's visit to Cairo was 'a novelty, it had never happened before', the official's colleague said. 'I do not rule out that it may lead to a cooperation between Frontex and the Egyptian authorities, although the relations between Egypt and the EU, which are not ideal, will need to be improved before that.'[37]

Hence, in February 2017 the EU quintupled the budget for the Egyptian fund 'Enhancing the Response to Migration Challenges in Egypt' (ERMCE) for migration-related development projects to €60 million. However, the Egyptian government halted the project, as it could not agree with EU on exactly which activities should be funded.[38]

By 2018, the parties were closer to a resolution: Frontex director Fabrice Leggeri traveled to Cairo and 'praised Egypt's regional role, affirming that the European Union considers Egypt as one of the main partners in the region, especially regarding hindering illegal immigration. He also hailed the efforts of the Egyptian military's border guards to stop illegal immigration across Egyptian borders with Europe'.[39]

That October, President al-Sisi visited German Chancellor Merkel in Berlin. 'Egypt secures its maritime borders so well that there is effectively no migration from Egypt to Europe, although many refugees live in Egypt,' Merkel said. 'This is worthy of great recognition, and so we are supporting Egypt with an untied loan of €500 million.'[40]

Antennas in the desert

Frontex is also increasingly active beyond the Maghreb these days. From September 2015 to January 2017, for example, there were 11 top-level diplomatic meetings between Niger and the EU, one of them being Merkel's visit to the Sahel state. The goal was always the same: The key transit country should cut off the trans-Saharan migration route.

This diplomatic marathon gave Frontex a growing influence in the country. In March 2017, Frontex Director Leggeri traveled to the capital, Niamey. Calling Niger 'an indispensable and pivotal partner' in the 'common challenges that are affecting our two continents', he opened the country's first AFIC meeting at the Hotel Soluxe with Niger's Minister of State for the Interior, Mohamed Bazoum.[41] Afterwards, Leggeri dispatched a liaison officer to Niamey, the first long-term posting to a sub-Saharan state. In November 2018, Frontex opened the first Risk Analysis Cell.

According to the US web portal 'Homeland Security Today':[42]

'The role of these cells, which are run by local analysts trained by Frontex, is to "collect and analyze strategic data on cross-border crime in various African countries and support relevant authorities involved in border management." The data can include information on illegal border crossings, document fraud, trafficking in human beings and other types of cross-border crime. It is shared with authorities at national and regional level to produce analysis and policy recommendations, as well as with Frontex. The Risk Analysis Cell in Niger is the first of eight such cells that was established in the framework of the Africa-Frontex Intelligence Community (AFIC). The remaining cells will be established in Ghana, Gambia, Senegal, Kenya, Nigeria, Guinea and Mali until the end of 2019.'

EU High Representative Mogherini met Nigerian Minister of Foreign Affairs Geoffrey Onyeama in Brussels in March 2016. Africa's most populous state was also the first to close a working arrangement with Frontex in 2012.[43] Mogherini negotiated permission for Frontex to continue intervening in Nigeria's border management, and call Nigerian officials to Europe on identification missions so that they could issue travel documents to repatriate large numbers of deportees.[44] After a visit by EU Commission Vice President Andrus Ansip in February 2017, Nigeria and the EU agreed to further active cooperation against people smuggling on the basis of the AFIC and on the new bilateral 'Cooperation Platform on People Smuggling'.[45]

A free hand with foreign policy

In December 2016, the EU provided €5 million for a project in Sudan: the 'Regional Operational Centre in support of the

Khartoum Process and AU-Horn of Africa Initiative' (ROCK)[46] at the Police Higher Academy in Khartoum. Its purpose is to bolster information exchange between the countries of the Khartoum Process on irregular migration and people smuggling networks. EU diplomats on the ground called this plan 'the most sensitive project in Sudan'.[47] ROCK will also serve to strengthen East African cooperation with Interpol, Europol and the AFIC.

Why is it even possible for an agency charged with guarding Europe's borders to send German police officers, Romanian customs officials or Finish passport falsification experts halfway around the world? By what right can the EU deploy Frontex so far outside its territory?

Frontex' major goal is to reduce the numbers of irregular migrants reaching European borders. To achieve this, the agency developed a multi-tiered model for 'integrated border management', as described in Article 4 of the 2016 Frontex Regulations.[48] One of its points is 'cooperation with third countries', particularly those 'which have been identified through risk analysis as being countries of origin and/or transit for illegal immigration'.

In these cases, EU law gives Frontex a relatively free hand. Article 54 states, in essence, that in 'cooperation with third countries', the agency must comply with EU foreign policy and observe refugees' basic rights, especially 'the principle of non-refoulement'.[49]

But if it does not – what then?

The only thing still gravely underfunded is an effective mechanism for supervision and complaints. Those who are illegally turned away or deported by EU border protection agents have little recourse. This complaint, raised by many refugee and human rights organizations, is now shared by members of the EU Parliament. Frontex must provide more staff and funding to protect basic freedoms and to handle asylum applicants' complaints, warns the EU Committee on Civil Liberties.

Particularly since the 2007 introduction of Rapid Border Intervention Teams (RABIT) – police officers from across the EU deployed to the external border – human rights organizations have severely criticized Frontex. They accused the agency of violating the rights of asylum and non-refoulement, the right to leave one's country of origin and the rights to privacy and personal data protection; even of flouting the ban on torture and degrading treatment. So Frontex came up with a fundamental rights strategy on 31 March 2011[50] and designated Spanish UN lawyer Inmaculada Arnaez Fernandez as Human Rights Officer one year later.[51]

Yet censure from human rights organizations continued. In particular, they denounced Frontex for tolerating fundamental rights violations in the brutal and sometimes deadly practices of national coast guards.[52] Corresponding reports came mainly from the Aegean – for example, a fatal incident off the Greek island of Farmakonisi, or direct refugee pushbacks by the Hellenic Coast Guard on the high seas. Moreover, Frontex reportedly violated human rights at the 'hotspot' registration centers in Italy and Greece.[53]

Today, within Europe, politicians, NGOs and the media are watching Frontex' every move. Yet, the farther from Europe the agency operates, the less intense the scrutiny. This is especially true of EU border protection missions in Africa, as shown by the Frontex 'Operation Hera' initiated at Spain's request. The agency's longest-running mission to date began at sea and by air on 17 July 2006. Frontex intercepted boats traveling from Mauritania or Senegal to the Spanish Canary Islands and escorted them back. Some of the passengers were brought to the Nouadhibou detention camp in Mauritania. Spain had wrested permission from the governments of Morocco, Senegal and Mauritania for the European coast guard to patrol in their territorial waters. After a while, hardly any refugees reached the Canaries anymore.

How did Frontex do it?

The Berlin-based European Center for Constitutional and Human Rights (ECCHR) believes that the border guards may simply have turned all intercepted migrants into Mauritanian and Senegalese citizens on the spot and skipped checking their asylum claims and the requirement of calling interpreters. In 2016, the ECCHR wants to investigate whether Frontex could thereby have violated fundamental rights and EU law.[54] That May, the legal nonprofit asks Frontex for access to 12 documents pertinent to Operation Hera.

Only after the ECCHR threatened legal action did Frontex provide the documents – 'heavily censored.' In the Handbook to the Operational Plan, for example, just 48 of the 99 pages were not blacked out; in an Evaluation Report on Hera, 21 of 26 remained uncensored. The internally documented 'List of potential fundamental rights violations within Frontex activities' was removed altogether. Frontex justified the censorship to ECCHR by arguing that 'publication would affect public security'. So it remains unclear what EU officers have been doing in African territorial waters all these years. The ECCHR concludes: Operation Hera is still 'opaque and unaccountable.'[55]

Notes

1. Visit on board the ship, November 2016

2. Jakob, Christian (2017) 'Schrecklicheres verhindert', *tageszeitung*, 17 April | http://bit.ly/2uRHwac

3. Frontex (2017) *Risk Analysis for 2017*, Warsaw, February 2017 | http://bit.ly/2lKrFIs

4. Frontex (2017) *Programming Document 2019 – 2021*, Warsaw, 7 November, p. 18| https://bit.ly/2ObkvZj

5. European Commission (2017) 'European Agenda on Migration: Commission reports on progress in making the new European Border and Coast Guard fully operational', European Commission press release, Brussels, 25 January 2017 | https://bit.ly/2jebvBF

6. Frontex (2015) *Single Programming Document 2016-2019*, Warsaw, 24 December 2015, p. 17 | https://bit.ly/2IQQ1wT

7. European Commission press release, Brussels, 25 January 2017 | https://bit.ly/2jebvBF

8. *Statewatch News* (2017) 'Malta Summit – External aspects of migration', 19 January | http://bit.ly/2v1gGzm

9. Frontex (2016) *Africa-Frontex-Intelligence Community Joint Report 2016*, Warsaw, April 2017, p. 8 | http://bit.ly/2vZi1nh

10. Ibid., p. 9

11. Frontex (2017) *Risk Analysis for 2017*, Warsaw, February 2017, p. 20 | http://bit.ly/2lKrFIs

12. Frontex (2016) *Africa-Frontex Intelligence Community Joint Report 2016*, Warsaw, April 2017 p. 9 | http://bit.ly/2vZi1nh

13. Ibid.

14. Ibid., p. 8

15. Ibid.

16. Frontex (2006) *Annual Report 2006*, Warsaw, 2007 | https://bit.ly/2SpgXTP

17. Frontex (2016) *Frontex Final Accounts 2016*, Warsaw, 30 June 2017, pp. 32-35 | https://bit.ly/2tGh3wm

18. Eder, Florian (2016) 'New border force guards Europe's "broken fence"', *Politico*, 10 June | http://politi.co/2dximHe

19. Frontex (2019) *Return*, Operations, Frontex, 2019 | https://bit.ly/2Ua2XyW

20. Frontex (2019) *Budget VOBU 2019* Warsaw, 1 January | https://bit.ly/2OeXiFO

21. Jakob, Christian (2017) 'Zwei One-Way-Tickets für 82.000 Euro', *tageszeitung*, 26 January | http://bit.ly/2hhMREp

22. Personal information/conversation, 24 January 2017

23. Afrique Europe Interact (2016) 'Video Amadou Ba Flugzeug', *YouTube*, 7 December | http://bit.ly/2vZoOgT

24. Personal interview, 25 January 2017

25. EU Fundamental Rights Agency (2016) *Opinion of the European Union Agency for Fundamental Rights on fundamental rights in the "hotspots" set up in Greece and Italy* Vienna, 29 November, p. 10 | https://bit.ly/2BT1PII

26. UN High Commissioner for Refugees (2016) *'Better Protecting Refugees in the EU and Globally: UNHCR's proposals to rebuild trust through better management, partnership and solidarity'*, December 2016, p. 17 | http://bit.ly/2h9FgXt

27. EU Commission (2017) *On a more effective return policy in the European Union. A renewed action plan*, Brussels, 2 March | http://bit.ly/2mi5oRR

28. EU Commission (2015) *Refugee Crisis: European Commission takes decisive action*, Strasbourg, 9 September | http://bit.ly/1iwsGOJ

29. UNHCR Operational Portal, Refugee Situations, *Italy* | https://bit.ly/2riHwgV

30. EU Commission (2017) *Migration on the Central Mediterranean route. Managing flows, saving lives*, Brussels, 25 January, pp. 5-7 | http://bit.ly/2kxOOc3

31. Ibid.

32. European Union External Action Service (2016) 'EUNAVFOR MED Op SOPHIA - Six Monthly Report 1 January - 31 October 2016, Council document 14978/16, RESTRICTED, 30 November 2016', *Statewatch News*, 28 February 2019 | https://bit.ly/2v9PSZK

33. EU Commission (2017) *Migration on the Central Mediterranean route. Managing flows, saving lives*, Brussels, 25 January 2017, pp. 11-14 | http://bit.ly/2kxOOc3

34. Ibid, p. 14

35. EU Presidency in agreement with the President of the European Council (2017) 'Malta Summit – External aspects of migration', *Statewatch News*, 19 January | http://bit.ly/2v1gGzm

36. European External Action Service and EU Commission (2016) 'Options on developing cooperation with Egypt in migration matters.' *Statewatch news*, 1 March 2019, p. 6 | http://bit.ly/2wf4yXX

37. Cuttitta, Paolo (2017) *Viewpoint Egypt: Europe's other north African border*, Vrije Universiteit Amsterdam, April 2017, p. 10 | http://bit.ly/2vY9u4g

38. Ibid.

39. *Egypt Today* (2018) 'EU's FRONTEX head praises Egypt's role in halting illegal immigration', Cairo, 27 June | https://bit.ly/2TdOzEH

40. Speech by Chancellor Merkel (2017) 'Pressekonferenz von Bundeskanzlerin Merkel und dem aegyptischen Präsidenten Abdel Fattah al-Sisi', Bundesregierung, Berlin, 30 October 2017, (accessed 1 March 2019) | https://bit.ly/2Xxwwg3

41. Mixed Migration Hub (2017) *February Trend Bulletin 2017*, Cairo, 28 February | http://bit.ly/2vZiwhd

42. *Homeland Security Today* (2018) 'Frontex opens first Risk Analysis Cell in Niger', 29 November | https://bit.ly/2TlXfgj

43. 'Frontex signs Working Arrangement with Nigeria', Frontex news release, 19 January 2012, (accessed 18 March 2019) | https://bit.ly/2W6ntkr

44. Ibid.

45. European Commission (2017) *Commission reports on progress under the migration partnership framework and increased action along the Central Mediterranean Route*, European Commission Fact Sheet, Brussels, 2 March | https://bit.ly/2TLjWeD

46. European Commission (2016) *Regional Operational Centre in support of the Khartoum Process and AU-Horn of Africa Initiative Action Document*, International Cooperation and Development, 19 December 2016 | http://bit.ly/2hhAzMf

47. Statewatch News (2017) *GUE/NGL Delegation (2017) EU and Italian cooperation with Sudan on border control: what is at stake? Report GUE/NGL Delegation to Khartoum, Sudan 19 – 22 December 2016*, GUE/NGL Delegation, p. 9, 2 March 2019 | https://bit.ly/2IO7K89

48. European Union (2016) *Regulation (EU) 2016 / 1624*, Official Journal, 16 September 2016, p.12 | https://bit.ly/2SEXwGt

49. Ibid., p.44

50. Statewatch (2011) *Frontex Fundamental Rights Strategy*, Frontex Management Board, Frontex Observatory, 31 March, (accessed 2 March 2019)| https://bit.ly/2BZjrms

51. Frontex (2012) 'Management Board designates Fundamental Rights Officer', *Euro-police*, Frontex press release, Warsaw, 27 September

2012, (accessed 2 March 2019) | https://bit.ly/2EIqBx3

52. Jakob, Christian (2013) 'Brutale Zurückweisung', *tageszeitung*, 7 November | http://bit.ly/2tSh1jx | and Jakob, Christian (2016) 'Rabiater Rechtsbruch', *tageszeitung*, 16 June | http://bit.ly/2tSfPwr

53. Amnesty International (2016) *Hotspot Italy – How EU's flagship approach leads to violations of refugee and migrants rights*, Amnesty Report Index EUR 30/5004/2016, London, October 2016 | http://bit.ly/2eCgnTE

54. Wriedt, Vera and Reinhardt, Darius (2016) *Analysis: Opaque and unaccountable: Frontex Operation Hera*, Statewatch Analyses, No. 307, February 2016, (accessed March 2, 2019) | http://bit.ly/2pZD0Ga

55. Ibid.

Technology:
New border facilities
subsidizing
Europe's arms industry

The propellers of the white UN plane whip up the fine desert sand. The aircraft takes off with a roar, carrying almost 100 Somali refugees: men, women, children, elderly. The safe neighboring country of Kenya has sheltered them for nearly a quarter of a century, but now the UN refugee agency UNHCR is taking them back to their homeland. Civil war is still raging in Somalia and the Islamist militia al-Shabaab controls large parts of the country, including the border region.

Until 2016, the world's largest refugee camp was not in Syria or Turkey, but in Kenya. The vast city of white plastic tents in the middle of nowhere was called Dadaab. Almost half a million people lived here at the height of the war and drought in Somalia in 2011 and 2012. Dadaab does not appear on any map, but it became notorious for photographs of emaciated children dying in the desert sand. Now it will be demolished. Kenya will build a border fence in its place.

In 2016, Kenya's government announced it would stop hosting refugees and set a deadline for Somali refugees to go home voluntarily.[1] The official reason was the terrorist threat. In 2013, gunmen in Nairobi killed at least 71 people and wounded up to 200 more, holding Westgate Shopping Mall under siege for several days. The attack decided the fate of Somali refugees: investigations led to Dadaab, 300 miles away, and framed refugees as the bad guys. Now the UNHCR is paying them $150 each to voluntarily board the plane. The authorities stress the term 'voluntary', since free choice is a condition for repatriation under the Geneva Refugee Convention.[2] But in reality, all sides are exerting pressure – particularly the Kenyan government, as the German daily *taz* describes.[3]

Somalis had once fled here on foot. The border is barely 60 miles from Dadaab: an invisible, perfectly straight line in the barren desert sand, no demarcation, no border posts, not even a barrier – a typical African border. Nomadic groups drive their cattle herds across these lines, which exist only on maps, especially during drought periods; herders must sometimes drive their cattle hundreds of miles to the nearest watering hole, across national borders, to keep them alive. Drought has haunted this region for centuries, most recently in spring 2017.

The days of free border crossings are over. 'Whatever it is going to cost us,' Kenya's Deputy President William Ruto emphasized, as he announced the construction of a wall along the border with Somalia in 2015 – almost 435 miles long, right through the desert.[4] Like many African borders, it is still disputed. On top of that, oil has been discovered in the disputed territory; every square foot could be worth a fortune and trigger a turf war. Kenya is getting down to business and staking its claim to a large part of the resources.[5] So refugees and terrorists from the neighboring country have to stay out. A wall solves many problems. Kenya follows the EU's example.

Just a few months after the Deputy President's announcement, the first excavators arrived, escorted by Kenya's counterterrorism units. It's a risky venture: al-Shabaab controls the region just across the border. Several attacks on engineers have halted the construction. The plans include fences and walls several yards high, surveillance cameras and patrol vehicles.[6] To cover the wall's construction costs, Kenya increased its 2016/17 defense budget to $2.6 billion. This budget has been growing for some years. Kenya now spends more than any other African state on security and defense.[7] It invested most of the money in technology. Today, surveillance cameras are mounted all over Nairobi, and even supermarket or bank entrances have full-body scanners. The international airport was upgraded with surveillance technology so that it could offer direct flights to the USA again, a business worth billions.

German companies have also been attracted by these major contracts for the new border facility and the airport. In 2015, the German Chamber of Commerce Abroad (AHK) in Nairobi organized a 'market reconnaissance trip' for civil security technologies to Kenya. The agenda included meetings with the defense minister and counterterrorism units. Germany's leading defense and security firms expressed their interest: Airbus Defence and Space (formerly EADS), Siemens and Rheinmetall.[8] In the end, however, Kenya awarded the contract to Israeli company Magal Security, which also offered to build the border wall with Mexico for President-elect Donald Trump.

When Trump announced during his campaign that he wanted to erect a barrier along the southern US border, many Europeans jeered. However, the EU is the border-building pioneer – even in other countries. Along the border between Afghanistan, Tajikistan and Uzbekistan, the EU has recently built ten 'border infrastructure sites' to stop drug trafficking.[9]

Saudi Arabia boasts one example of a high-tech border 'Made in the EU'. Three parallel fences supported by 21-foot-high sand walls run straight through the desert. Any approach is detected by underground motion sensors, cameras or one of the 50 radar systems in surveillance towers or patrolling jeeps. The system instantly sends all information to a control center; over 9,000mi of fiber-optic cable ensure fast data connections, and 3,400 border guards are on duty.[10]

The European defense corporation EADS (now Airbus) delivered this luxury border gear to the kingdom in 2009. It upgraded the 560-mile border with Iraq to an anti-terrorist wall for about $2.3 billion in an all-inclusive package spanning requirements analysis to border guard training by the German Federal Police. The officers' allowances and travel costs were paid by the German Corporation for International Cooperation (GIZ), which received Saudi funds through EADS.[11] The close ties between the development agency GIZ and the armaments industry are no coincidence: after leaving the Cabinet in 2013, German Development Minister and GIZ client Dirk Niebel became chief lobbyist of the Düsseldorf-based arms maker Rheinmetall. This company is expanding its portfolio of border control, sensor systems and surveillance drones. 'I can't use foot patrols to secure miles of borders between Libya and Egypt. They need protection technology as well,' Niebel says in a February 2018 interview. The defense lobbyist explains: 'Protection technology does not always mean erecting walls or fences. It can also be sensors, ground penetrating radar, flying objects – depending on the topography and general conditions, the possibilities are very diverse.' Niebel asserts: 'The technology is available. It just has to be paid for. And that's usually the bottleneck you can't get through. The countries that need these technologies often don't have the means for what they would require to really do the job effectively. And if it's in Europe's and in Germany's interest to implement such protective measures, then it must also be in their interest, first, to finance these measures where necessary, and second, to train the people who will work with them.'[12]

Fortified border fences with automatic firing systems

The EU has already penetrated Africa with the fences around the Spanish exclaves in Morocco, Ceuta and Melilla. Migrants have stormed the fences often over the years, usually injuring themselves severely. The Spanish company ESF is regarded as the leading manufacturer of NATO wire worldwide. Its razor-sharp blades can sever human tendons effortlessly. ESF tested its deadly wire on the fences of Ceuta and Melilla and later sold it to Greece, Hungary and Turkey.[13] The Turkey deal was not just a political move; it was also a technical upgrade to the EU's anti-migration shield. The border wall with Syria is monitored by drones and reportedly equipped with smart watchtowers. When they sense an approach within 300 yards, the towers first emit a warning in three languages and then fire automatically.[14] This equipment was manufactured by the emerging Turkish armaments company Aselsan, whose research budget for border fortifications comes from the European innovation fund Horizon 2020.[15]

In the 2017 Africa-Frontex Intelligence Community Joint Report, the European border control agency lists all African border fences fortified so far. In the 1980s, Morocco built around 1,700mi of border walls, secured with landmines and high watchtowers, against the Polisario Front rebels. There are already about 90mi of fence between Morocco and Algeria. Over 100mi of fence reinforce the border between Tunisia and Libya. With US aid, a wall is currently being erected between Niger and Nigeria to fend off the Boko Haram militia. According to Frontex, all these high-tech facilities are meant to protect against terrorists and smugglers, but also against migrants: 'This artificial border also affects the migratory movements to the northern shores of Morocco towards Spain,' states the report.[16] What the EU justifies as counter-terrorism combats all forms of migration in many places.

From 'Central Asia ... to Central Africa', the EU is expanding its fortress by investing all the way to the equator in the 'resilience of states', according to the June 2016 EU strategy paper for its new common foreign and security policy to 'guarantee Europe's security' and 'sustainable peace'. As 'crises' plague the EU's neighboring states, the EU 'must counter the spill-over of insecurity'.[17]

In April 2016, Europe's foreign and defense policymakers met for their annual conference in Paris. It was a symbolic location;

the French capital had been under a state of emergency since the November 2015 terrorist attacks. The EU could no longer regard itself as a protected island in world affairs, warned the French Foreign Minister Jean-Marc Ayrault. Europe had enemies, Europe had opponents, he thundered,[18] and added Europe would finally have to face this. He pinpoints the opponents not only in Syria, but also in Libya and the Sahel: in Africa. There, the EU should fight against people smugglers, human traffickers, passport forgers, and open or non-existent borders. The new EU defense strategy demands 'homeland security' – just like the USA after the September 11 attacks.[19]

To European policymakers, the neighboring continent is full of dangers. This shows in Frontex' annual risk analyses, as well as the 'African intelligence community' reports, which focus mainly on migration flows.[20] Frontex Director Fabrice Leggeri opens the 2016 Risk Analysis by citing '1.8 million detections of illegal entries into Europe'. The migration 'chaos' of 2015, he writes, was 'unlike almost any other year since World War II'.[21]

A fundamental pillar of the EU is the Schengen Agreement. However, when hundreds of thousands of refugees entered the Schengen Area via Greece and the Balkan route in 2015, EU member states were forced to close their national borders again. This shook the Union's foundations. 'Our aim is to lift all internal border controls as quickly as possible, and by December 2016 at the latest,' states an internal Commission paper to the EU Parliament in March 2016.[22] However, this implies that the EU's external borders need more protection, so Fortress Europe's walls are now cutting into Africa.

What's more, the Defence Action Plan drawn up by the EU Commission in November 2015 after the Paris attacks sees the real danger in Europe's limited military capacity. National armies throughout Europe maintained 19 different types of infantry combat vehicles, the document states. The USA, by contrast, deployed only one type of tank, which was cheaper. EU states had cut defense budgets too far; they no longer invested in research and development of new security technologies. A secure Europe could only succeed if everyone worked together – to build a common defense industry.[23]

Europe's leading military powers, especially Germany, France and the United Kingdom had so far been reluctant to join in. The German government had stuck to its principle that the Bundeswehr should buy from German manufacturers only. The scandal around the faulty G36 assault rifle, however, changed this attitude. Defence Minister von der Leyen and her French counterpart signed a declaration of intent for a joint air transport squadron in October

2016. The Bundeswehr is now supplying helicopters for Frontex to track down smuggler boats in the Mediterranean. 'This shows how cooperation can work in Europe,' said von der Leyen.[24]

Smart turnstiles and satellites over Africa

The common key technology of the future is Integrated Border Management (IBM), which the EU developed and first used in the Balkan states and later in Afghanistan.[25] It refers to 'intelligent' border posts, which let travelers with electronic identity papers pass easily and quickly, since their databases are connected to all relevant authorities: immigration, security, customs. Border control turnstiles scan the biometric passport and match the chip's stored data real-time with global databases such as INTERPOL in order to track down potential terrorists or forged identity documents. IBM is also supposed to make customs processing simpler and safer. Border guards can use heartbeat monitors, breath scanners and x-rays to detect stowaways in trucks. The small but highly sensitive devices are expensive: a single truck scanner can cost a good $1.7 million.

Europe's top defense and security companies have discovered IBM as a new, almost civilian market. Unlike major military projects, European suppliers work closely together here. Over 40 companies were involved in the construction of the border barrier in Calais, France alone – and it is barely over three miles long.[26] Beyond the barrier, all other possible ways across the border are sealed off by miles of fences and also monitored from the air.

The power behind EU border surveillance is the European Border Surveillance System (EUROSUR). Since December 2013, drones have been monitoring the southern EU borders, supported by geostationary satellites over the Mediterranean. Boats along the coasts, trucks in the desert or wandering migrants – Frontex can watch them all live at its headquarters in Warsaw. Spain operates a smaller satellite monitoring system, Seahorse, in cooperation with Mauritania, Morocco, Senegal, Gambia, Guinea-Bissau and Cape Verde.[27] A joint system is currently being set up with Tunisia, Algeria and Egypt. According to the European Commission, EUROSUR cost the EU over $380 million.[28] However, a study by the Heinrich Böll Foundation of Germany estimates that it cost at least $994 million, including development costs.[29]

Since 2002, the EU has funded 56 projects with $359 million for border technology research. Leading defense companies such as Airbus Defence and Space, Thales of France, BAE Systems of the

UK, the Italian group Leonardo-Finmeccanica, the Spanish company Indra, as well as the German Fraunhofer Institute, and even Israeli and Turkish companies had access to EU funds. They equipped the EU borders in Bulgaria and Hungary with the latest technology, like a high-precision Airbus radar system that can detect even the smallest objects 137 miles away.[30] Not even a fly can get through.

Dominant lobby groups based in Brussels are the force that drives EU investments in new technologies like border security. The most powerful lobbyist is the European Organisation for Security (EOS), headed by ex-Thales manager Luigi Rebuffi. There is also the AeroSpace and Defence Industries Association of Europe (ASD), whose chairperson Mauro Moretti was also the head of Leonardo SpA (then Finmeccanica), as well as the think tank Friends of Europe. In recent years, these influential lobbyists have set up 'working groups': within the EOS, the Intelligent Borders Working Group, led by French companies Safran and Thales, or the Border Surveillance Working Group, headed by Italian electronics firm Selex. Technology partnerships link these working groups indirectly to Europe's major corporations. For example, Mercedes-Benz and Volkswagen developed off-road vehicles that can be upgraded for border patrols. Over the past five years, Airbus has invested at least $8.5 million in lobbying; Finmeccanica and Thales each invested over $1 million.[31] Now this must pay off. The new technology has to go somewhere, preferably outside of Europe.

The African continent with its thousands of miles of invisible borders is the ideal market. With the escalating threat of terrorism, many African governments are following Kenya's example: they want support to combat it, preferably in the form of EU equipment and training. By the same token, they are awarding contracts to international companies. Whether at the Airbus-sponsored Border Management & Technologies Summit in Ankara in March 2016, the annual Border Security Conference in Rome or the World Border Security Congress in Morocco in March 2017, Africans number increasingly among the participants, for example, the ECOWAS migration department director, as well as representatives of the Nigeria Immigration Service and the Ghanaian National Identification Authority.[32]

At the same time, the EU ensures that African governments must adhere to the logic of intelligent border controls, if necessary by force. 'Integrated border management would benefit both the prevention of irregular migration and the fight against all types of trafficking,' says a European Commission internal strategy paper on negotiations with Nigeria. Further, it states that money from the Emergency Trust Fund for Africa can be used to this end.[33] Hence,

EU development funds may be spent to arm African states. The EU had already supported the establishment of a Nigerian migration police force. 'Security and border control' are major interests of the EU in Côte d'Ivoire, according to another internal Commission document.[34] The EU also suggests integrated border management for Mali as a transit country. 'Support in the area of border management and control' was important to Mali, and 'equipment is a frequent request',[35] writes the Commission to the Committee of Permanent Representatives of the Member States, which prepares EU Council meetings.

Upgrading borders with high-tech equipment is expensive, and hardly any African state can afford it. So EU member states pay out of their own pockets, motivated to secure lucrative contracts for domestic defense companies. In 2016, for example, the German Ministry of Defence and the Foreign Office provided nearly $14 million from their joint budget for 'strengthening partner countries in the area of security, defence and stabilisation',[36] which is also used to fund security projects in Iraq, Jordan, Mali and Nigeria. A further $45 million were planned for Tunisia in 2017, according to a speaker for the Ministry of Defence. The EU is also contributing almost $16 million for Tunisian border upgrades. German Federal Police are training Tunisian border guards, while the Bundeswehr is providing speedboats and armored trucks. In 2017, the German government promised mobile surveillance systems with ground reconnaissance for the Tunisian-Libyan border. Airbus has supplied five night surveillance systems, 25 thermal imaging cameras, 25 optical sensors and five radar systems to Tunisia for training purposes. The German government paid for the devices with taxpayer money.[37] Tunisia gets its high-tech border virtually free.

The EU has earmarked more than $6.8 billion through 2020 to protect its external borders. Of this, $3.2 billion comes from its Internal Security Fund (ISF) and $1.9 billion from the EU Security Research Programme (ESRP). Around $1.7 billion are estimated for Frontex and EUROSUR. In addition, there are cash injections for non-member states: around $75.6 million to Libya, $18 million to Mauritania, $16 million to Lebanon and $26 million to Tunisia, according to a study by the Transnational Institute and the Dutch NGO Stopt Wapenhandel.[38]

Europe also financed border security measures in Mali and Niger. In 2016, the Cabinet of Germany decided to send up to 20 officials to Niger, a major transit country in the Sahara, as part of the Federal Foreign Office's 'Police Programme Africa' implemented by GIZ. Niger received nine police stations on the border with Nigeria for around $1.6 million, three of which were paid for by the German Foreign Office and the other six by the EU. Germany donated nine pickup trucks costing $307,000 and 12 motorcycles costing $11,400 each to Niger's border force, plus border police training sessions. In Chad, a facility was built on the border with Cameroon. The third phase of the police program, which was to run until 2018, planned to support police structures in Mauritania, Côte d'Ivoire, Niger, the Democratic Republic of Congo, Cameroon, Nigeria and South Sudan. The German government also funded INTERPOL's Operation Adwenpa II, which trained border guards in 14 West African countries from 2016 to 2018.[39]

'The African market is definitely interesting, because there's a demand there,' an Airbus spokesperson stated on enquiry. But the company found access difficult because Africa lacked 'responsible local business partners who meet our high standards'. It was much easier for corporations to supply individual products like radar technology or cameras. Therefore, border security programs paid for by the German Foreign Office or the EU ensure companies' access to African markets. 'Generally, we consider all states facing the problem of illegal border crossings to be potential users of border security systems. We are also talking with individual African states in this direction,' confirms a Rheinmetall spokesperson. But it was 'still too early to speak of concrete projects'. As usual, when it comes to lucrative contracts, European security and defense companies are reluctant to show their hand. A spokesman for Airbus DS Electronics and Border Security (Germany) says: 'Our customers insist that we not talk about their procurement projects.' In 2016, Airbus announced its intention to open a subsidiary in Nigeria.[40]

Airbus delivered a Heron 1 surveillance drone to German armed forces stationed in Mali as part of MINUSMA, the UN mission there.[41] The Italian company Leonardo-Finmeccanica provided 15 surveillance helicopters to Algerian border troops. Airbus boasts on its website that it has supplied its Spexer radar, specially developed for border surveillance, to three West and North African countries. In 2015, a Dutch offshoot of French armaments giant Thales equipped the Egyptian navy with radar technology worth $38.7 million. Aerodata, a Braunschweig-based aircraft technology specialist, outfits aircraft and helicopters with radar systems worldwide. The Maltese air force ordered three systems at once and the EU's ISF paid part of the cost. Aerodata has also become interested in Africa recently: the company promoted its products in Kenya and Tanzania in 2015, when airports there planned security technology upgrades.

Development aid on the wrong track

The German GIZ was founded as a state corporation for technical development cooperation. Its main clients so far have been the Federal Ministry for Economic Cooperation and Development (BMZ), the Federal Ministry for the Environment (BMU) and the Federal Ministry of Education and Research (BMBF). Back in 2011, GIZ and the Federal Ministry of Defence (BMVg) closed an agreement on cooperation at home and abroad.[42] GIZ still hesitates to accept contracts directly from the BMVg. Lately, however, GIZ has been handling an increasing number of contracts for the Federal Foreign Office in which the BMVg is closely involved. The major aim of these programs is to support partner countries in the fight against terrorism and drug trafficking, according to an internal paper from the two ministries dated May 2016.[43] In March 2017, GIZ held a conference with the BMVg in Berlin. It was their first public presentation of the joint projects consisting primarily of programs in Africa.

Hence, GIZ is now improving border security in Mali, Niger and Burkina Faso. In Burkina Faso it provides 'expert advice on developing an integrated border management policy', and it advises Mali 'on revision of national border policy', states the German government. In Chad and Mauritania, GIZ also supports the equipment and training of border guards and construction of border stations. In Niger, GIZ supports the EU training mission EUCAP with 'border protection and the fight against criminal smuggling'. German funds finance navy training in the Gulf of Guinea in cooperation with ECOWAS.[44]

Development can occur only when security is established, German Chancellor Merkel had declared in her opening speech at the G20 Partnership with Africa Conference in June 2017 in Berlin. This precondition was largely absent in Africa. She warned that new thinking would be necessary: 'For a long time, we felt virtuous when we were not dealing with military equipment.'[45] This means that security and military training will now become essential components of Germany's development policy. Europe's defense industry is delighted.

In November 2017, African states were well represented at the world's largest trade fair for security and border technology, the Milipol in Paris. Niger's top generals came; delegations from African state ministries of interior and defense showed interest in the latest surveillance devices being promoted there. The industry is enjoying a hearty upswing. Lionel Le Cleï of French arms contractor Thales praises the newest smart border surveillance technologies at the Milipol. 'If you want to prevent border crossings, there are diverse possibilities for surveillance, control and alarm,' Le Cleï states in an interview. 'The solution is like a Swiss Army knife, you can select what you need,' he says, adding that Thales expects contracts from Frontex.[46]

Thanks to all these programs financed with European tax money, the market for border technology is estimated to grow from around $17 billion in 2015 to almost $40 billion by 2022, predicts the market research company Frost & Sullivan.[47] At the moment, American and Israeli companies still dominate this sector. Europe's leading defense companies want to catch up – in Africa.

Biometrics: transparent Africans

European security corporations are at the fore in another lucrative area on the African continent: the market for biometric ID cards and travel documents. Biometric documents are an element of border security programs, as they enable rapid passage through modern border posts. According to 2016 World Bank statistics, around one-third of the estimated 1.2 billion Africans had never been officially registered.[48] There are various reasons: Many African countries have no civil registry since their last census was decades ago, or the government has not issued any identity cards. In the DR Congo, for example, a driver's license or an election card, just laminated scraps of paper, serve as ID cards. Without digital databases at the civil registry office, the colorful paper files and blue-checkered register books typical of African authorities stack to the ceiling in damp cellars. Centralized data storage systems, networked computers, servers, fingerprint scanners, digital cameras, reading devices: high-tech border equipment costs a fortune. Once installed, it still often fails due to a lack of electricity in the desert. But there is international pressure to change this. The International Civil Aviation Organization (ICAO), a specialized UN agency, set a deadline: since 2015, international travelers have been required to carry machine-readable passports. Morocco, Senegal, Ethiopia, Sudan, Kenya, Uganda and Liberia have thus introduced biometric identity documents in recent years. The six-country East African Community (EAC) is investing in an ePassport project. Scanners are already operating at international airports in Cairo, Nairobi and Accra in Ghana.[49]

The global biometrics market is booming. The research institute MarketsandMarkets assumes an annual growth rate of 19.9 percent through 2023.[50] Africa is the ideal market: over one billion people will be needing digital ID cards, passports or driving licenses. African states often award contracts to security document makers such as Bundesdruckerei in Berlin, which prints blank passports for Libya's transitional government, for example.[51] Sudan has also declared interest.

'Modern travel documents have a built-in microchip which stores the bearer's biometric characteristics,' explains IT expert Eric Töpfer of the German Institute for Human Rights.[52] Fingerprints, face shape, iris scans will soon be centrally stored and retrievable. EURODAC is one of the four EU biometric databases soon to be merged into one. According to the European IT agency EU-LISA, the fingerprints of more than 2.7 million asylum seekers across Europe were stored in EURODAC at the end of 2014, and the trend is rising.[53] 'Currently the EU is working intensively on merging its databases. Since July 2015, police and law enforcement authorities of EU member states and Europol have also been able to access EURODAC for investigations,' says Töpfer. Groups already marginalized would thus be profiled as suspects in the name of fighting terrorism. 'The fact that the other databases also serve mainly to control migration shows how important biometric technology has become in this field.'

According to Frontex, more than 9,400 people were caught entering the EU with forged or borrowed travel documents in 2014 alone. In addition, there were almost 10,000 arrests at borders within the Schengen area that year. The EU border agency, which will be responsible for repatriations across Europe, called the identification of asylum seekers one of its 'most pressing challenges' in its 2016 risk analysis.[54] The European Commission, citing information from the European Police Office (Europol), speaks in a September 2016 paper of 'increased document fraud in high-risk areas'. The document speaks of 'threats to internal security'. Secure travel and identity documents 'are crucial whenever it is necessary to establish without doubt the identity of a person'.[55]

Biometric identification is essential for deportation. Many migrants cannot prove their identity or have gotten by with forged passports. Hence, authorities cannot determine to which country they should be deported. In Germany, over 70 percent of asylum procedures handle seekers 'without any identity documents', according to January 2015 statistics[56] from the Central Register of Foreign Nationals. This has led to massive complications: 'The lack of proof of identity among asylum seekers and persons obliged to leave the country is still quantitatively the most significant problem in implementing measures to terminate residence.'[57] Deportation to 'countries without a functioning registration system' is particularly 'difficult', states a 2013 study by the German Federal Office for Migration and Refugees (BAMF). A deportation delay of one year can quickly add up to over $13,000.[58]

An imminent 'system collapse' would be 'unavoidable' without appropriate precautions, warns the Federal and State-level Workgroup on Repatriations (AG Rück) in an April 2015 evaluation of German repatriation practice.[59] Hence, at the November 2015 Valletta Summit on migration, the EU and over 30 African states adopted an Action Plan.[60] The plan announced extensive EU support for the 'modernisation' of civil registries and secure identity documents: biometric development aid, so to speak.

The EU has invested $5.7 million to develop the West African Police Information System (WAPIS).[61] The idea is that up to 17 states between Mauritania and Nigeria should store fingerprints collected by police in a central database, which INTERPOL could access in the future. This means that African biometric data could also be accessed in Europe. Pilot projects have been running in Ghana, Mali, Niger and Benin since 2015. The system is also intended for border controls and identifying forged documents. 'This brings mass matching of data from undocumented African migrants for deportation purposes within reach,' says Töpfer of the German Institute for Human Rights.

On his trip to the Maghreb in early 2016, German Interior Minister Thomas de Maizière proved that these are not just tales spun by privacy activists. Morocco had already agreed to biometric data matching for deportations, he announced.[62] About two weeks later, Veridos, a joint venture of the German Bundesdruckerei GmbH and Giesecke&Devrient (G&D) based in Munich, publishes a press release stating that Morocco has awarded it the contract to 'develop and implement a national border control system'. The contract includes biometric scanners, passport readers, automated gates and servers for 1,600 checkpoints.[63]

Contracts like these are a strategically valuable investment for African states to control their own populations, but they are expensive. Introduction of biometric databases usually goes hand in hand with a switch to electronic voting systems. Before voters are allowed to cast their ballot, they must provide their fingerprints or undergo an iris scan. This is supposed to prevent duplicate votes and facilitate voter turnout surveys. Yet, it opens the door to electoral fraud.

In many African countries, these e-systems tend to work poorly. Registered voters do not appear in the databases, or the devices fail on election day. Electronic voting systems have not necessarily increased confidence in election transparency, which is often controversial in Africa. On the contrary.[64] Rwanda is one example:

in the August 2017 elections in this small country of just 10 million inhabitants, voters do not mark a cross on a ballot but leave their fingerprint next to their candidate's photo. Civil society voices criticize that the vote is no longer anonymous, since the intelligence service can now conduct a mass comparison of fingerprints.[65] In 2015, Rwanda's President Paul Kagame won 98 percent in the referendum on amending the constitution to permit him a third term in office. Only around 100,000 voted against this – with their fingerprints.[66] 98.6 percent voted for him in the presidential elections in August 2017. Human rights organizations describe Rwanda as a surveillance state, but this complete control would not be possible without biometrics.

Since biometric technologies are key to retaining power, it is no surprise that these contracts are awarded by top-level officials, usually without a tendering procedure. Back in 2010, the German family enterprise Mühlbauer of Bavaria made headlines due to a shady deal. As the leader in the African ID document market, it supplies six African states. Its African base is in Uganda. In the middle of a night in 2010, company head Josef Mühlbauer met with Ugandan President Yoweri Museveni to close a contract worth over $70 million.[67] This disregarded Ugandan public procurement law, which requires a public tender. Mühlbauer later faced corruption allegations, and Uganda's government canceled the deal.[68] In 2016, Uganda awarded a contract to the German company Veridos, which is partly a subsidiary of identity document manufacturer Bundesdruckerei. The contract encompassed printing all of Uganda's security-relevant documents and proofs of identity, including passports, driving licenses, ID cards and bank notes.[69] Here, too, the government ignored its own procurement law.

In Cameroon, a similar case of corruption arose with G&D, one of Veridos' parent companies.[70] G&D was already involved in a scandal in Zimbabwe when it printed banknotes for the country's dictator Robert Mugabe during hyperinflation.[71] Mühlbauer's biggest African customer is now Algeria, where lucrative contracts await. A European Commission internal strategy paper states that the country was 'highly skeptical' about a readmission agreement with the EU as a whole. Only a quarter of planned deportations of Algerians had been successful in 2014. Aiming to increase the state's compliance, the EU Council proposed financial and technical support for 'the further development of a biometric database'.[72]

The largest market in Africa is Nigeria. With 182 million inhabitants, Africa's most populous country ranks second on the list of irregular migrants to the EU and is a hub for passport forgers. In March 2015, the EU signed a mobility agreement with Nigeria that envisions biometric technology to make identification documents more secure.[73] In February 2016, a European Commission internal paper proposed expanding a civil registry with biometric information.[74] Seven months later, Nigeria's President presented a new eID. The catch is that US company MasterCard has turned the IDs into bank cards, locking in 100 million Nigerians as potential long-term customers. The cards are printed by Dutch chip card manufacturer Gemalto.[75] Africa's market truly offers boundless opportunity.

Notes

1. *The Nation* (2016) 'Decision to close Dadaab refugee camp final, Ruto tells UN boss', 23 May | http://bit.ly/2vgmpQY

2. UNHCR (2011) *Convention and Protocol Relating to the Status of Refugees*, Geneva, April 2011 | https://www.unhcr.org/3b66c2aa10

3. Schlindwein, Simone (2016) 'Abschied von Dadaab', *tageszeitung*, 3 December | http://bit.ly/2uRiGHj

4. IRIN (2015) 'Kenya's anti-terror border wall sparks heated debate', 27 April | http://bit.ly/2hhUM4u

5. Müller-Jung, Friederike (2016) 'Kenia oder Somalia: Wem gehört das Öl unterm Meer?' *Deutsche Welle*, 19 September | https://p.dw.com/p/1K31f

6. Nkala, Oscar (2016) 'Kenya Begins to Build Wall Along Somali Border' *DefenseNews*, 26 April | https://bit.ly/2CkHv3i

7. *Business Daily* (2017) 'Nairobi leads EA arms race with Sh96 (3 million) billion military budget', 25 April | http://bit.ly/2uRx81T

8. Press briefing with trip participants, Berlin, 14 October 2016

9. 'EU-Border Management in Northern Afghanistan (BOMNAF)', European Commission, International Projects and Development, Brussels (accessed 17 March 2019) | http://bit.ly/2vZASPg

10. Blechschmidt, Peter (2011) 'Hart an der Grenze', *Süddeutsche Zeitung*, 15 July | https://bit.ly/2ObuWw6

11. *Bundestags-Drucksache 17/10358*, Berlin, 20 July 2012 | http://bit.ly/2wrSxCC

12. Interview with Dirk Niebel, Berlin, 9 February 2018

13. Monroy, Matthias (2015) '"Klingendraht 22" aus Spanien: Das Symbol der Festung Europa', *Heise Online*, 14 September | http://bit.ly/2vgXuN2

14. *Yeni Şafak* (2016) 'Turkey starts building automatic shooting gun towers at Syrian border', 30 May | http://bit.ly/1NYMGZc and: Arkin, Dan (2017) 'Turkey to Install New Air Defense Systems on Syria Border', *IsraelDefense*, 6 February | https://www.israeldefense.co.il/en/node/28443

15. ASELSAN (2017) *Annual Report 2016*, Ankara, February 2017, p. 23 | http://bit.ly/2v8vOqK

16. Frontex (2017) *Africa-Frontex Intelligence Community Joint Report 2016*, Warsaw, April 2017, p. 39 | http://bit.ly/2vZi1nh

17. European External Action Service (EEAS) (2016) *Shared Vision, Common Action: A Stronger Europe. A Global Strategy for the European Union's Foreign And Security Policy*, Brussels, June 2016 | http://bit.ly/2kvZ73G

18. European Commission EUISS Annual Conference (2016) 'Towards an EU Global Strategy: the final stage', speech by French Foreign Minister Jean-Marc Ayrault, Déclarations officielles de politique étrangère du 22 avril 2016, *France Diplomatie*, 22 April | https://bit.ly/2KAOJXs

19. European External Action Service (June 2016) p. 53

20. Frontex (2016) *Africa-Frontex Intelligence Community Joint Report 2015*, Warsaw, 28 January | http://bit.ly/2ucN8tm

21. Frontex (2016) *Risk Analysis for 2016*, Warsaw, March 2016, p. 5 | http://bit.ly/1qmFE5Y

22. European Commission (2016) 'Back to Schengen – A Roadmap, Communication from the Commission to the European Parliament, the European Council and the Council' Press release, Brussels, 4 March | http://bit.ly/1RsMcWk

23. In the authors' archives: European Commission (2016) 'European Defence Action Plan: Towards a European Defence Fund', Press release, Brussels, 30 November | http://bit.ly/2vZgrBP

24. Jungholdt, Thorsten (2016) 'Von der Leyen leistet gleich zwei Offenbarungseide', *N24*, 6 October | http://bit.ly/2vbVuWX

25. European Commission (2010) *Guidelines for Integrated Border Management in European Commission External Cooperation*, Brussels, November 2010, p. 14 | https://bit.ly/2FijNGU

26. 'Calais Research 40 companies profiting from the eviction and border violence', Calais Migrant Solidarity, 17 October 2016 | https://bit.ly/2Tcd5FV

27. '"Seahorse" Projects: Present and Future', Presentation by Lt. Eduardo León, Guardia Civil, Project on Integrated Maritime Policy in the Mediterranean (15 March 2019) | http://bit.ly/2uduQsa

28. European Commission (2011) 'EUROSUR: Providing authorities with tools needed to reinforce management of external borders and fight cross-border crime', Press statement, Brussels, 12 December | https://bit.ly/2HrtGnI

29. Hayes, B. and Vermeulen, M. (2012) *Borderline: The EU's New Border Surveillance Initiatives – Assessing the Costs and Fundamental Rights Implications of EUROSUR and the "Smart Borders" Proposals'*, Heinrich Böll Stiftung, Berlin, June 2012 | https://bit.ly/2Huj9s6

30. Akkerman, Mark (2016) *Border Wars – The arms dealers profiting from Europe's refugee tragedy*, Transnational Institute and Stop Wapenhandel, 4 July | http://bit.ly/2wfectE

31. Grieger, Fabian and Schlindwein, Simone (2016) 'Das Geschäft mit Hightech-Grenzen', *tageszeitung*, 15 December | http://www.taz.de/!5363960/

32. World Border Congress (2017) *Programme and List of Presenters, World Border Congress, Morocco*, 21-23 March | http://bit.ly/2uRw3Hj

33. EU Council and EEAS (2016) *Joint Commission-EEAS non-paper on enhancing cooperation on migration, mobility and readmission with Nigeria*, Brussels, 24 February, p. 6 | http://bit.ly/2g0amS8

34. EU Council and EEAS (2016) *Joint Commission-EEAS non-paper on enhancing cooperation on migration, mobility and readmission with Côte d'Ivoire*, Brussels, 24 February, p. 5 | http://bit.ly/2uOzFvr

35. EU Council and EEAS (2016) *Joint Commission-EEAS non-paper on enhancing cooperation on migration, mobility and readmission with Mali*, Brussels, 24 February, p. 5 | http://bit.ly/2fZzpVF

36. Author's archive, German Ministry of Defence (BMVg) and Federal Foreign Office (2016) 'Projektliste Ertüchtigung', Letter from the respective State Secretaries Drs. K. Suder and M. Ederer to committee representatives, listing planned reinforcement initiatives, 17 May, and: German Corporation for International Cooperation (GIZ) 'Working with GIZ' (accessed 17 March 2019) | https://bit.ly/2L7DtlR

37. Author's archive, "Deutschlands Beitrag zur Unterstützung des Transformationsprozesses in Tunesien''', *Bundestags-Drucksache 18/4550*, 2 April

38. Akkerman (2016) pp. 26-29

39. Deutsche Gesellschaft für Internationale Zusammenarbeit (GIZ) 'Programm: "Stärkung der Funktionsfähigkeit von Polizeistrukturen in Subsahara-Afrika''', 'Fachexpertise: Ergebnisse', (accessed 15 March 2019) | https://bit.ly/2TfkLap; and: GIZ (2017) 'Police Programme Africa' | https://bit.ly/2CndD6m; and: *Bundestags-Drucksache 18/11307*, 20 February 2017 | http://bit.ly/2wyiot4

40. Company speakers quoted from interviews conducted by Fabian Grieger for the tageszeitung article: Grieger, F. and Schlindwein, S. (December 2016)

41. Federal Ministry of Defense (BMVg) (2017) 'Aufklärungsdrohne Heron: Das fliegende Auge über Mali', BMVg press statement, Berlin, 1 February | http://bit.ly/2uZTIsr

42. *Bundestags-Drucksache 17/10721*, Berlin, 23 October 2012 | https://bit.ly/2F8Ybvq

43. From the authors' archives

44. *Bundestags-Drucksache 18-5895*, Berlin, 1 September 2015 | https://bit.ly/2TJwKSX

45. Speech by German Federal Chancellor Angela Merkel at the 'G20 Africa Partnership – investing in a common future', conference, Berlin, 12 June 2017 | https://bit.ly/2Iljm1W

46. Interview with Lionel Le Cleï, Paris Milipol, 21 November 2017

47. Proctor, Keith (2015) 'Europe's Migrant Crisis: Defense contractors are poised to win big', *Fortune*, 10 September | http://for.tn/2ubplKD

48. Identification for Development (ID4D) (2016) *ID4D Country Engagement*, Updated version, World Bank, 31 January | http://bit.ly/2fi9Qmy

49. This and the following citations from research by: Welch Guerra, Paul (2016) 'Durchsichtige Afrikaner', *tageszeitung*, 9 December | http://www.taz.de/!5361733/

50. MarketsandMarkets (2018) Biometric *System Market by Authentication Type*, July 2018 | http://bit.ly/1vGshYo

51. Gieseke&Devrient (2013) *Geschäftsbericht G&D 2013*, Annual Report 2013 | https://bit.ly/2W7hexd

52. Interviewed by Paul Welch Guerra, Berlin, 21 November 2016

53. EU Agency for the Operational Management of Large-Scale IT Systems in the Area of Freedom, Security and Justice (eu-LISA) (2010) *Biometrics in large-scale IT: Recent trends, current performance capabilities, recommendations for the near future*, 6 October | http://bit.ly/2weVUsp

54. Frontex (2016) *Risk Analysis for 2016*

55. European Commission (2016) *Enhancing security in a world of mobility: improved information exchange in the fight against terrorism and stronger external borders*, Communicaton from the Commission to the Institutions, Brussels, 14 September, p. 10 | https://bit.ly/2HDLRpQ

56. Ibid., p. 11

57. Arbeitsgruppe Rückführung (AG Rück) (Federal- and State-level Workgroup on Repatriations) (2015) *Bericht der Unterarbeitsgruppe*

Vollzugsdefizite, April 2015, p. 11 | http://bit.ly/2uMGZId

58. Ibid.

59. Ibid.

60. EU Council (2015) *Valletta Summit Action Plan*, 11-12 November 2015, p. 8 | http://bit.ly/2iligGJ

61. European Commission (2016) 'EU Trust Fund Action Document for operational committee decisions', Annex document, 4 October | http://bit.ly/2vepW26

62. 'Marokko, Algerien und Tunesien sagen Rücknahme ihrer Staatsbürger zu', German Federal Ministry of the Interior (BMI) press release, 29 February 2016 | http://bit.ly/2vXiQNp

63. 'Veridos Supplies Innovative Border Control Solution to the Kingdom of Morocco', Veridos press release, Berlin, 21 March 2016 | http://bit.ly/2vkzWaU

64. Mungai, Christine (2016) 'Dirty hands: Why biometric voting fails in Africa – and it doesn't matter in the end', *PaZimbabwe*, 28 December | https://bit.ly/2ufpkYt

65. *Rwanda News Agency* (2010) 'Local observers cite intimidation in presidential polls', Kigali, 11 August | https://bit.ly/2UHM5jl

66. *BBC* (2015) 'Rwanda vote allows Kagame to extend term in office', 19 December | http://bbc.in/1IeraNc

67. Knaup, Horand (2010) 'Um Mitternacht im Palast', *Der Spiegel*, 26 July | http://bit.ly/2hfEs40

68. Kalungi, Nicholas (2013) 'The national ID scandal', *Daily Monitor*, 9 March | http://bit.ly/2foe2Ty

69. State House Uganda (2016) '"Uganda being liberated from slavery of importing security documents" – President', State House press release, Kampala, 12 June | http://bit.ly/2vXs78e

70. *I-Cameroon* (2012) 'G & D au centre d'une controverse', Douala, 25 October | http://bit.ly/2vemsN8

71. Grill, Bartholomäus (2008) 'Blutgeld aus Bayern', *Die Zeit* No. 25/2008, 12 June | http://bit.ly/2uO4MqY

72. EU Council and EEAS (2016) *Joint Commission-EEAS non-paper on enhancing cooperation on migration, mobility and readmission with Algeria* Brussels, 9 February 2016, p. 11 | http://bit.ly/2ikcwwN

73. *tagezeitung* (2015) 'Joint Declaration on a Common Agenda on Migration and Mobility between the Federal Republic of Nigeria and the European Union and its Member States.' Brussels, 12 March 2015, p. 6 | http://bit.ly/2xlxaPB

74. EU Council and EEAS (2016) *Nigeria*, 24 February 2016 p. 6 |

http://bit.ly/2g0amS8

75. Gemalto (2017) 'Nigerian national ID program: an ambitious initiative', Press release, 14 May 2017 | http://bit.ly/2vaLYTY

The Mediterranean: Dying where others take vacations

Matteo Salvini, head of Italy's far-right Lega Nord (LN), made good on his most crucial election promise just days after taking office as deputy prime minister and interior minister. In June 2018, he declared that Italy's ports would no longer allow ships to enter if they carried migrants rescued at sea. The only way that sea rescue NGOs would see Italy would be 'on a postcard'.[1] He would prohibit fuel supplies to these organizations' ships. Foreign naval ships carrying rescued refugees would also be denied entry. The previous administration had agreed to accept all migrants rescued by EU patrol vessels. That was no longer the case, said Salvini. 'With our government, the music has changed.'[2] This was the escalation of a decade-long policy dispute, in which the EU had consistently abandoned Italy for too long.

Italy's Ambassador to the EU, Maurizio Massari, had already threatened to enact this measure a year earlier on 28 June 2017. If the EU wished to avoid closed ports, it must pay for Libya to expand its coast guard, Massari urged. Above all, he demanded, the other EU states should accept significantly greater numbers of refugees from Italy and ships carrying refugees should call at the ports of other EU states in the future.

Berlin, Paris, Brussels, Amsterdam and Madrid respond at the EU summit in Tallinn a few days later.

They say no.[3]

But the interior ministers agree to a plan presented by the EU Commission in Tallinn. Apart from the objectives for Italy, the plan comprises 19 points, 11 of which do not affect the EU per se. These are border management measures in African countries such as Libya, Tunisia, Egypt, Mali or Niger.[4]

Europe's migration policy in Africa shows its inability to create collective internal regulations. That is the cause of the ongoing decades of tragedy in the Mediterranean.

After Spain closed the western Mediterranean route, from 2005 onwards, increasing numbers of refugees arrived mainly in Malta and Italy, as well as Greece. The clique around Prime Minister Silvio Berlusconi and his two right-wing coalition partners, Gianfranco Fini, then head of the post-fascist National Alliance (Alleanza Nazionale), and Umberto Bossi of the then-separatist Lega Nord who had ruled Italy since 2001, took a hardline stance. In 2003, Bossi called for the use of cannons against 'illegal immigrants': 'After the second or third warning – boom. Without any more talk, the cannon fires. The cannon kills. Otherwise we'll never see the end of this.'[5] Later, in an interview with the renowned Milanese daily Corriere della Sera, Bossi claimed it was just a 'joke'.[6]

It was clearly no laughing matter when the Italian government took Tunisian fishermen such as Abdel Basset Zenzeri to court for bringing 44 shipwrecked migrants to Italy.[7] For the same reason, Italy seized the ship of the German aid organization Cap Anamur in 2004. Italy then showed no intention of rescuing shipwrecked refugees.[8] They often drifted at sea for days on end. Many died of thirst instead of drowning.[9] Tineke Strik, a Dutch professor of migration law, has investigated for the Council of Europe (CoE) why NATO and the EU watched 61 refugees drift for two weeks on the heavily monitored Mediterranean Sea in March 2011. In the end, 50 of them were dead. 'Nobody helped them,' says Strik.[10]

Nobody was counting the dead, either. Unlike today, with statistics provided by IOM, in the past decade no one kept official statistics, even though thousands were dying. The only people who felt responsible were volunteers. A group led by Italian journalist Gabriele del Grande of Lucca spent years painstakingly analyzing newspaper reports from around the Mediterranean. Their blog 'Fortress Europe'[11] tries to document the scope of the tragedy. At the same time, the Amsterdam NGO United for Intercultural Action collected reports of a total of 34,361 people who died trying to enter Fortress Europe from 1993 until mid-2018.[12] Had it not been for the volunteer efforts of both groups, the death toll at Europe's gates would never have been recorded.

Since 2003, a fundamental imbalance in Europe's asylum law has determined the situation in Italy: Regulation 343/2003, commonly known as Dublin II, in force since 1 March 2003.[13] It essentially states that the country through which refugees enter the EU is responsible for them. If refugees or migrants go to another EU country nevertheless, they will be deported back. This is obviously unfair not only towards the refugees, but also towards the states at the EU's external borders. Ever since arrivals began to rise around 2003, the government in Rome has been calling for compensation, but without success. After 2010, the asylum system collapsed, primarily in Greece, Malta and Italy, which had disastrous consequences for the reception of refugees. But countries such as Germany stuck to the procedure anyhow. 'Dublin II remains unchanged, of course,' declared Hans-Peter Friedrich (CSU), the German Federal Minister of the Interior, in 2013.[14] He stated that critics had a 'lack of expertise'.[15]

The day that changed everything

Since the 1990s, an estimated 20,000 refugees had already died in the Mediterranean when an especially grim catastrophe strikes on 3 October 2013. Over 360 people, most from Eritrea, drown within sight of the island of Lampedusa when their boat catches fire. Not all of the bodies can be recovered. The disaster is a turning point in the debate. A few days later, 280 dark wooden coffins, each bearing a long-stemmed red rose, are displayed in a corrugated metal hangar near the port of Lampedusa. 'I will never forget the sight of 280 coffins today. I will bear this with me for the rest of my life,'[16] says EU Commissioner for Home Affairs Cecilia Malmström. 'This isn't the European Union we want.' Malmström visits the Mediterranean island together with President of the European Commission José Barroso. Hours after the photo session in front of the coffins, Malmström announces the creation of a 'task force'.

Public opinion also changed in Italy. In February 2013, Enrico Letta (Partito Democratico, PD) becomes prime minister. Letta orders a national day of mourning for the deaths near Lampedusa – the first time ever for dead refugees. On 18 October 2013, he launches the naval mission Mare Nostrum (Our Sea) under Admiral Guido Rando's leadership to rescue shipwrecked people and escort refugee boats to the mainland. An entire naval unit is deployed close to Libyan territorial waters. Within a year, navy personnel rescue some 150,000 people, more than ever before. At the same time, 3,165 people drown in the central Mediterranean.[17] Without Mare Nostrum, the toll probably would have been much higher. 'We applaud,' says the International Organization for Migration (IOM), and 'pay tribute to the heroic work of Italy's maritime forces'.[18]

Saving lives as a 'pull factor'

Applause came, but money did not. The EU pays only about one-sixth of the monthly expenditures of about \$12.2 million.[19] Italy is not just left to pay the remainder in accordance with the Dublin Regulation; it also is solely responsible for all the rescued migrants. In February 2014, Matteo Renzi (PD) becomes prime minister of Italy. His plea for a fair distribution of the burden falls on deaf ears. To build some pressure, Renzi orders Mare Nostrum units to pull back a bit from the Libyan coast. The death toll skyrockets: from January to April 2014, 60 deaths had been recorded; in the months following the retreat, there are between 314 and 839.[20] The fatal demonstration leaves Europe unimpressed. Unlike the 2013 disaster, people are now dying slowly, one by one, not all at once. Hence the media pays little attention.

The EU does not want to pay for Mare Nostrum – it wants to end the mission. 'Mare Nostrum was meant as emergency aid and has turned out to be a bridge to Europe,'[21] says German Minister of the Interior Thomas de Maizière. In the first nine months of 2014, the number of new asylum seekers in Germany rose by almost 60 percent to around 116,000.[22] Many domestic politicians saw this as a result of Italy's rescue policy.

The EU border protection agency Frontex also views Mare Nostrum as a 'pull factor',[23] an invitation to refugees in Libya to embark, because they would not need to get far before they had a chance of rescue. If this prospect no longer existed, then 'considerably fewer migrants'[24] would risk a departure, states Frontex in leaked meeting minutes from this period. The EU agency wants to halt the Italian navy operation and the monitoring of Libyan territorial waters. Instead, Frontex wants to launch its own 'Triton' mission to guard only Italy's coastal waters.

Frontex knows what this would mean. In a concept paper written in August 2014, the agency warns that it was 'likely' that the withdrawal of Italy's navy would increase the death toll.[25] 'The priority for the EU and Frontex is clearly deterrence. That took precedence over human life,' says Lorenzo Pezzani, a researcher at Goldsmiths' College, London. The EU decision-makers were 'aware of the risk in detail'.[26]

On 3 September 2014, the EU Parliament's Committee on Civil Liberties and Internal Affairs invites Frontex Executive Director Gil Arias-Fernández to a hearing. MEP Barbara Spinelli asks him if he was 'aware that more people will be dying again in the Mediterranean'[27] if Mare Nostrum is discontinued. Arias-

Fernández simply replies that the Triton mission will not replace Mare Nostrum, neither its mandate nor its available resources.[28]

Nevertheless, Mare Nostrum is officially phased out on 31 October 2014 and Operation Triton takes its place. Italy remains uneasy about this decision: Initially, Rome still lets some of its ships cruise near Libya for rescue operations. Frontex tries to prevent this. Klaus Rösler, head of the Frontex Operations Division, writes a letter to Giovanni Pinto, director of the Italian border police. Rösler criticizes Italy for continuing to respond to emergency calls outside the 30-mile zone. This was not in line with the operative plan, he warned.[29]

In the following months, 1,450 people drown in the Mediterranean.[30] Two weeks after another serious ship accident, on 23 April 2015, EU Commission President Juncker addresses the EU Parliament: 'It was a serious mistake to bring the Mare Nostrum operation to an end. It cost human lives.'[31] He increases the budget for Triton to $135 million a year, which was exactly what Mare Nostrum had cost. This was intended as a 'return to normality. It was not right to leave the financing of the Mare Nostrum operation to Italy alone'. But the mistake cannot be undone. For years, the EU will not be able to build the rescue capacities to replace Mare Nostrum.

Germany and a few other states now send naval units. The EU extends Triton's area of operations: Instead of 30 miles, the ships now patrol up to 138 nautical miles south of Italy – but still a long way from Libya. This is the critical difference to the Italians' previous activities. They had sailed close to the Libyan coast, since most of the accidents happened there. The EU, on the other hand, now follows the Frontex dictum that a strong rescue force near Libya 'triggers emigration',[32] as Rösler later puts it.

In the ensuing years, the number of deaths keeps rising: From January 2015 to February 2019, at least 12,046 people drown off the Libyan coast.[33] This far exceeds the death toll from some African civil wars.

Not everyone is willing to just let this happen. What follows is the finest hour of Europe's civil society. More than a dozen private NGOs appear on the scene. Organizations of a type which never existed before.

The finest hour of Europe's civil society

The NGOs are backed by people like Marcella Barocco of Nijmegen, Netherlands. On 10 April 2015 she begins her shift: eight hours staffing the Alarm Phone hotline for refugees in distress at sea. The NGO has no office; Barocco works from home, just like some 80 other activists.[34] 'Our aim is to help to change things in real terms,' she says.[35]

Since October 2014, volunteers from Europe, Tunisia and Morocco have been running the project every day, around the clock. Some of the activists came to Europe as boat refugees themselves. They spread the hotline number through the Internet, refugee organizations, migrant communities and social media. The idea is that refugees who get into trouble should first make an emergency call and then inform the Alarm Phone initiative.

Alarm Phone, which is funded by donations, went into action on 11 October 2014. This was the first anniversary of a terrible accident: In 2013, more than 260 Syrians drowned off Lampedusa as Italian and Maltese coast guards argued back and forth over who should be responsible.[36] This was the first time that German, Italian and Swiss activists documented in such detail how organized irresponsibility leads to the death of hundreds of refugees at sea. 'We want to make sure that this won't happen anymore,' says Barocco.[37]

They found the Alarm Phone, create a detailed manual and train volunteers. The first thing is to tell callers that they are not connected to a rescue service, and then to ask for as much information as possible, as quickly as possible: the callers' position, size of the boats, size of the group, are there any sick people, are there any pregnant women, is the engine still running, is water leaking into the hull?

Alarm Phone is a success. On 10 April 2015 at 7.15am, for example, a boat set out from Zuwara, Libya. More than 600 people, many from Eritrea, are on board. From there it is 184mi to Lampedusa, about 10 hours if things go well. There is hope of leaving the horrors behind: the journey through the desert, the abuse and chaos in Libya. But things are not going well.

At the time, smugglers usually give the refugees satellite telephones made by Thuraya. They look like mobile phones from the late 1990s: a bit clunky, but they fit into your pants pocket. They are the life insurance for many boat refugees. The boats they board may be falling apart, but the Thuraya phone lets them make emergency calls even if they are far away from a cellular network. Most importantly, the satellite phone pinpoints their position. These coordinates allow rescuers art least a chance to reach the small boats.

The boat that sets out from Zuwara on 10 April 2015 also carries a satellite telephone. That morning, the passengers notice that their boat is shipping water. They have just left Libyan territorial waters. They do not have an emergency number, only the one of Eritrean priest Mussie Zerai. He has been taking care of Eritreans arriving in Italy for years. Every Eritrean who sets out has heard of him. Latitude 33'20" north, longitude 12'13" west, the refugees read the coordinates to Zerai. He forwards them to the Maritime Rescue Coordination Centre (MRCC) in Rome, the control center of the Italian coast guard, and hands over the case to Barocco. At 1.04pm Barocco can make contact with the refugees. 'Communication was difficult,' she says. Most of the refugees speak only the Eritrean language Tigrinya. Alarm Phone has a pool of translators, but on this day the time pressure is immense. 'We understood that water was coming into the boat and it was an emergency,' she says. The activists turn to the MRCC. 'They said they would look into it.' In fact, the refugees were about 28mi from the Libyan coast and thus outside of Italy's mandatory rescue zone.

Barocco speaks with the passengers five times. Her eight-hour shift is long over. 'They told us there was no rescue in sight, but the boat was still filling with water.' She has called the Italian coast guard several times, but they make no promises. Neither does the Maltese coast guard. 'Then we decided to sound the alarm,' Barocco remembers. At 5.16pm the initiative sends a multilingual message across Europe through mailing lists and social media: '600 people are in danger. Write emails now, as many as possible.'

Meanwhile, the boat's coordinates have changed. Barocco passes the new information to the coast guard. At 6pm, the UN refugee aid organization UNHCR receives a message from the MRCC: rescue ships and helicopters are on their way. The public pressure seems to have worked. Around 7pm the rescuers reach the refugee boat. In the meantime, one person has died. The rescuers can save about 600 people. They are taken to the Italian ports of Augusta and Porto Empedocle.

From October 2014 to December 2018, Alarm Phone volunteers receive emergency calls like these from 2,591 boats with a total of over 100,000 passengers: an average of more than two emergency calls per day.

At the start of the project, the activists wrote a letter to the rescue control centers. 'We announced what our role would be, that we see it as our duty to build up pressure, if we feel that a rescue is not undertaken immediately,' says Barocco's fellow volunteer Maurice Stierl.[38] This 'may be somewhat unwelcome', but rescue services would have to learn to cope with it. In fact, activists were convinced that rescue services were 'not always doing everything' possible. At the moment, said Stierl in May 2015, this has improved: 'Right now there is a great willingness among the Italian rescue services, but there is far too little rescue capacity, and that is a political decision.'

A new breed of NGOs

Official rescue capacities fall short, but others step in to help: people like Harald Höppner. On 19 May 2015, the small business owner from the German state of Brandenburg registers the nonprofit association Sea-Watch under the number VR 34179 B at the district court in Berlin-Charlottenburg. Three weeks later, a converted fishing cutter that Höppner bought for $112,000 leaves from Hamburg for Malta. On the boat, which is also named *Sea-Watch*, a crew of volunteers aims to keep an eye out for refugees on the Mediterranean and help them. They carry drinking water and life rafts for up to 500 people. The ship is not meant to take on refugees, but to alert the coast guard in emergencies. A 'complicated undertaking', says Höppner. But 'doing nothing is not an option for us'.[39]

Many people share his attitude and follow Höppner's example: By 2018, the NGOs Doctors Without Borders and Save the Children (both international), SOS Méditerranée, Jugend Rettet IUVENTA, LifeBoat, Mission Lifeline, Sea-Eye, CivilFleet (all based in Germany), Migrant Offshore Aid Station (Malta), Proactiva Open Arms (Spain), Stichting Bootvluchteling (Netherlands), Mediterranea and Mayday Terraneo (Italy) have sent rescue boats to the Mediterranean – all are funded by donations.

Their goal is to rescue the living and recover the dead. Where the EU states fail to meet the need, alternative communities emerge to rescue shipwrecked people. They buy ships and drones and lease planes. Growing numbers of volunteers join them to meet the boats full of refugees and distribute life jackets, pint bottles of water and emergency blankets. These volunteer groups shoulder state tasks, but unlike official welfare organizations, they get no state funding, because their work undermines state policies. They do not just reject these policies, they resist by fulfilling their own demands. Although they first stepped up in response to an emergency, in time they build solid professional structures, adapt to circumstances and seek pragmatic solutions. They change state institutions. And they change themselves.

For a long time, refugee groups held all authorities equally responsible for the high death toll. Yet, since forming working relationships with state rescue organizations through their activities, some refugee activists are now more discerning. In June 2016, the activist Tamino, who organizes the Sea-Watch base camp in Malta, says, 'The Italians are tops.'[40] The Italian sea rescue center in Rome, MRCC, also dropped its initial mistrust. 'When we're on the phone, we are put through directly to a certain line, and the person there is always very friendly,' says Tamino. Since spring

2016, the MRCC has been inviting private sea rescuers to regular meetings.

The sea rescue community wishes to become redundant at some point, hoping the navy and coast guard will eventually start doing their job again.

Ferries not Frontex, demands Sea-Watch, safe and legal routes to Europe.[41] Nobody should be forced onto the smuggler boats; nobody should need to be pulled from the water by volunteers or Italian navy forces. Above all, sea rescue NGOs want to draw attention to the ongoing catastrophe at the fringes of Europe. Their activists seek to break through the indifference and the numbing of public empathy: if need be, with the photo of the dead baby recovered by Sea-Watch on 27 May 2016. The NGO shared the image with news agencies to show the world, once again, the fate of one in 23 refugees trying to reach Europe via Libya at that time.

No luck with the failed state

While Harald Höppner of Brandenburg was buying his first ship and thus catalyzing the growth of a whole generation of new NGOs, the EU was increasingly looking to Libya. To Europe, the country is the key to gaining control over irregular migration. Almost all migrants who come to Italy by sea set out from Libya. But since the fall of Gaddafi in 2011, turmoil has spread throughout the country. Can a state like this be a partner?

In May 2015, EU Foreign Affairs Commissioner Mogherini travels to the UN Security Council in New York. She wants a mandate to use military force against the smugglers.[42] The EU is considering using combat helicopters to destroy smuggler boats along or off the Libyan coast, before they take refugees on board. This proposal has no precedent. Multiple groups and militias are vying for power in the oil-rich state, which is dominated by tribal structures. The interim Government of National Accord (GNA) around Prime Minister Fayez al-Sarraj was internationally recognized in 2015,[43] but it controls only part of Libya's territory. The Libyan National Army (LNA), commanded by General Khalifa Haftar, is supported by the parliament, the Libyan House of Representatives (HoR) in the East Libyan city of Tobruk. The parliament, in turn, declared itself a rival government to the Islamist General National Congress (GNC) in Tripoli, which rejects cooperation with the EU. Islamist groups controlled several Libyan coastal cities temporarily but were later driven out. So they moved to the south of the country, which was already overrun by militias from neighboring countries, mercenaries, smugglers and other criminals. In short: in 2015, al-

Sarraj is politically too weak to allow the EU to take action against people smugglers in Libya. And Europe has no other allies there.

In June 2015, a month after Mogherini's trip to New York, the EU must accept that a military operation is out of the question for now. The UN has given a mandate only for 'phase one' of the operation: reconnaissance on smugglers. 'We view every landing attempt in Libya as an attack,' says Khalifa Ghwell, prime minister of the Islamist Fajr Libya (Libya Dawn) rebel government. 'After all, we haven't even been consulted about the plan.'[44]

Hence, the EU navy mission EUNAVFOR MED starts off without teeth in June 2015. 'The target is not the migrants. The target is those who make money with their lives and, far too often, with their deaths,' Mogherini explains.[45] The Italian aircraft carrier Cavour leads the operation, which includes five ships, two submarines and drones, three aircraft and three helicopters. 1,000 soldiers are deployed.

But almost nothing happens. Despite its diplomatic efforts, the EU is unable to quell the chaos in Libya. It does not even dare to open an embassy for security reasons. And the EUNAVFOR MED soldiers are not allowed to approach the Libyan coast. So the smugglers go on about their business.

The EU interior ministers meet on 13 October 2016. German Minister of the Interior Thomas de Maizière demands once more that refugees rescued in the Mediterranean be returned to North Africa. He says that asylum claims should be examined while the seekers wait there, in 'safe accommodations'.[46] His Austrian colleague, Wolfgang Sobotka, wants 'an agreement by which Europe can send refugees back to Libya immediately'.[47] Hungary wants similar conditions. But the EU is still divided on the Libya option.

Phase 2: 'Less aggressive behavior'

Phase two of the navy mission begins on 24 October 2016. EUNAVFOR MED is now renamed Operation SOPHIA, after a baby born on the German frigate Schleswig-Holstein. A Dutch and an Italian training ship leave the port of Catania in Sicily. For months, the EU has searched Libya for participants to join its upcoming training measure. Candidates must have served two years in the Libyan Coast Guard, commit for another two years, and be loyal to Prime Minister al-Sarraj's government. A security check is supposed to prevent jihadists from joining.

On 26 October 2016, 89 selected Libyan coast guards board the vessels for an 84-hour cram session: the course schedule includes human rights, maritime law, maritime safety, marine conservation, sea rescue, fishery monitoring and English, a full twelve hours per subject. The instructors come from Belgium, Greece, Germany and the Netherlands. The UNHCR and Frontex are also sending experts.

Some of the coast guards still came from the Gaddafi era, says SOPHIA commander Manlio Scopigno. They were 'well organized, eager to learn and teachable'.[48] However, they had 'no knowledge of human rights or maritime law' and were 'not at the standard of Western coast guards'. They stood out for their 'very aggressive demeanor', says Scopigno. Hence, the goal of the training course was 'less aggressive behavior'. The EU has trained a total of 237 Libyan Coast Guard members as of 2018.

The Libyans are supposed to catch the smugglers; sending refugees back to Libya is still a taboo subject at this time.

In early February 2017, an internal situation report becomes public. It was written by the German embassy in Niger's capital Niamey and deals with conditions in Libyan prisons, where smugglers detain migrants who intended to leave the country. 'Executions of migrants who cannot pay, torture, rape, blackmail and abandonment in the desert are the order of the day there,'[49] states the wire report to the Federal Foreign Office in Berlin. It tells of 'the most severe, systematic violations of human rights'. The following words make the public listen up: 'Authentic cell phone photos and videos document concentration camp-like conditions in the so-called private prisons.' Later, the diplomats explain that they chose the drastic phrasing because they learned of regular, fixed times for shootings in the camps. Some of these private prisons are in the hands of militias who control parts of the country. Islamists, militia fighters and state actors are equally entangled in the smuggling business.

The agreement: 'Null and void'

Nonetheless, EU Commission President Juncker allocates around $225 million for border protection in Libya in late January 2017.[50] This is not enough for Fayez al-Sarraj, the powerless prime minister in Tripoli. He demands nearly $900 million from the EU to stop migrants; General Heftar even calls for $20 billion a few months later.[51] There is nothing al-Sarraj can offer in return, since the smugglers' bases are out of his reach.

Italy does not want to accept this. Since the EU has not helped Italy, it is counting on cooperation with Libya. Italy is the only EU state with an embassy in Tripoli. At a meeting on 3 February 2017, al-Sarraj promises Italy's Prime Minister Paolo Gentiloni to better control the borders and to set up camps from which refugees are to be returned to their home countries. Italy offers money.

One the same day, the EU heads of state meet in Malta. For the first time, they question the taboo against sending people back to Libya. They decide that Libya should now have more border guards, more training and new camps, which they call 'adequate reception capacities and conditions for migrants'.[52]

Within a few months, everything is set in motion. Italy's EU ambassador Maurizio Massari had threatened the EU with closing Italy's ports but achieved nothing, so Europe probes the Libyan option, which it had avoided until then. The Libyan coast guard receives inflatable boats, jeeps, buses, bulletproof vests and communication equipment from the EU Emergency Trust Fund for Africa (EUTF). The consequences are fatal.

On August 15, 2017, the Golfo Azzurro, a boat of the Spanish sea rescue NGO Proactiva Open Arms, nears the Libyan coast. Around 5pm, a Libyan Coast Guard boat arrives. Its identification number '654' is visible on photos: it is one of six ships of the Bigliani V series that Italy supplied to Libya in recent years. It heads towards the Golfo Azzurro. Ricardo Gatti, 39, formerly a social worker on Mallorca, now commander of the boat, summons the crew below deck. The Libyan boat heaves to. Men with guns are on board. They make radio contact in English, demanding an 'authorization' from the Libyan government. 'We don't have one and we don't need one,'[53] Gatti replies. The Libyans want to come aboard; Gatti refuses. Then the Libyans order the Golfo Azzurro to follow them, to Tripoli. Or 'we will target you,' they threaten, as Gatti reports. The Golfo Azzurro complies. 'We knew that once we got to Libya, our ship would be gone,' says Gatti.

Gatti uses a satellite telephone to call the Spanish and Italian Ministries of Defence, the EU Operation SOPHIA headquarters and the assistant to the President of the European Parliament Antonio Tajani. Finally, after about an hour, the Libyans stop. The Golfo Azzurro is allowed to turn north. "'If you come back, we'll shoot," they said,' Gatti reports.

It is the second incident of this kind within a few days. On 8 August, the Libyan boat '654' had approached another Proactiva Open Arms rescue ship. A video shows the coast guards firing a machine gun into the air, obviously to drive off the sea rescuers. According to Gatti, this incident also occurred in international waters. 'We're really disturbing the EU, but we're not leaving. So now they're sending the Libyans,' Gatti says.

A short time earlier, the International Maritime Organization (IMO) in London received a letter from the Libyan government.[54] The letter declares that Libya will now be responsible for emergencies in the southern half of the maritime area between Libya and Italy. While this is the international standard, Libya has been unable to comply, so Italy coordinates rescue operations up to the 12-mile limit off Libya's coast. That was to end now. 'No foreign ship has the right to enter' the area without authorization, said General Abdelhakim Bouhaliya, commander of the Tripoli naval base.[55]

His forces will now cruise the Libyan coast. When they spot refugees, they stop them and bring them back. After a brief treatment by the UN organizations UNHCR and IOM, the refugees go straight back to hell: to the internment camps of the Libyan interior ministry's Department for Combatting Illegal Migration (DCIM). Reports of 'extremely serious human rights violations' are credible, states the German Federal Foreign Office. The camps are characterized by 'heavy overcrowding, poor sanitary conditions, food and drug shortages'.[56] Journalist Michael Obert reported on inmates' horrifying descriptions from one of the camps near Zawiya. Bloodstained women told him about mass rapes, he writes.[57] The German Foreign Office states that it is 'not possible' to track what happens to people after they enter the DCIM camps. Amnesty International estimates that about 20,000[58] people were returned in 2017. As of August 2018, the figure had already reached 29,000,[59] according to a report by the UN mission in Libya. Images of torture or mock shootings in the camps surface repeatedly. In November 2017, CNN released a video[60] recorded undercover at a slave auction in Libya. Young Black men and women from the internment camps are for sale.

Blaming the rescuers

But the Libyan Coast Guard does not stop all the refugees. So now Italy in particular starts targeting the sea rescuers, who are bringing the rest of them to Italy. At first, everyone underestimated the private initiatives, which were mostly crowdfunded. But from January 2016 through May 2018, according to an IOM count, 301,491 people were rescued in the Central Mediterranean and brought to Europe – and 97,236[61] of them were taken on board by sea rescue NGOs. They are one of the major actors in the Mediterranean.

And they have upgraded: A civil air reconnaissance mission off the Libyan coast is launched in April 2017. A search aircraft, type Cirrus SR22, funded mainly by the Evangelical Church in Germany (EKD), Germany's official Protestant federation, is stationed on Malta and named after the migratory 'Moonbird'. It is the latest project of the NGO Sea-Watch, which just recently introduced an app which is supposed to let refugees make emergency calls. This technology reinforces the NGOs in the moral trench war along the EU's external border.

This war now has NGOs coming under fire. Frontex director Fabrice Leggeri claims that their activity 'leads smugglers to force even more migrants onto unseaworthy boats than in previous years. Therefore, we should put the current concept of rescue measures off Libya under scrutiny'.[62] Sebastian Kurz (Austrian People's Party), Austria's Minister of Foreign Affairs, calls it 'NGO madness'.[63] Stephan Mayer, Home Affairs spokesman for the CDU/CSU parliamentary group in the Bundestag, speaks of a 'shuttle service'[64] to Italy.

The Italian government demands that the eight maritime rescue NGOs then active in the Mediterranean sign a code of conduct. This would make their work much more difficult. The German NGO Jugend Rettet IUVENTA is one of five NGOs who refuse to sign at a meeting at the Ministry of the Interior in Rome in early August 2017. On the following day, the rescue control center in Rome calls the Jugend Rettet ship IUVENTA to the port of Lampedusa. There, state prosecutors seize the boat. The charge: 'Encouraging illegal entry.'[65] Human rights organizations expect the trial against the 12 crew members to start in Agrigento, Italy in 2019. They face up to 15 years in prison. Additionally, Italy could charge fines of nearly $17,000 per person brought into the country – and the IUVENTA has rescued just over 14,000[66] people.

From early 2013 to mid-2018, some 681,000[67] refugees and migrants arrived in Italy. Had Europe shared the load fairly, Italy, according to its size and economic power – about one-ninth of the EU's – would have had to take care of about 75,000 in those five and a half years. With such a small load, the Italian mayors who started sit-ins or even hunger strikes so that their municipalities would not be assigned any more refugees would have been considered Nazis, or insane. But the real imbalance allows politicians like Simone Dall'Orto, the Lega Nord mayor of Traversetolo near Parma, to blame the EU and threaten to go on hunger strike against more migrants. Many local politicians followed his example.

By 2015, the EU agreed to take on a total of 160,000[68] refugees from Greece and Italy in the following years, 45,000 of which were to come from Italy. Even that would have been insufficient, but the EU never followed through. Hungary and Slovakia took legal action against the agreement and lost – but still refused to take a single refugee from Italy. Seven other states did not appeal, but also did not accept a single refugee by the end of the program in October 2018. Overall, the so-called relocations to other EU states reduced

Italy's burden by just 12,706[69] refugees – only about a quarter of the paltry number promised.

In the Italian parliamentary elections of March 2018, the populist Five Star Movement (Movimento Cinque Stelle, M5S) and the far-right Lega Nord both win a narrow majority. Soon afterwards, the interior ministers Horst Seehofer of Germany, Matteo Salvini of Italy and Herbert Kickl of Austria meet in Innsbruck. They discuss matters that would have been utterly impossible until recently: Austria wants to ensure that no more asylum applications can be filed on European soil. Salvini asserts that he will reject all ships with rescued refugees. The main goal is 'to reduce arrivals and increase the number of deportations',[70] he says. This is all that matters now.

If 2015 was the summer of migration, then 2018 is the summer of isolation. An axis of far-right governments, from Rome through Vienna to Budapest, is now in power. And the media are playing into it. The German weekly Zeit publishes a pros & cons essay titled 'Or should we just keep out of it? Private helpers rescue refugees and migrants at sea. Is this legitimate?'[71] This question, in one of the most reputable newspapers on the continent, shows how low the debate has sunk.

'Suddenly, there are two opinions on whether to save people in mortal danger or to just let them die,'[72] writes the Süddeutsche Zeitung, and calls it 'the first step towards barbarism'. The words quickly cause a stir, but they miss the mark. The debate is not new, but now those who prefer not to rescue are in power. They have created conditions that allow them not only to flaunt this view, but also to brazenly act upon it.

On 1 July 2018, Captain Pia Klemp of the vessel *Sea-Watch* receives an email from the Maltese Port Directorate: the boat is forbidden to sail. The ships *Lifeline* and *Seefuchs* and the search plane Moonbird are also banned from setting out. The Maltese government briefly explains that it must 'verify that all who use our ports comply with national and international standards'.[73] Why is there any doubt? And why now? At the same time, Mission Lifeline captain Claus-Peter Reisch is accused of not registering his ship properly in Malta. Reisch's attorneys reject the charge. Other ships abruptly lose their flags' registration.

For a long time, Malta struggled with the mass arrivals of refugees. The number of people taken in by other EU states was insignificant. In 2014 Italy finally promised the island state to take in those picked up in Malta's rescue zone. The two countries never officially confirmed this agreement.

But now this arrangement is over. In June 2018, Italy turns away the Aquarius from the German NGO SOS Méditerranée. After an odyssey lasting for days with 629 people on board, the boat is allowed to dock in Spain on 17 June. Next, Italy rejects the *Lifeline*, which is carrying 233 people. Italy wants the shipwrecked migrants returned to Libya. But the rescue groups strictly refuse to expose the ships' passengers to the abuse and imprisonment in Libya. The *Lifeline* has to dock in Malta. The island's government fears a precedent.

In the 72 hours before the *Lifeline* arrived, Maltese politicians made every effort to ensure that the refugees could travel on to other EU states. Malta, a country of 122sq mi, population 432,000, had to negotiate on its own what the entire EU has failed to achieve for years: an effective distribution system. 'It was an insane challenge,'[74] says an official on staff for Prime Minister Joseph Muscat. Alone, Malta probably could have accommodated the *Lifeline*'s 230 people, maybe even another thousand, but not many more.

There were days in 2018 when rescue ships pulled 5,000 people from the Mediterranean and brought them to Italy. 'Now everyone in Europe is saying: Our country first. What are we supposed to do?'[75] asks a Maltese official. According to government insiders in Valletta, Italy used to be the biggest ally, but not anymore. Though nobody says it openly, this is the real reason why Malta is blockading the sea rescuers, not some faulty registrations. Malta was the rescuers' base as long as the refugees could go somewhere else: to an Italy under social democratic rule. But now, others are running not just Rome.

So the rescuers are chained up in port. There are times when no rescue ship is at sea. Italy now frequently refuses responsibility for emergency calls and refers them to the Libyan Coast Guard.

The death toll in the Central Mediterranean among those who reach Europe is still rising. In the first half of 2017, one person drowned for every 38 who made it. In the first half of 2018 it was one in 19 and in June it was one in seven.

On 25 August 2018, Italian prosecutors opened an investigation against Minister Salvini for kidnapping, illegal detention and abuse of power. On his personal orders, refugees had been detained on the *Diciotti*, a ship belonging to the Italian Coast Guard. On 16 August 2018, the ship had rescued 190[76] migrants from the Mediterranean Sea in compliance with international sea rescue rules. Salvini's office head is also under investigation, because the *Aquarius*, with 629[77] rescued passengers, had been denied entry to an Italian port.

Civil society is not giving up either. In summer 2018, the German Seebrücke (Sea Bridge) solidarity movement brings hundreds of thousands of people to the streets against Salvini's policies. Following appeals from celebrities, NGOs receive six-figure donations – and can afford new ships. The pressure forces Malta to let the ships go. In early November the new private rescue ship *Mare Ionio,* sailing under the Italian flag, reaches Libyan coastal waters. The Bavarian-based NGO Sea-Eye acquires a bigger ship for new rescue missions. The *Sea-Watch 3* is also sailing again, as is the Spanish NGO Open Arms. Even the Jugend Rettet IUVENTA activists, whose ship was confiscated by Italy and who are facing heavy fines, want to continue: 'We are now considering options for a new deployment,' says spokesperson Kira Fischer.[78]

But where the rescuers can take their passengers remains to be seen. Over the winter, rescue ships have to cruise the sea again, sometimes for weeks, because no country will let them dock with the refugees. Now the European Commission wants to set up 'regional disembarkation platforms' in North Africa – but no country is willing to host these camps. The EU keeps mentioning Tunisia, but President Béji Caïd Essebsi calls it 'out of the question'.[79] His country 'does not have the capacity to set up such centers and to carry Europe's burdens', Essebsi says. 'Here everyone must bear their own burden.'

But nobody in Europe wants to do that anymore.

In March 2017, when Italy was still under social democratic rule and receiving refugees but demanding relief, a high-level EU official explained to a group of journalists how Europe intended to deal with Italy's complaints: For the time being, everything would remain the same. There was 'no majority' for other options.

This is exactly why Italy no longer has a pro-EU majority. The EU's third-largest economy post-Brexit is governed by racists who equally despise the EU and the migrants crossing the sea. This could have been prevented. The rest of Europe betrayed and thereby weakened the pro-Europeans in Italy. The Lega Nord/M5S government could be the EU's third disaster after the Greek crisis and Brexit. We all should have shared the responsibility of migration to build the trust needed to bring Europe closer together. The price would have been manageable. The opposite has happened, and so we have risked further disintegrating the EU and causing irreparable damage to this unique intergenerational project.

Notes

1. *Tagesschau* (2018) 'Innenminister Salvini: "NGOs werden Italien nur auf Postkarte sehen"', 29 June | https://bit.ly/2TUmQoH

2. Crolly, Hannelore and Reuscher, Constanze (2018) 'Salvini treibt es

sogar für die eigene Regierung zu weit', *Welt Online*, 10 July | https://bit.ly/2OmqbQ9

3. Barigazzi, Jacopo (2017) 'Germany rejects Italian proposal to open EU ports to migrants', *Politico*, 7 June | https://politi.co/2HB3asq

4. European Commission (2017) 'Central Mediterranean Route: Commission proposes Action Plan to support Italy, reduce pressure and increase solidarity', Press release, Strasbourg, 4 July | http://bit.ly/2tnTE1T

5. *Spiegel Online* (2003) '"Peng – feuern wir die Kanone ab"', 16 June | http://bit.ly/2ve9zmg

6. Ibid.

7. Personal interview, Taboulba, Tunisia, July 2009

8. Jakob, Christian (2013) 'Die Angst vor dem Asylantrag', *tageszeitung*, 29 November 2013 | http://bit.ly/2hhxcoA | and '23 Tage ohne Hilfe', *tageszeitung*, 7 October 2011 | https://bit.ly/2Ub5cW8

9. Shenker, Jack (2012) 'Migrants left to die after catalogue of failures, says report into boat tragedy', *The Guardian*, 28 March | http://bit.ly/2tWoIWQ

10. Personal telephone interview, March 2012

11. Del Grande, Gabriele, 'Fortress Europe' Blog, (accessed 20 March 2019)| http://fortresseurope.blogspot.com

12. United for Intercultural Action (2017) '33.305 documented refugee deaths since 1993', Press release, 20 June | http://bit.ly/2tQiW87

13. 'EU Council Regulation (EC) No. 343/2003 of 18 February 2003' *Official Journal of the European Union*, Brussels, 25 February | https://bit.ly/2HPghpd

14. *Die Zeit* (2013) 'Deutschland blockiert Änderung der Flüchtlingspolitik', 8 October | http://bit.ly/2vetd1j

15. Ibid.

16. European Commission (2013) 'Commissioner Malmström's intervention during the press conference in Lampedusa', Press release, 9 October 2013 | http://bit.ly/2tWeTeA

17. International Organization for Migration (IOM), Missing Migrants Project (accessed 20 March 2019) | http://bit.ly/2fQfnJ1

18. IOM: UN Migration (2014) 'IOM Applauds Italy's Life-Saving Mare Nostrum Operation: "Not a Migrant Pull Factor"', 31 October | http://bit.ly/2hfb526

19. European Commission (2014) 'Frontex Joint Operation "Triton" – Concerted efforts to manage migration in the Central Mediterranean', Press memo, Brussels, 7 October | https://bit.ly/

1LGPced

20. IOM, Missing Migrants Project (accessed 20 March 2019)

21. *Deutschlandfunk* (2014) 'Italien beendet Rettungsaktion "Mare Nostrum"', 31 October | http://bit.ly/2vlcyKp

22. Bundesamt für Migration und Flüchtlinge (BAMF) (2014) *Asylgeschäftsstatistik*, September 2014

23. Jakob, Christian (2016) 'Sie wussten, was sie tun', *tageszeitung*, 18 April | http://www.taz.de/!5292921/

24. Ibid.

25. Frontex Operations Division, Joint Operations Unit (2014) 'Concept of reinforced joint operation tackling the migratory flows towards Italy: JO EPN-Triton', Classified document, Warsaw, 28 August

26. Telephone interview, April 2016

27. EU Parliament (2014) 'Committee on Civil Liberties, Justice and Home Affairs (LIBE) Committee Meeting.' EU Parliament (EPTV), 4 September 2014, 00:39 | https://bit.ly/YdCzXU

28. Ibid.

29. Liberti, Stefano (2015) 'Quando Frontex ammoniva l'Italia: troppi salvataggi', *Internazionale*, 11 February | http://tinyurl.com/y2w4pmcg

30. IOM, Missing Migrants Project (accessed 20 March 2019)

31. European Commission (2015) 'Speech by President Jean-Claude Juncker at the debate in the European Parliament on the conclusions of the Special European Council on 23 April: "Tackling the migration crisis"', Press release, Strasbourg, 29 April | https://bit.ly/1OD7eWm

32. *Spiegel Online* (2016) 'Frontex rechnet mit 300.000 Bootsflüchtlingen aus Libyen', 18 June | http://bit.ly/1YyxunC

33. IOM, Missing Migrants Project (accessed 20 March 2019)

34. 'Watch the Med: Alarm Phone Initiative' | https://alarmphone.org/en/

35. Telephone interview, 17 April 2014

36. Kopp, Hagen (2013) 'Überleben Glückssache', *medico international Newsletter 4/2013*, 25 November | http://bit.ly/2vayRCl

37. Telephone interview, 17 April 2014

38. Personal interview, May 2015

39. Christine Xuân Müller (2015) 'Brandenburger startet Flüchtlingshilfe', *Potsdamer Neueste Nachrichten*, 12 June | http://bit.ly/2wdejWs

40. Personal interview, 2 June 2016, Valletta, Malta

41. Sea-Watch (2019) 'FAQ' (accessed 20 March 2019) | https://bit.ly/2HzFioQ

42. *EEAS news* (2015) 'Federica Mogherini at the UN Security Council on migration crisis', 12 May | https://bit.ly/2OocmAG

43. UN Security Council (2015) 'Unanimously Adopting Resolution 2259 (2015), Security Council Welcomes Signing of Libyan Political Agreement on New Government for Strife-Torn Country', Press release, 23 December | http://tinyurl.com/y4zhu8x4

44. Bonse, Eric; Jakob, Christian, and Keilberth, Mirco (2016) 'Noch wird nicht geschossen', *tageszeitung*, 23 June | http://bit.ly/2varquB

45. *Süddeutsche Zeitung* (2015) 'EU billigt Militäreinsatz gegen Flüchtlingsschleuser', 22 June | http://bit.ly/2uPHMGC

46. *Die Zeit* (2016) 'De Maizière fordert Aufnahmelager für Flüchtlinge in Nordafrika', 13 October | http://bit.ly/2foZfYz

47. *Die Welt* (2016) 'De Maizière will gerettete Flüchtlinge in Aufnahmelager in Nordafrika bringen', 13 October | http://bit.ly/2vaFgxk

48. Personal interview, Rome, November 2016

49. Bewarder, Manuel (2017) 'Auswärtiges Amt kritisiert "KZ-ähnliche" Verhältnisse', *Die Welt*, 29 January | http://bit.ly/2vXtUdv

50. European Commission (2017) 'Managing migration along the Central Mediterranean Route', Press release, Brussels, 25 January 2017 | http://bit.ly/2jQZVhx

51. Sarzanini, Fiorenza (2017) 'Gommoni, elicotteri e la sala-radar Per la Libia piano da 800 milioni', *Corriere della Sera*, 20 March | http://bit.ly/2mGr4Uf; *Fatto quotidiano* (2017) 'Migranti, il generale libico Haftar: "Con 20 miliardi dall'Europa fermiamo il flusso. Sarraj ha violato gli accordi di Parigi"', 12 August | http://bit.ly/2x6lgKf

52. EU Council (2017) 'Malta Declaration by the members of the European Council on the external aspects of migration: addressing the Central Mediterranean route', EU Council press release, Valletta, 3 February | https://bit.ly/2QH8oVI

53. Jakob, Christian (2017) 'Wer rettet die Retter?' *tageszeitung*, 24 August | http://www.taz.de/!5436108/

54. Ibid.

55. *Arab News* (2017) 'Libya navy bars foreign ships from migrant "search and rescue" zone', 10 August | https://bit.ly/2OkKuO7

56. Jakob, Christian (2017) 'Vom Mittelmeer zurück in die Hölle', *tageszeitung*, 20 September | http://www.taz.de/!5445531/

57. Obert, Michael (2018) 'Gefangen in Libyen', *medico international Newsletter* 1/2018, 26 April |https://bit.ly/2HUos3D

58. Amnesty International (2018) 'A year after Italy-Libya migration deal,

time to release thousands trapped in misery', Press release, 1 November | https://bit.ly/2un8uqH

59. Laessing, U. and Elumami, A. (2018) 'Libyan coast guard says it has intercepted 15,000 migrants in 2018', *Reuters UK*, 20 December 2018 | https://reut.rs/2Bu8Sqg

60. 'Libya migrant slave auction', CNN World International Edition video, 13 November 2017 | http://tinyurl.com/y4j8zpy6

61. Internal document, in the authors' archives

62. Bewarder, Manuel (2017) 'Einsätze vor Libyen müssen auf den Prüfstand', *Die Welt*, 27 February | http://bit.ly/2vXiczr

63. *Die Presse* (2017) 'Kurz: "Der NGO-Wahnsinn muss beendet werden"', 24 March | http://bit.ly/2tWjzkQ

64. Meisner, Matthias (2017) 'Ermittlungen gegen Dresdner Seenotretter', *Tagesspiegel*, 26 June | http://bit.ly/2tfoPvQ

65. Gümpel, Udo (2018) 'Retter oder Helfershelfer? Die "Iuventa" und die Menschenschmuggler', *N-TV*, 4 August | https://bit.ly/2US99vX

66. Jugend Rettet-IUVENTA, 'About us', (accessed 21 March 2019) | https://jugendrettet.org/

67. Statistica, 'Number of migrant arrivals to Italy from 2014 to January 2019', (accessed 21 March 2019) | https://bit.ly/2FsXsVJ

68. European Commission (2016) 'Relocation and Resettlement: Member States need to sustain efforts to deliver on commitments', Press release, Brussels, 9 November | https://bit.ly/2eD4ojH

69. European Commission (2018) 'Member States' Support to Emergency Relocation Mechanism (As of 30 October 2018)', Press material (accessed 21 March 2019) | https://bit.ly/2ifnGlx

70. *Focus Online* (2018) 'Seehofer spricht mit Salvini über Asylpolitik - der stellt erneut drastische Forderungen', 12 July | https://bit.ly/2WmLWSR

71. Lobenstein, Caterina and Lau, Mariam (2018) 'Seerettung: Oder soll man es lassen?', *Die Zeit*, No. 29/2018, 12 July | https://bit.ly/2KvM7Vz

72. Leuf, Wolfgang (2018) 'Der Untergang', *SZ Magazin: Süddeutsche Zeitung*, 5 July | https://bit.ly/2IXygXq

73. Bartsch, Michael and Jakob, Christian (2018) 'Retter in Not', *tageszeitung*, 9 July | https://bit.ly/2U7eJNK

74. Ibid.

75. Ibid.

76. *Zeit Online* (2018) 'Migranten verlassen italienisches Rettungsschiff', 26 August | https://bit.ly/2HQ8bfQ

77. *France24* (2018) 'L'Aquarius: l'odyssée de 629 migrants face au bras de fer européen', 17 June | https://bit.ly/2YiI872

78. Personal interview, November 2018

79. Tarhini, Dima (2018) 'Essebsi: Flüchtlingsabkommen "kommt nicht in Frage"', *Deutsche Welle*, 31 October | https://p.dw.com/p/37UVp

Opening the markets

Aid to fund migration control: The 'Merkel Plan' with Africa

Berlin's downtown streets are blocked off as the column of black diplomatic limousines moves from the Chancellery through the Tiergarten on 12 June 2017. The German government has invited more than 10 African heads of state; Christine Lagarde, director of the International Monetary Fund, has come from Washington. German Chancellor Merkel, Federal Development Minister Müller, Economic Minister Brigitte Zypries (SPD), Finance Minister Schäuble and many ambassadors arrive at the Gasometer in the Schöneberg district. The German hosts have chosen the former site of Berlin's main natural gas provider GASAG, because it stands for economic development and energy production. GASAG was the 19th century's largest gas provider in Western Europe, when gas lanterns lit the fast-growing cities. Today, the listed landmark with its towering gas tank is an event venue.

Germany's government has convened the G20 Africa Partnership Conference here just weeks before the actual G20 Summit in Hamburg in July 2017. As Germany holds the G20 presidency for 2017, it has declared this the Year of Africa. 'Investing in a common future' is the motto for the Berlin conference. In her opening speech, Merkel warns: 'We know that pan-global development can only succeed if all continents share in such development.' Many speakers that day will repeat her description of Africa as a continent of 'opportunities'.[1]

Just in time, on that same morning the Organization for Economic Co-Operation and Development (OECD) delivered its prognosis for Africa: growth would double to 3.4 percent in the coming year.[2] Like a good weather forecast before a trip, this news should have lifted the mood. 'Even today,' says Merkel, 'dynamic economic developments in Africa 'reveal the potential that lies in African countries.' Standing onstage, she raises her index finger in her own peculiar way: 'But much still remains to be done.'

That day, the Chancellor calls for a new era of German development aid. 'We have to consider whether we have always taken the right path in providing our traditional development aid,' she says, warning: 'There too, we have to learn to think anew.' This meant that Germany will rely more on military power: For many years, Merkel says, 'we felt virtuous when we were not dealing with military equipment.' Those days were over. 'We have to be more honest and admit that only where security is given can development take root. If hopelessness is too widespread in Africa, young people are also more likely to seek a better life elsewhere in the world.' Therefore, the Chancellor demands an education offensive for the African youth. 'By working together with you for your countries, we are also enhancing our own security,' she says.[3]

Continent of opportunities

The African leaders thank Merkel for her words. 'We appreciate that very much,' says Alassane Ouattara, President of Côte d'Ivoire, taking the podium after Merkel.[4] His state's economy, having grown over nine percent in 2015, numbers among the most dynamic worldwide. The country is one of the largest cocoa producers globally and the strongest economy within the ECOWAS.

Twenty-six percent of Côte d'Ivoire's population were foreigners, most of them labor migrants from surrounding countries, Ouattara says. 'Migration can also be a positive factor.' The migrants were sending money back to their families. But for that, they needed jobs, so his country hoped that Germany would invest more in ports, streets and railways. 'I spoke with the head of Siemens and he has promised to open a subsidiary in Abidjan,' Ouattara rejoices.

Côte d'Ivoire is one of the states in which German businesses now want to invest more. Earlier, German Development Minister Müller had called for a 'Marshall Plan with Africa.' In his speech, Ouattara bluntly renames it the 'Merkel Plan' to loud applause. Merkel laughs and seems moved.

However, at this point in June 2017, there is no real plan yet. What the Germans are presenting to the Africans in Berlin are three different, though similar-sounding concepts developed independently by three different ministries. Journalists in the press section at the Gasometer are cursing: 'Who still understands all this?'

Much has happened since Merkel's Africa trip in October 2016. Launched in late 2015, the first phase of Europe's new Africa policy – not new in content, but in scope – had relied on directly strengthening border controls. Money for stopping refugees; that was the plan. But the EU found the results insufficient. So the second phase of the policy relies on economic aid. The EU will invest billions in Africa, not for mere profit, but also to create jobs for young Africans, so they will stop leaving for Europe.

'This continent's population will double by 2050. Every year, 20 million new jobs are needed,' states Development Minister Müller, without revealing how he reached this estimate.[5] One June 2017 study even speaks of 50 million jobs needed in Africa by 2040.[6] German companies should therefore help out by investing in jobs. 'If we don't help this continent, millions will leave and set off a new mass migration for Europe,' Müller warns.[7]

At the same time, German industry has a lot of catching up to do in Africa. Eleven of the world's twenty fastest growing economies are in Africa. In Berlin, the presidents of Ghana, Rwanda and Côte d'Ivoire boast of growth rates of over seven percent. 'Lions on the move,' as management consultancy McKinsey calls them,[8] on the 'continent of opportunities' according to the Federation of German Industry (BDI).[9] Besides China and Israel, Turkey, South Korea and India are also investing in infrastructure and agricultural projects, as well as in banks and telecommunications.

German businesses are still hesitant: About 1,000 German companies do business in Africa, 600 of them in South Africa and most of the rest in the Maghreb. The enormous area in between looks like a wasteland to German investors. 'The German industry is missing out on a market,' Müller warned recently.[10] 'Africa has been off our radar for decades,' confirms Christoph Kannengießer,[11] CEO of the German-African Business Association. He blames 'mental', but also structural causes: most German companies were medium-sized, risk-averse family businesses and still viewed Africa as too volatile. German companies also tended towards the high-tech sector and supplied the machines instead of building roads and factories. 'Companies tend to go where it's profitable,' says Kannengießer, 'VW will build cars wherever they see customers.' Drawn by Africa's new purchasing power, Volkswagen has already built factories in Kenya and Rwanda.[12] Germany's government now wants to secure the field for German companies entering this risky market. Investment aid as development aid – that is the idea.

A Marshall Plan with Africa

The idea was a Marshall Plan *with* and not *for* Africa. Minister Müller introduced the 33 pages to African diplomats at his ministry's conference hall in central Berlin in November 2016.[13] After the end of World War II, the USA helped devastated economies in Western Europe recover with this program. The plan, named after US Secretary of State George Marshall, included loans, raw materials, food and manufactured goods. However, the US attached conditions to this aid package. Most of the funds were direct subsidies and had to be spent on US products to boost the American economy.

In Germany, a significant legacy of this era is the *Kreditanstalt für Wiederaufbau* (KfW), today the world's largest development bank. It was founded in 1948 in Frankfurt with startup capital from the USA. At first, the KfW primarily granted loans and risk protection to German companies domestically. Since 1961, it has also had the task of managing financial cooperation with developing countries. The KfW remains the major instrument of German development cooperation and hence is to play a key role in the Marshall Plan with Africa.

In November 2016, Müller explained to the African ambassadors in Berlin: 'Clearly, Africa's challenges are not comparable to Europe's after World War II, but the necessary efforts certainly are.' He defined three focal points: industry, trade and employment. His plan was designed foremost as a 'Future Pact for Africa's Youth', who 'need jobs and prospects!'[14]

President of the European Parliament Antonio Tajani liked the idea. The conservative Italian followed suit in late February 2017 and demanded that the EU also develop a 'Marshall Plan with Africa'. Europe must invest several billion euros there now, he warned. Otherwise, millions of Africans would come to Europe over the next 20 years. However, Tajani failed to reveal his sources for this scenario. This problem concerned all EU states, not just Italy or Germany, he claimed.[15]

The current Marshall Plan barely mentions migration. To the contrary, it focuses on creating jobs on the ground for Africa's youth.

For 2017, the German government increased the Development Ministry (BMZ) budget by over €1 billion, to €8.5 billion. 'We are investing the major share in Africa,' Müller proclaimed generously.[16] In early 2017, the German government boasted that this increase marked its first-ever achievement of the OECD's 1970 target for official development assistance (ODA): 0.7 percent of gross national income (GNI). International NGO Oxfam criticized this calculation as a sham: 'The German government reached the international target only by adding in the costs of housing refugees. Those now account for 25.2 percent of all German development aid,' Oxfam states. 'This welcome increase in the development budget in recent years must be followed by further increases of at least €1.5 billion a year.'[17] Far from being a raise, Müller's vaunted offer falls even below previously set targets.

Initially, the 'Marshall Plan' did not include a single euro. Only on the eve of the G20 Africa Partnership Conference did Müller rectify this. He quickly freed up another €300 million and picked Ghana, Côte d'Ivoire and Tunisia as his first 'reform partners', countries that met the German requirements for direct investments in terms of anti-corruption efforts and rule of law.[18]

Pro! Africa – Germany's business plan

In early February 2017, Germany's Minister for Economic Affairs, Brigitte Zypries, brought a delegation of top executives to the German-African Business Summit (GABS) of the Sub-Saharan Africa Initiative of German Business (SAFRI) in Kenya. Representatives of Volkswagen, Deutsche Bank, Siemens, SAP, pharmaceutical company Braun Melsungen and technology group Voith came along. Kenyan President Uhuru Kenyatta gave the opening speech at Nairobi's Hotel Intercontinental to over 400 participants from across the continent. With a trade volume of €533 million, Kenya is Germany's most important economic partner in East Africa. Here, Germany maintains one of eight Delegations of Industry and Commerce (AHK) south of the Sahara.

At the summit, Zypries presented the *Pro! Africa* initiative, to which her ministry had allocated €100 million.[19] She too speaks of Africa as a 'region of opportunity' and a market ready to develop its full potential. German-African business relations were good, but could be expanded, she said.

In fact, Germany's bilateral trade volume with sub-Saharan Africa in 2015 was just €26 billion. This roughly corresponds to Germany's trade with the Slovak Republic. Yet Africa showed great demand for 'Made in Germany' know-how said Zypries, and German companies were ready to invest in Africa's youth and promote technology transfer.

Pro! Africa promotes German companies' entry into Africa's alternative energy markets, more trips to Africa for the German AHK, new jobs within the AHK and the embassies to promote economic partnerships. Dual vocational programs aim to train young Africans on German machines, preparing them to work at German companies. Even in the African healthcare sector, so far funded by development aid, the initiative plans to 'introduce German products and services' to African doctors.[20]

'Everyone envies our dual training system,' says Kannengießer of the German-African Business Association. Not for the curriculum itself, but because the companies finance it, so 'they train for their exact needs', Kannengießer explains. This system does not qualify workers just to build up a labor reserve. Therefore, he expects little from the proliferation of vocational schools in Africa. 'Basically, the investment comes first, then the training; it won't work the other way around.' For example, he thinks that using aid money to build company-specific schools would be a good mix of development cooperation and foreign trade promotion.[21]

Schäuble's Compacts

As if two plans were not enough, the German Ministry of Finance under Wolfgang Schäuble (CDU) also drafted the Compacts with Africa. Just like the two plans, these Compacts promote German direct investment in Africa. However, Schäuble got the G20 on board for his Compacts: member states will offer loans, and African countries can apply by submitting project plans. They should also make their legal and tax systems more investor-friendly. The Compacts with Africa represent a 'completely new approach in business cooperation', states the Ministry of Finance: 'The countries themselves must take more responsibility.'[22] Whoever offers the best conditions gets the biggest investment package, so African countries will compete for funding.

Some African governments were allowed to speak directly to Schäuble. In March 2017, he invited Côte d'Ivoire, Morocco, Rwanda, Senegal and Tunisia to meet with G20 finance ministers and central bank executives in Baden-Baden.

Hardly any place on Earth is as far removed from the reality of an African village as this posh town in the northern Black Forest, where the richest of the rich promenade past the jewelry shops and enjoy evenings in one of the world's most famous casinos. Just as the African delegations sit at the table, a scandal erupts among the G20 states: For the first time, the 20 leading industrial nations cannot agree on expanding free trade and climate protection in their final statement. US President Donald Trump's 'America First' calls for more protectionism, and the climate is not really his issue anyway. Two months later he announces the USA's withdrawal from the Paris Climate Agreement of 2015.

The final statement from Baden-Baden vexed policymakers in Rwanda's capital Kigali. For decades, big business had demanded that small African economies dismantle their tariffs and open up to free trade. Just when they were about to, thought the Rwandans, came this international turnaround. Whether America First or Brexit, isolationism sends the wrong signal to African countries, says Fred Nkusi, Rwanda's leading international law expert. EAC states were just learning that 'regional integration is the best approach for development and growth of the country's economy', [23] he commented in the state-owned *New Times* on the Baden-Baden meeting attended by Rwanda's delegation.

The small state in the heart of Africa has high hopes for the Compacts. Loans are needed to build housing and connect the small, landlocked country to the East African railway line, which is planned to connect the interior to the ports of Mombasa, Kenya and Dar es Salaam, Tanzania. Construction would cost as much as $900 million.[24] So Rwanda needs loans urgently. In Berlin, President Kagame campaigned for rapid investments. His country already was business-friendly, he said, and not prone to long discussions. Kagame's hurry was no coincidence: elections were coming up in August 2017. Kagame's goal was to bring home loan commitments from Berlin to secure his power. In 2018, he was still sulky that Germany had not approved a single loan for his country.

The German-African Business Association thinks it is not such a bad idea that the Compacts focus on the 'reform champions'. After all, the Compact states were selected as model countries within their regions – with an eye on preventing or redirecting labor migration, says the Association's CEO, Kannengießer.[25] The notion is simple: If Ghana's business booms and creates jobs, Togolese jobseekers may go there – and not to Europe.

There's profit in Africa

'If the world is to become more stable, we must reduce the gap between the richest and poorest,' Finance Minister Schäuble explains his Compacts at the Baden-Baden summit.[26] Yet a deeper look shows that the Compacts would primarily benefit investors in developed countries, criticizes the association Jubilee Germany (Erlassjahr), a development policy alliance between churches, politics and civil society. Since the G20 offer Africans states loans at market conditions, i.e., with short 25-year maturities and interest rates between 5 and 15 percent, they are expensive and risky – unlike the low-interest loans with maturities of over 50 years that are common in development aid. The Compacts ignore that 'the downside of this funding is escalating debt and, in extreme cases, state bankruptcy', says Jürgen Kaiser of Jubilee Germany.[27]

The German NGO World Economy, Ecology and Development (WEED), which advocates for fair financial, economic and environmental policy, shares this criticism. It fears that in the long run, corporate investments in projects like road or power plant construction could put Africa's entire infrastructure into private hands. In developed countries, privatizing public services like water and power has come at a great cost for citizens, states the NGO. The Compacts allowed G20 governments to '"preach" to the African countries that development is just a side effect' of profiteering, says Markus Henn of WEED. He warns that the Compacts could 'become the starting point of the next African Debt Crisis'.[28] Today, the Global South already spends far more on debt service than it receives in development aid.[29]

Those who profit from these loans are the small depositors who make up Schäuble's core constituency, wealthy private investors in Baden-Baden, big banks, hedge funds and insurance companies in Frankfurt, as well as major pension funds, including Germany's subsidized private pension scheme (Riester pension). Investors have a hard time finding profitable ventures in Germany or the G20 countries. Their savings earn hardly any interest, so they scour the globe. 'The German government openly declares its aim to open up Africa for Western pension funds,' states Jubilee Germany's position paper. 'Allianz and others urgently need these returns of 5 to 15 percent, which are still achievable in Africa, to meet their obligations towards customers holding subsidized pensions and other types of old-age provision.'[30]

'It's not about wanting to help Africa, it's about business and making profits,' summarized Morocco's Finance Minister Mohamed Boussaid at the Partnership Conference in Berlin in June 2017.[31]

After Bundestag elections in September 2017, German politicians rarely mentioned any of the business promotion concepts they had developed for Africa. At the big EU-AU summit in Côte d'Ivoire in November 2017, the Marshall Plan no longer plays even a minor role. The final statement only echoes the issues of education and jobs. At the end of 2017, the German government passed the G20 presidency to Argentina, which had little interest in the Compacts with Africa and set its own G20 priorities.

Nevertheless: 'One year after presenting the Marshall Plan with Africa, Development Minister Müller sees positive interim results,' declared the BMZ website in January 2018. In February, it published a 'state of affairs' report on the Marshall Plan's implementation, while noting that it 'contains no detailed information on the Plan's financial resources'.[32]

The Ministry's budget grew steadily from 2018 to 2019. For 2019 it even exceeds €10 billion.[33] This major increase is clearly not enough for Müller: 'I say to everyone calling to combat the causes of migration: I lack funding for some urgent programs,' he complains to the Bundestag during the September 2018 budget debates. 'There were simply too many crises in the world,' he says.[34] So while the Marshall Plan appears as a financial instrument in the draft budget, there is not one single euro allocated to it. By contrast, defense spending for 2019 was to increase 15 times more than development aid, which development politician Helin Sommer (The Left) criticized in the Bundestag debate: '15:1 might be a great result for an international football match, but in this case, it's morally wrong and economically unwise.'[35]

Notes

1. Speech by German Federal Chancellor Angela Merkel at conference 'G20 Africa Partnership – investing in a common future', Berlin, 12 June 2017 in | https://bit.ly/2Iljm1W

2. AfDB/OECD/UNDP (2017) *African Economic Outlook 2017: Entrepreneurship and Industrialisation*, OECD Publishing, Paris, 22 May | https://bit.ly/2V8KItW

3. Merkel Speech (12 June 2017)

4. This quotation taken from the authors' notes and descriptions of the event, Berlin, 12 June 2017

5. Ibid.

6. Said, Jonathan et al. (2017) 'The Jobs Gap – Making inclusive growth work in Africa', *Tony Blair Institute for Global Change*, 26 June 2017 | https://bit.ly/2zbw79k

7. Authors' notes of event (12 June 2017)

8. Roxburg, Charles et al (2010) 'Lions on the move: The progress and potential of African economies', *McKinsey Global Institute/ McKinsey&Company*, June 2010 | https://mck.co/2qGbXhZ

9. 'Africa – continent of crises or land of opportunity?' *Federation of German Industry (BDI)*, 2 May 2016 | https://bit.ly/2DXfU8f

10. Kroll, Katharina (2018) 'Entwicklungsminister Gerd Müller – Afrika ist Chancenkontinent', *Deutsche Welle*, 17 February | https://p.dw.com/p/2sruV

11. Personal interview with Christoph Kannengießer, CEO of the German-African Business Association, Berlin, 19 June 2017

12. Menzel, Stefan (2016) 'Volkswagen entdeckt Afrika', *Handelsblatt*, 21 December | http://bit.ly/2tQxXXo

13. Federal Ministry for Economic Cooperation and Development (BMZ) (2016) 'Speech by Development Minister Müller in dialogue with African ambassadors in Germany: "Cornerstones for a Marshall Plan with Africa"', Berlin, 24 November 2016 | https://bit.ly/2j9hRTJ

14. Ibid.

15. *Tagesschau* (2017) 'Entweder wir handeln, oder Millionen kommen', 27 February | http://bit.ly/2wdfrJz

16. Müller, 24 November 2016 | https://bit.ly/2j9hRTJ

17. Oxfam (2017) '0,7 Prozent für Entwicklungshilfe ist mehr Schein als Sein', OECD press release, Berlin, 11 April | http://bit.ly/2tQxRPw

18. *Die Welt* (2017) '"Merkel-Plan": 300 Millionen Euro zusätzlich für Afrika', 12 June | http://bit.ly/2vm2tgq

19. BMWi - Federal Ministry for Economic Affairs and Energy (2017) 'Pro! Africa: Promoting the prospects, taking the opportunities, strengthening the economies', Strategy paper, Berlin, 4 May |https://bit.ly/2VaBHQL

20. Ibid.

21. Kannengießer (2017)

22. 'Federal Ministry of Finance (2017) 'Partnerschaft mit Afrika: Startschuss für G20-Afrika-Konferenz in Berlin', press release, Federal Ministry of Finance, Berlin, 12 June | http://bit.ly/2vlWUOS

23. Nkusi, Fred (2017) 'Why protectionism is a threat to integration?' *New Times*, 27 March | http://bit.ly/2hfZNus

24. *New Times* (2017) 'Rwanda Won't Opt Out of Northern Corridor Standard Gauge Railway Project. – Govt', 19 May | https://bit.ly/2ElulEJ

25. Kannengießer (2017)

26. Schäuble, Wolfgang (2017) 'Nationale Alleingänge sind keine Antwort', *Die Zeit*, 2 March | http://bit.ly/2vaZlDu

27. Erlassjahr (Jubilee Germany) (2017) 'G20-Finanzministertreffen in Baden-Baden: Drohende Schuldenkrisen ignoriert', press release, Baden-Baden/Düsseldorf, 18 March | http://bit.ly/2vXidmY

28. Henn, Markus (2017) 'The G20's Compact with Africa: Some disastrous recipes for sustainable development', *WEED - World Economy, Ecology and Development*, press release, Berlin, 28 April 2017 | http://bit.ly/2x6MHDS

29. Obenland, W. (2016) 'Europas Einfluss auf die globale Ungleichheit', in Braunsdorf, F. (ed.) *Fluchtursachen 'Made in Europe'*, Friedrich Ebert Stiftung, Berlin, November 2016 | https://bit.ly/2V9agaa

30. Erlassjahr (Jubilee Germany) (2017) *Der Compact with Africa: Nord-Süd-Initiative der G20 mit gefährlicher Kehrseite*, position paper, Baden-Baden/Düsseldorf, 13 April |http://bit.ly/2vXQAuf

31. Authors' notes of event (12 June 2017)

32. Ministry of Economic Cooperation and Development (2018) 'Ein Jahr Marshallplan mit Afrika Reformpartnerschaften erfolgreich gestartet – nächster Schritt: Europäisierung', Press statement, *BMZ*, Berlin, 18 January | https://bit.ly/2DY3ux4

33. Source missing.

34. Bundestag (2018) 'Minister Gerd Müller hofft auf weitere Aufstockung seines Etats', Bundestag budget debates, Berlin, 12 September | https://bit.ly/2CotEiz

35. *Deutsche Welle* (2018) 'Bundeshaushalt 2019: Zu wenig Geld für Entwicklung?', 14 September 2018 | https://bit.ly/2F7vctj

Free Trade:
Euro-African café latte

When Germany's Development Minister Müller visited Côte d'Ivoire in March 2017, he was astounded: 'It can't be right that cocoa and coffee growers cannot live off their hard work, and that instead of going to school, children have to slave on the plantations,' he railed. The country is the world's largest cocoa producer, and European chocolate manufacturers are among the main purchasers. Yet a cocoa farmer earns only about 50 cents per day. To help the country progress, the minister urged for more local processing. The EU, for its part, should help by dismantling trade barriers. Müller calls fair trade between the continents 'a modern policy for Africa's future'.[1]

Since colonial times, trade ties between Europe and Africa have depended on African small farmers planting tea, coffee, cotton, cocoa or vanilla – commodities consumed by Europeans, not Africans. Africans earn more by exporting these goods. These small farmers use only a small fraction of their fields for subsistence. They plant foodstuffs high in calories and protein but low in vitamins: beans, cassava or plantains. This food is usually just enough to feed a family, but not really healthy. If the weather goes crazy, as during the 2016-17 drought in East Africa, the yield will be too poor to feed their kids a decent lunch.

Since the 1970s, African countries have exported these commodities duty-free to the EU,[2] including coffee, the continent's second major global export after crude oil. Small farmers from West to East Africa have been planting coffee bushes for centuries – European colonial powers once forced them to. The Africans export the green coffee duty-free to EU companies, who then roast, package and sell it. If African coffee cooperatives were to invest in their own roasting plants to create jobs and obtain a higher selling price, the EU would charge import duties on the refined product. Therefore, shipping pure green coffee is cheaper for trading companies.

This has absurd consequences: Until just a few years ago, Rwandan restaurants would serve anyone ordering coffee a packet of Nescafé powder from Swiss producer Nestlé and hot water in a thermos jug, while coffee beans grow on bushes just outside. With increasing urbanization and globalization, the African middle class has developed a taste for coffee. In the cities, coffeehouses are opening for the middle classes to meet for cappuccino. However, the drink costs more in Rwanda than at Starbucks in downtown Berlin[3] – even though the world's largest coffeehouse chain gets some of its coffee from Rwanda, whose beans now rank among the best in the world.

The second-largest Ugandan coffee producer, Good African Coffee, which supplies Ugandan coffee houses, drove this absurdity to extremes: For years, it shipped green coffee duty-free from Uganda over 3,700 miles to Ireland to be roasted and ground in Dublin – and then shipped back to Uganda vacuum-packed. A pound of roasted ground coffee costs less than 3 euros. In 2009, Good African Coffee opened its own roasting plant in Uganda. The price for this coffee far surpassed that of green coffee,[4] but this also raised the price for European coffee drinkers.

Latte lovers in Africa usually have to make do with powdered milk produced by the Dutch-British food giant Unilever. African supermarkets sell this item many times cheaper than fresh milk – although in many African countries, cows outnumber people. However, massive subsidizing of agricultural subsidies in the EU generates huge food surpluses through factory farming, high-yield breeding and feed supplements. In recent years, these surpluses have caused milk prices to hit rock bottom. The same has happened to meat production, for example chicken; and also, to wheat for baguettes and sandwich bread, which has long since displaced traditional millet varieties in Africa.

For this reason, the 2015 export strategy by German Agricultural Minister Christian Schmidt plans to process European cows' milk into powder in Europe and export it cheaply to Africa. In countries like Burkina Faso or Nigeria, for example, where cows traditionally belong to extended families, supermarket refrigerators offer the choice between yogurts from French food corporation Danone made with powdered milk from the EU, or a yogurt from the milk cooperative around the corner. The EU yogurt is cheaper, although its ingredients were produced over 3,000 miles away.[5]

Those who claim that more European corporations in Africa could create more jobs there fail to recognize that they are causing African small farmers to lose their livelihoods. Large European dairy corporations like Arla, FrieslandCampina and Danone recently invested in West African companies or formed joint ventures. They get rid of their milk powder by turning it into yogurt in Africa.

NGOs like Germanwatch, *Brot für die Welt* and *Misereor* warned back in 2015 that Schmidt's export offensive could lead to significant 'market disruptions' in developing countries. Milk and whey powder make up 60 percent of EU dairy exports, and Africa is the most important market.[6] 'Especially in West African countries, cheap imports prevent domestic dairy farmers from gaining access to the growing urban markets in their own country,' says Kerstin Lanje of *Misereor*. 'We fear that in the near future, more EU imports will worsen the economic situation of herder families, who make up about a third of the population.'

Africa risks becoming a 'clearance section for EU exports', says Francisco Marí of *Brot für die Welt*. 'Skimmed milk powder enriched with vegetable fat and aimed at the lowest market segment is seen as the EU's new best-selling export to Africa. In the last 10 years the EU has more than doubled its exports there.'[7]

The 2014 study *Honest Accounts? The True Story of Africa's Billion Dollar Losses*, conducted by 14 international NGOs, calculated: Sub-Saharan Africa receives $134 billion a year from the West in development funding, investments and loans – while $192 billion flow out of Africa. Of this figure, major corporations take $46 billion as profit. Another $35 billion vanish into tax havens, mostly invested in mailbox companies by corrupt state employees. The assumption that the West is helping Africa has created a 'perverse reality in which the UK and other wealthy states celebrate their generosity whilst simultaneously assisting their companies to drain Africa's resources', the researchers write.[8]

EU-Africa free trade: the art of the foul deal

In his Marshall Plan for Africa, German Development Minister Müller speaks of 'fair trade': that is, free trade agreements on a fair basis, so cocoa and coffee growers can soon earn sufficient incomes. He is referring to current negotiations on Economic Partnership Agreements (EPAs) between the EU, individual African states, and blocs such as the East African Community (EAC), the Economic Community of West African States (ECOWAS) and the South

African Development Community (SADC), which are highly controversial in Africa.

For almost 20 years, the EU has been insisting that African markets open up to EU imports and eliminate their protective tariffs. The Europeans argued that opening their markets unilaterally, that is, maintaining the duty-free regime for African products entering the EU but not vice versa, would be incompatible with the rules of the World Trade Organization (WTO). Hence, back in 2000 in Benin's capital Cotonou, the negotiating partners decided to set up EPAs. The resulting plan accounted for African concerns and included a developmental policy component on paper: The Africans were to open their markets to 80 percent of the EU's products gradually over the next 15 years, while 20 percent would be protected from EU competition. Negotiations began in 2002.

At the same time, the EU guaranteed continued duty-free access to Africa's 49 low-income countries through its *Everything But Arms* initiative [9] which came into force in 2001. Hence, the EU's potential punitive tariffs would affect only the continent's 'middle-income countries': Kenya, Botswana, Ghana, Cameroon, Namibia, South Africa and Côte d'Ivoire. Protests erupted over the initiative: in Kenya, demonstrators took to the streets in Nairobi during the 2007 World Social Forum, an alternative event to the WTO summits;[10] in Ghana the labor unions protested in 2008.[11] The partners have since extended negotiation deadlines several times.

In 2014 the EU put the gun to Kenya's head and imposed import duties on Kenyan products for three months. Kenyan farmers who grow cut flowers for the European market threatened their government in 2016, saying they would emigrate to Ethiopia or Tanzania if the 6 percent punitive tariff remained in place. Thousands of jobs were at risk, which raised pressure on Kenya's government to finally accept the deal. In September 2016, Kenya and Rwanda signed the EPA.[12] Rwanda is about to ratify it. Günter Nooke, the German Chancellor's G8 Personal Representative for Africa, said about Kenya, 'No, the way we handled it in the EU Commission, there was no choice. We left them no other option to keep their access to Europe.'[13]

Since then, the EAC has been deeply divided: Burundi vehemently refuses to join talks with the Europeans.[14] After the post-election political crisis in Burundi in 2015, the EU stopped development cooperation with the country and imposed sanctions against the new regime. As a result, Burundi has no interest in accommodating the EU. Tanzania is resisting as well. A parliamentary declaration cites the disadvantages of liberalization for Tanzania's industry and development.[15] While the country planned to push ahead with industrialization, domestic products would not withstand European competition, which would threaten jobs and investments, the declaration states.[16]

At the 2016 annual conference in the Kenyan capital Nairobi, Patrick Gomes, Secretary General of the African, Caribbean and Pacific Group of States (ACP), warned of heavy-handed threats from Brussels: Countries should recognize that 'EPA comes not only with trade options with Europe', urged Gomes. Those who did not sign the agreements 'could end up losing important development aid from the EU'.[17]

For a long time, it seemed that the EAC would fall apart over the issue of EPAs. After all, the EAC is a free trade zone, like the Schengen Area. If EPAs allowed Europeans to import products duty-free to Kenya, what would prevent those goods from reaching Uganda or Rwanda? EAC countries would have to restore their customs borders.

A study commissioned by the EAC and conducted by the United Nations Economic Commission for Africa (UNECA) found that East Africans would be the biggest losers in the EPAs. Kenya, a relatively developed country, would suffer the greatest damage and lose about $45 million annually in customs, while the EU, the clear winner, would gain $212 million.[18] 'Local industries will struggle to withstand competitive pressures from EU firms, while the region will be stuck in its position as a low value-added commodity exporter,' the study found.[19] Further, East Africans fear for their good trade ties with India and China, from where they import far more, if they were to grant Europe duty-free import for competing goods.

In late May 2017, the EAC heads of state met for their annual summit in Tanzania's largest city, Dar es Salaam. They had long postponed this top-tier meeting because their negotiators could not agree on the EPAs. For days, the leaders conferred behind closed doors. Uganda's President Museveni delivered the closing statement. The region's oldest president proudly announced their new consensus: no country would sign the outstanding EPAs until the EU could dispel the concerns of Burundi and Tanzania. He added that the EU should negotiate a trade deal with the EAC, not with individual states, and that the EAC had charged him with clarifying these points with Brussels.[20] At this summit, the East Africans dared to stand up together to the European economic superpower.

West Africa was a different story. The region with its economic community ECOWAS is the EU's major trading partner in Africa – so an agreement is all the more important.[21] In July 2014, the EU completed its negotiations with the West African states and

ECOWAS, and in December 2015 they signed the EPAs. The individual countries were to ratify them as soon as possible. Yet it emerged that Nigeria, Africa's largest economic power and biggest oil producer, would refuse – and thereby prevent the ECOWAS partners from ratifying the EPAs as a bloc. At last, ECOWAS managed to levy a 35 percent import duty on all 'sensitive' food products such as beef, chicken, yogurt, eggs, cocoa powder, chocolate, tomato paste and print fabrics to protect domestic products.[22]

However, the EU found loopholes. Threatening punitive tariffs, it pressured the developed states Ghana and Côte d'Ivoire, who make up the lion's share of trade with Europe, to accept the bilateral EPAs. They are the two largest global cocoa exporters. Both states closed interim agreements with the EU that have regulated their trade since 2016. Since then, they have been accessing the EU market free of customs and quotas. In return, the EU requires them to open their markets to 80 percent of EU imports within 15 years.[23]

However, these individual agreements specify different tariffs than the ECOWAS agreement. For example, ECOWAS levies an external tariff of 35 percent on European chicken, while Ghana and Côte d'Ivoire levy only 20 percent. Although Ghana can initially protect its local milk production with a higher tariff of 20 percent – the ECOWAS common external tariff (CET) allows only 10 percent – it has to eliminate this tariff altogether by 2022.[24] As a likely result, European export companies will ship their goods to West Africa via the ports of the capitals Accra and Abidjan, and from there across the duty-free internal borders of ECOWAS to other countries.

'And so after 14 years of negotiations, the EU's trade policy is leaving behind a wreck in West Africa,' comments the German NGO *Brot für die Welt*.[25] Its advisor for global nutrition, agricultural trading and ocean policy, Francisco Marí, concludes in his December 2016 blog entry on the EPA deal with Ghana: 'People in Africa are aware that the soapbox speeches by EU politicians, such as Federal Chancellor Merkel's on her recent Africa trip, are only lip service. It is time to throw poverty-producing partnership agreements between the EU and Africa into the dustbin of history and see them as they are: a failed attempt to carry on the neo-colonial relationship with the neighboring continent. This is not what partnership looks like.'[26]

Notes

1. *Bild* (2017)'Entwicklungsminister Müller wirbt für fairen Handel mit Afrika', 1 March | http://bit.ly/2tWrrCG

2. In 1963 the states of the European Economic Community (EEC) met with 17 African states in Cameroon's capital for the so-called First Yaoundé Convention. They signed an agreement by which the least developed countries of Africa could import raw materials duty-free into the Schengen area. In 1969 the 'Second Yaoundé Convention' renewed this agreement.

3. Schlindwein, Simone (2016) 'Not my cup of coffee', *Fluter*, 9 September | http://bit.ly/2cySRSV

4. *Uganda Radio Network* (2009) 'Uganda's First Local Coffee Processing Plant Opens', Kampala, 17 July | http://bit.ly/2x6EvmM

5. *Der Irrsinn mit der Milch*. ZDF television documentary film, 25 January 2017 | http://bit.ly/2vaQ3aN

6. Reichert, T. and Leimbach, J. (2015) *Billiges Milchpulver für die Welt – Das Auslaufen der EU-Milchquote und die Milcherzeugung und -exporte in Deutschland und der EU*, October 2015 | https://bit.ly/2N7R221

7. Sarmadi, Dario (2015) 'NGOs: Deutsche Milchexport-Offensive bedroht Entwicklungsländer', *Euractiv*, 14 October | http://bit.ly/2uMDNfE

8. *Honest Accounts? The true story of Africa's billion dollar losses*, Curtis Research Report, p.7. July 2014 | https://bit.ly/2VoEuvV

9. EU Commission (2013) 'Everything But Arms (EBA) – Who benefits', Strategy paper of the EU Commission, Brussels, 30 April 2013 | http://bit.ly/2tQtJ2d | http://www.trade.ec.europa.eu/doclib/docs/2013/april/tradoc_150983.pdf (This document has since been removed from this website)

10. *Africa Renewal* (2007) 'Africans fear "ruin" in Europe trade talks', July 2007 | http://bit.ly/2ubqOAq

11. *BBC* (2008) 'EPA protests in Ghana', 30 September | http://bbc.in/2uMIBSd

12. *The East African* (2016) 'Kenya, Rwanda sign East Africa trade deal with Europe', 1 September | http://bit.ly/2ct243j

13. *Deutsche Welle* (2017) 'EU-Freihandel mit Afrika: Unfairer Deal?', 11 January | http://bit.ly/2hfWvHK

14. *The East African* (2016) 'Burundi says will not sign EPAs; Dar mulls decision as Uganda backs Kenya, Rwanda', 4 September | http://bit.ly/2cncOfR

15. 'Tanzanian parliament advises government not to sign EPA with EU', *International Centre for Trade and sustainable Development*, 17 November 2016 | http://bit.ly/2hfIp9l

16. Mwambe, Geoffrey (2014) *Analysis of the Economic Partnership Agreement between the East African Community and the European Union: A Gravity Model Approach*, Macroeconomic and Financial Management Institute for Eastern and Southern Africa (MEFMI), December 2014 | https://bit.ly/2BFK2oj

17. *The Citizen* (2016) 'Report: EAC members risk losing Europe aid over EPA', 25 December | http://bit.ly/2vkFYsa

18. *The East African* (2017) 'EPA: To sign or not to sign? That is the question for EAC partners', 21 May | http://bit.ly/2uPGziy

19. ibid.

20. *The East African* (2017) 'EAC-Europe trade deal signing put on hold', 27 May | http://bit.ly/2uMDr8R

21. EU Commission (2017) 'Economic Partnership Agreement with West Africa – Facts and figures', 29 November | https://bit.ly/2SkxckZ

22. Ibid.

23. Official Journal of the European Union (2016) *Internationale Partnership Agreement with Côte d'Ivoire*, Brussels, 7 October | https://bit.ly/2ToX9uW -The specifics can be found following the source document (1)ABl. L 287 vom 21.10.2016, S. 1. –CJ

24. Official Journal of the European Union (2016) *Internationale Partnership Agreement with Ghana*, Brussels, 15 December | http://bit.ly/2uMe8DG

25. European Union (2016) *How can the EPA help Ghana's sustainable development?*, June 2016 | https://bit.ly/2g5dibd

26. Marí, Francisco (2016) 'EPA-Handelsabkommen EU-Ghana ratifiziert!', Blog entry by NGO expert in world nutrition, agricultural trade and ocean policy, *Brot für die Welt*, 5 December | http://bit.ly/2uZOQDG

Conclusion

Conclusion:
Europe's dreams, Africa's dreams

Humanity's oldest migration route leads through the deserts of Africa, along the Nile to the north, across the Sinai Peninsula to the Middle East and Turkey, then on via the Balkans to Central Europe. A few thousand Africans traveled to Europe on this route during the momentous 2015 summer of migration. Among the Syrians and Afghans who marched across the Balkans at that time, Africans were just a small minority.

Today this historic route is closed. Israel had already built a fence along the border with Egypt. After the 2016 refugee deal with the EU, Turkey closed its southern border with Syria. Earlier, Spain sealed off its two North African exclaves Ceuta and Melilla with razor wire. The two neighboring continents of Africa and Europe are now artificially separated.

Europeans are sending Africans the message: 'You cannot get in here.' If you try, you could die. And if you do arrive, you must live in misery. The fate that awaits you here are camps like those on the Greek islands.

To make sure that the 'KEEP OUT' message reaches Africans, EU states hire ambassadors like Hervé Tcheumeleu, a Cameroonian based in Germany. He receives $50,000 from the German Foreign Office to tour schoolyards in Cameroon and make young girls say sentences like 'Illegal emigration is not good,' and then ask for 'Applause for this clever girl!' His audience is supposed to believe what he says: 'Anyone who travels without the necessary papers has no rights. And this has nothing to do with racism. That's just the way it is.'[1]

The EU has spent billions buying African leaders as gatekeepers, including dictators and suspected war criminals. European border guards train their African counterparts to stop migrants and refugees. At the EU's request, key transit states have passed laws against people smugglers.

The smuggling rings often bring together gangsters and corrupt state employees, who also get money from the EU to stop smuggling. So they earn double.

Migrants and refugees, on the other hand, are criminalized. Irregular border crossings are punishable offenses. People who try are hunted by well-equipped border guards in the desert, arrested, put in camps or prisons, or sent back to their state or some other country; 'encouraged,' voluntary – or not. And that is still the good side of the story.

The other side is murderous: thousands of people from Africa perish in this new world of fences and mobile border troops; dehydrated in the desert, drowned in the Mediterranean Sea, force-recruited by Islamist militias, enslaved, tortured, beheaded or bled to death in the razor wire.

The death toll is rising. At least 12,046 people drowned off Libya between January 2015 and February 2019 alone.[2] Some African civil wars are less deadly. However, the EU is pleased with the sinking number of arrivals: registered unauthorized border crossings fell from 204,000 to 151,000 in 2018.[3] This was 27 percent less than in the previous year and a decline for the third year in succession. 'Regarding irregular arrivals, we're not facing a burning crisis right now,'[4] said Frontex Director Fabrice Leggeri at the presentation of his latest risk analysis in Brussels in February 2019.

A growing number of African heads of state are publicly criticizing the EU for letting people die at its gates. Mali's President Ibrahim Boubacar Keïta addressed Merkel at the G20 Africa Partnership Summit in Berlin in June 2017: 'Every time a young African dies in the Mediterranean, we get sick – honestly, Madam Chancellor.'[5] A year later, the EU-Africa summit in Abidjan collapsed and ended with a diplomatic scandal. There was no joint final declaration. The views on migration remain too different.

Today, any person lucky enough to get from Africa to Europe must undergo a lengthy procedure to obtain asylum. Deportation is a frequent outcome: often by brute force, in handcuffs, possibly not even to the person's country of origin. Perhaps the EU decides that a deportee is not from Sierra Leone, but from Nigeria, as in the case of Joseph Koroma. Frontex may leave deportees in a country where they know no one and no one wants them. African countries who enter such deals benefit from EU equipment and training for their security forces. From here, it is no big step towards Israel's forced, systematic deportation of Eritreans via Rwanda to Uganda.

The EU has been negotiating with African governments since the 2015 escalation in the Balkans. Europe is trying to buy Africa's willingness to serve European interests. By threatening to cut aid, the EU has subdued African states Niger, Sudan, Ethiopia, Senegal or Morocco – sometimes against the will of their own populations.

Negotiations often took place behind closed doors so as not to alert civil society. For example, in December 2016 Mali's President Keïta signed a communiqué on readmissions and then denied it after protests in Bamako. Many African citizens still do not know what their governments are doing to serve the EU. This is not in line with the original aim of European development aid: to promote democracy in Africa.

The most cooperative regimes are the authoritarian or even totalitarian ones, as in Eritrea. These regimes profit most from the new EU migration policy. Europeans are now reaching out to long-isolated dictators. Like Sudan's alleged war criminal General Hametti, they play Europe's accomplice and then make demands on Berlin and Brussels, blackmail the EU or, like Eritrea's dictator Isaias Afewerki, fool it with empty promises. European aid allows them to expand their power, supported by a security apparatus now professionalized with European programs.

Some other states, such as Niger, are too poor to turn down a cash injection from Brussels. Some, like the state of Cape Verde, which was the first to sign many EU agreements, are too small to refuse the EU anything. Others, like Africa's most populous country Nigeria, are big enough that the EU has to make them large offers. By focusing on selected transit states north of the equator, European diplomats have managed to divide Africans who were striving for common positions in the African Union (AU) or in regional associations, such as the Economic Community of West African States (ECOWAS) and the East African Community (EAC).

Migration is something fundamentally human. A primary instinct once caused the earliest people to migrate north along the Nile, leaving the continent via the Sinai. There are many reasons to go elsewhere: Natural disasters, hunger, finding better arable land, work, happiness, or sometimes just curiosity or wanderlust. In African societies, people who have seen much of the world are considered wise. When they return to their village they are treated like heroes: neighbors and relatives come to hear stories of the wider world.

Earlier communities in Europe were also like this, in the days before package vacations. Traveling, let alone emigrating, was costly and terribly risky. Only in recent decades have cheap airlines and mass tourism enabled Europeans to lie around tanning half-naked by the millions on Mediterranean beaches, while thousands are drowning in the same sea.

In autumn 2015, at the peak of the Balkan crisis, the image of a drowned Syrian child on a Turkish beach horrified the European media. 'The fall of Europe,' wrote the Spanish newspaper *El Periódico*. The photo triggered compassion and benevolence. The picture also influenced how people in many European cities responded to Merkel's saying, 'We can do it,' as they volunteered to help the arriving refugees. The image created solidarity, something Europe is missing right now.

The EU pushes for readmission agreements with African governments to get rid of Africans already in Europe. This is a job for Frontex, which ensures cheaper mass deportations of migrants from across the EU. Increasingly stricter laws and a pool of specially trained experts will support the border control agency.

Hardly any pictures exist of the African tragedy in the Nigerien desert. People there die unobserved by cameras. Only Frontex is watching on its flat-screen monitors. It collects information with satellites and drones to combat smugglers and human traffickers. But the more roads Europe blocks, the more modern slave traders earn. If there were more legal ways into the EU, smugglers would lose their business, which also funds terrorism.

Diplomat Vincent Cochetel is the Special Envoy for the Central Mediterranean Situation at the UN refugee aid agency UNHCR. As an observer, he has witnessed many negotiations between the EU and African countries. His summary is grim: 'If you just say that the problem has been solved because fewer people arrive in Italy, or because more people from Libya are returning home, then you're wrong. The problem is still there.' There are hardly any figures about the deaths in the Nigerien desert, but by the end of 2017, Cochetel is certain: 'We now have many more people dying in the desert – probably even more than in the Central Mediterranean.' He states that the EU should not 'expect everything from Africa, without offering people other opportunities.'[6]

But that is precisely where the EU balks. Its promises of creating 'legal ways for migration' remain largely unfulfilled.

This failure to act conflicts with Europe's historical responsibility towards Africa. Europe's colonial period in Africa is not that far in the past. African grandparents still remember their countries' often bloody struggles for independence. Their memories are generally better than European seniors' recollections of World War II and the resulting refugee treks through Europe. A few centuries ago, Europeans dragged enslaved African onto boats and shipped them across the Atlantic to work on the plantations of a continent that the Europeans had just conquered in their migration frenzy. Millions of people were stolen from the African continent; Europe was one of the causes of the 'underdevelopment' it now tries to amend with expensive development aid.

Only a few centuries later, Europeans now want the Africans to stay home. They are no longer welcome to get on board, nor to explore a new world – and no jobs await them. Europe fears Africa's fast population growth. In July 2017, Denmark's development minister Ulla Tornaes demonstrated this when she announced her intention to chip in $14 million for birth control in Africa: 'Part of the solution to reducing migratory pressures on Europe is to reduce the very high population growth in many African countries.'[7]

Yet, migration is the simplest way to compensate for the unequal distribution of global wealth. The enormous sums African migrant workers remit to their families show this. In Niger, remittances exceed tax revenue from the provinces; in Mali they make up a large part of the gross national product; in Eritrea they finance the state apparatus; in Nigeria remittances are nine times higher than the country's development aid.[8]

Migration drives development in Africa. Similar to the EU, African states join to form regional economic communities. They eliminate customs tariffs, visas and work permits in order to facilitate the free movement of goods, services and labor on a regional basis. They value Africa's strong population growth, as it increases the number of consumers and demand, which is good for the economy. Foreigners are welcome. At the beginning of 2019, the African Union presented its common African passport – biometric, of course – for visa-free travel throughout the continent. Whether this is realistic, and how the EU will handle it, remains to be seen.

So far, the EU has only managed to impose some of its migration demands on Africa. European deportation papers, called *laissez-passers*, are still not recognized by any African state. At the beginning of 2019, only Ethiopia has signed a readmission agreement with the EU as a whole, despite the billions spent to build political pressure on this issue. In return, African states want simpler access to EU visas for their citizens, but European governments reject migrant workers from Africa, with very few exceptions.

Anyone standing at the visa counter of the German consulate in an African capital today gets mixed messages: The bulletin board displays posters of blooming landscapes along the Moselle and Rhine rivers and advertisements to study medicine in Heidelberg or mechanical engineering in Munich, just next to warnings against smugglers and human traffickers who scam people with phony promises of work in the EU. Between these posters is an armored glass pane with a narrow gap for visa applications: the needle's eye to a work permit for Europe.

Africans seeking visas or asylum must be ready to disclose their entire lives, financial status and wider family relations to the European authorities. Databases and biometric detection are making it easier for the EU to monitor migration. Not all African borders have computers and Internet access yet. Many demarcations between states are still not fortified and not all passports are biometric. However, the EU makes great efforts to ensure that African states record fingerprints from Cairo to Cape Town, from Dakar to Dar es Salaam and finally send them to the European authorities – using security technology provided by Europe.

These so-called intelligent borders offer rich profits for European security and defense companies and their suppliers, who formerly viewed the African market as irrelevant or too risky. Germany aims to facilitate its companies' access to Africa and subsidizes exports while calling it 'combating the root causes of migration'. These concepts are sold to Africans as 'job initiatives' for a young 'continent of opportunity'. As German Chancellor Merkel put it during her G20 presidency at the Berlin Partnership Conference with Africa: fewer migrants from Africa also mean 'more security for us'.[9]

Many recent EU attempts to control migration within Europe were not new in content, but in scope. Brussels has redirected billions from development aid to migration prevention. Domestic policy concerns drive these strategies. Virtually all elections in the EU today depend on the question of immigration and border control. Rising right-wing populists have successfully dictated their agenda to everyone else.

One could think the common fight against migration was bringing Europe closer together. Yet the opposite is true; the discord could not be greater. The new Common European Asylum System, which has been in planning for years, is deadlocked. This shows the EU's profound crisis. It is not a refugee crisis, but a crisis of internal solidarity. Unable to agree on the necessary distribution of refugees, the EU is drifting further apart. The EU's only consensus on migration is that refugees should be stopped within Africa. This lowest denominator offers a miserable image of a Union that has always claimed to want to grow closer.

In Europe, Africa is not a foreign policy issue, but a domestic one. The vast African continent, which often appears chaotic and threatening to Europeans, serves as a projection target for all their fears, as it has since colonial times. In June 2017, Development

Minister Müller spoke of '100 million Africans' coming to Europe.[10] That is how Europeans play up their own fear of a Black planet.

With increasing economic development, more and more people from the 'continent of opportunity' will be looking for work beyond their home countries. The population will continue to grow, but not as fast as currently feared. The expanding African middle class tends to have fewer children – usually only two or three, because they fit into a car. Europe experienced a similar pattern: birth rates declined with increasing industrialization and urbanization. In many African countries, where education is expensive, the middle class considers how much school tuition they can afford to ensure education for all of their children.

Meanwhile, Europe's free trade agreements are threatening the livelihoods of African small farmers, while global warming will destroy the arable land of millions. The EU bears a great deal of responsibility for this.

The EU should work towards a rational, development-friendly joint foreign and security policy to bring the world's conflicts under control, instead of hiring dictators as gatekeepers to its fortress.

There are reasons why people radicalize or flee. Authoritarian and corrupt regimes, some of which the EU is now courting, are partly to blame for people leaving their homes. Many are also fleeing from European weapons.

In today's world, security, just like wealth, is distributed more unequally than ever before. Migration would be one of the easier fixes to global inequality. Europe's fight against migration is a massive, costly effort to uphold global inequality and defend Europe's prosperity. One African border guard commander, whose unit's training was funded by the German Corporation for International Cooperation (GIZ), put it like this: Donating a high-tech fence to a country where people starve to death and children are chronically underfed and do not go to school is like handing a cap to a freezing naked child.[11]

This raises the risk for young Africans to join jihadists. Terrorist attacks like the one in Berlin prove only that there will always be loopholes to get to Europe.

The EU is drafting generous Marshall plans and granting loans that benefit Europe's depositors and pension funds and draw German companies to Africa. These programs are supposed to create jobs and keep young job seekers at home. African states and regional organizations are invited to join free trade deals – played by Europe's rules. These agreements force Africans to open their markets to European products, which destroys jobs. Then development aid comes in to recreate these jobs elsewhere. This is what happens when migration is treated as a crisis.

The EU dreams of protected borders and open markets. Africa dreams of protected markets and open borders. Until this dilemma is resolved, there will be no real partnership.

Notes

1. Frenzel, Veronika (2019) 'Europa hat dichtgemacht', *SZ-Magazin*, issue 7/2019, *Süddeutsche Zeitung*, 14 February | https://bit.ly/2HOOq99

2. International Organization for Migration (IOM), Missing Migrants Project (accessed 28 March 2019) | https://bit.ly/2K6KuNZ

3. Frontex (2019) 'Frontex publishes Risk Analysis for 2019', Frontex news release, 20 February | https://bit.ly/2Te0y52

4. Jakob, Christian (2019) 'Flüchtlingskrise ist nicht', *tageszeitung*, Berlin, 20 February | https://bit.ly/2HNh1vS

5. Authors' notes from the 'G20 Africa Partnership – investing in a common future' conference, Berlin, 12 June 2017

6. Interview with Vincent Cochetel, Director of the Bureau for Europe at the United Nations High Commissioner for Refugees (UNHCR), Geneva, 16 February 2018

7. *BBC* (2017) 'Denmark's contraception aid to Africa "to limit migration"', 12 July | https://bbc.in/2HVoXKJ

8. Adegbesan, Elizabeth (2018) 'Nigeria tops remittances to Sub-Saharan Africa with 22bn- World Bank', *Vanguard Media Nigeria*, 24 April | https://bit.ly/2vHjxhR | and OECD (2018) 'Aid at a glance charts' (accessed 28 March 2019)| https://bit.ly/2tDi9et

9. Speech by German Chancellor Angela Merkel at the G20 Africa Partnership Conference, Berlin, 12 July 2017

10. *Die Welt* (2017) 'Entwicklungsminister warnt vor riesiger Fluchtbewegung aus Afrika', 18 June | https://bit.ly/2tBYbfT

11. Press briefing with border force commander in East Congo whose troops were trained by the German Corporation for International Cooperation (GIZ) border management program, Goma, 14 February 2017

Further reading

'Aiding Surveillance – An exploration of how development and humanitarian aid initiatives are enabling surveillance in developing countries', *Privacy International*, September 2013 | http://bit.ly/2udRDnN

Akkerman, Mark (2016) *Border Wars – The Arms Dealers Profiting from Europe's Refugee Tragedy*, Report by StopWapenhandel, 4 July | http://bit.ly/2wfectE

Andersson, Ruben (2016) 'Hardwiring the frontier? The politics of security technology in Europe's "fight against illegal migration"', *Security Dialogue*, 47 / 2016, p. 22–39 | http://bit.ly/2tYTYYt

Andersson, Ruben (2014) 'Time and the Migrant Other: European Border Controls and the Temporal Economics of Illegality', *American Anthropologist*, Vol. 116, No. 4 / 2014, p. 1–15 | http://bit.ly/2tT7BnD

Baldo, Suliman (2017) *Border Control from Hell – How the EU's migration partnership legitimizes Sudan's 'militia state'*, Report by the Enough Project, April 2017 | http://bit.ly/2wo8SL4

Betts, A., Collier, P., Dierlamm, H. and Juraschitz, N. (2017) *Gestrandet: Warum unsere Flüchtlingspolitik allen schadet – und was jetzt zu tun ist*, Munich, Siedler

'Biometrics: Friend or foe of privacy?', *Privacy International*, December 2013 | http://bit.ly/2hiyuzB

'Bis an die Zäune bewaffnet', *Heinrich Böll Foundation*, January 2015 | http://bit.ly/2uepNrb

Buckel, Sonja (2013) Welcome to Europe – *Die Grenzen des europäischen Migrationsrechts. Juridische Auseinandersetzungen um das 'Staatsprojekt Europa'*, Bielefeld, transcript, 2013

Burgis, Tom (2016) *Der Fluch des Reichtums: Warlords, Konzerne, Schmuggler und die Plünderung Afrikas*, Frankfurt, Westend, 2016

Braunsdorf, Felix (Hrsg.) (2016) 'Fluchtursachen "Made in Europe" – Über europäische Politik und ihren Zusammenhang mit Migration und

Flucht', *Friedrich Ebert Foundation*, November 2016 | http://bit.ly/
2hnyARN

Castles, S., de Haas, H. Miller, Mark J. (2013) 'International Population
Movements in the Modern World', in *The Age of Migration*, Basingstoke,
Palgrave

el Gawhary, Karim (2015) *Auf der Flucht: Reportagen von beiden Seiten des
Mittelmeers*, Wien, Kremayr & Scheriau

Frankenhaeuser, Malin (2015) 'Mapping Migration & Development in six
regional migration dialogues', *International Centre for Migration Policy
Development*, Vienna | http://bit.ly/2wfrOoz

'Grenzwertig – Eine Analyse der neuen EU-Grenzüberwachungsinitiativen
EUROSUR und "intelligente Grenzen"', *Heinrich Böll Foundation*, June
2012

Heimeshoff, Lisa-Marie (2014) '*Grenzregime II: Migration – Kontrolle – Wissen.
Transnationale Perspektiven*', Berlin, Assoziation A

Hess, S.; Kasparek, B. and Kron, S (2016) *Der lange Sommer der Migration:
Grenzregime III*, Berlin, Assoziation A

'Human Trafficking and Smuggling on the Horn of Africa-Central
Mediterranean Route', *Sahan Foundation and IGAD Security Sector
Program (ISSP)*, February 2016 | http://bit.ly/2uepIUp

'Im Schatten der Zitadelle – Der Einfluss des europäischen Migrations-
regimes auf Drittstaaten', *medico international, Brot für die Welt* and *Pro
Asyl*, November 2013 | http://bit.ly/2hixuMb

Johnson, Dominic (2011) *Afrika vor dem großen Sprung*, Berlin, Wagenbach

Mbolela, Emanuel (2014) *Mein Weg vom Kongo nach Europa. Zwischen
Widerstand, Flucht und Exil*, Wien, Mandelbaum

'The Global Surveillance Industry', *Privacy International*, July 2016 |
http://bit.ly/2uOYC9Z

Tinti, Peter and Westcott, Tom (2016) 'The Niger-Libya corridor – the
smuggler's perspective', *Institute for Security Studies*, Paper 29,
November | http://bit.ly/2h2beBR

Van Reisen, M. Estefanos, M. and Rijken, C. (2012) '*Human Trafficking in the
Sinai: Refugees between Life and Death*, Brussels | http://bit.ly/2vbE9x9

Acknowledgements

Thanks to all interview partners and people who helped with the research including:

Samir Abi – Observatoire Migration / Visions Solidaires (Lomé)

Luise Amtsberg (MdB) – member of the Bundestag for The Greens (Berlin)

Ingo Badoreck – German Africa Foundation (Berlin)

Marcella Barocco – Alarm Phone (Nijmegen)

Cheikh Ould Baya – Valletta Process Focal Point Mauritania – (Zouérat Mauritania)

Olaf Bernau – Afrique Europe Interact (Bremen)

Inge Brees – CARE (Brussels)

Sean Burke – Statewatch (London)

Tony Buyan – Statewatch (London)

Jean-Pierre Cassarino – Institut de recherche sur le Maghreb contemporain (Tunis / Perugia)

Sékou dit Gaoussou Cisse – Ambassador Extraordinary and Plenipotentiary Head of the Mission of the Republic of Mali to the European Union (Brussels)

Albert Chaibou – Alternatives Espaces Citoyen (Niamey)

Claudia Charles – Groupe d'information et de soutien des immigrés (Paris)

Ulrich Delius – Society for Threatened Peoples (Göttingen)

Alpha Abdoulaye Diallo – Réseau Afrique Jeunesse de Guinée (Conakry)

Alassane Dicko – Afrique Europe Interact (Bamako)

Helmut Dietrich – Forschungsgesellschaft Flucht und Migration (Berlin)

Stephan Dünnwald – Bayerischer Flüchtlingsrat (Munich)

Hans-Georg Eberl – Afrique Europe Interact (Vienna)

Sabine Eckart – medico international (Frankfurt)

Musa Ecweru – State Minister for Relief and Disaster Preparedness Uganda (Kampala)

Meron Estefanos – Eritrean Initiative on Refugee Rights (Oslo)

Michael Flynn – Global Detention Project (Geneva)

Ralph Genetzke – International Centre for Migration Policy Development (Brussels)

Jürgen Gottschlich (Istanbul)

Andreas Grünwald – staff member of the parliamentary group of the The Left (Berlin)

Mohamed Ibn Chambas – Head of the United Nations Office for West Africa (UNOWAS; Dakar)

Milka Isinta – Panafrican Network in Defense of Migrants Rights (Nairobi)

Cooper Inveen (Freetown Sierra Leone)

Dominic Johnson – tageszeitung (Berlin)

Chris Jones – Statewatch (London)

Thomas Hohlfeld – staff member of the parliamentary group of the The Left (Berlin)

Christoph Kannengießer – German-African Business Association (Berlin)

Uwe Kekeritz (MdB) – member of the Bundestag for The Greens (Berlin)

Ska Keller (MdEP) – Member of the European Parliament for The Greens / EFA (Brussels)

Jakob Kießling – staff member of the parliamentary group of The Greens (Berlin)

Gerald Knaus – European Stability Initiative (Berlin)

Martial Tetenyo Kodah – World Infant Alliance (Accra, Ghana)

Hagen Kopp – Alarm Phone (Hanau)

Judith Kopp – Pro Asyl (Frankfurt)

Karl Kopp – Pro Asyl (Frankfurt)

Andie Lambe – International Refugee Rights Initiative (Kampala)

Ramona Lenz – medico international (Frankfurt)

Barbara Lochbihler (MdEP) – The Greens / EFA

Carlos Lopes – University of Cape Town

Sabine Lösing (MdEP) – The Left / EL

Christian Manahl – EU delegation to Eritrea (Asmara)

Katja Maurer – medico international

Matthias Monroy – staff member of the parliamentary group of The Left (Berlin)

Niema Movassat (MdB) – member of the Bundestag for The Left (Berlin)

Melanie Müller – German Institute for International and Security Affairs (Berlin)

Ruben Neugebauer – Sea Watch e.V. (Berlin)

Carolin Njuki – Intergovernmental Authority on Development (Nairobi)

Neda Noraie-Kia – staff member of the parliamentary group of The Greens (Berlin)

Olawale Maiyegun – Director for Social Affairs African Union (Addis Ababa)

Rex Osa – Refugees for Refugees (Stuttgart)

Marina Peter – Brot für die Welt (Berlin)

Liepollo Pheko – International Network on Migration and Development (South Africa)

Martijn Pluim – International Centre for Migration Policy Development (Vienna)

Claire Rodier – MIGREUROP (Paris)

Marina Schramm – IOM Niger (Agadez)

Benjamin Schraven – German Development Institute (Bonn)

Christoph Strässer (MdB) – member of the Bundestag for the SPD (Berlin)

Ninja Taprogge – Care Deutschland (Nairobi)

Ralph Töpfer – German Institute for Human Rights (Berlin)

Jerome Tubiana – Small Arms Survey (Paris)

N'Faly Sanoh – Director Free Movement and Tourism ECOWAS (Abuja)

Maurice Stierl – Alarm Phone (Berkeley)

Zafira Sukee – Statewatch (London)

Mirjam van Reisen – Europe External Policy Advisors (Brussels)

Pierre Vimont – Carnegie Europe (Brussels)

Lydia Wamala – World Food Programme Uganda
Bruno Watara – Afrique Europe Interact (Berlin)
Sophie Wirsching – Brot für die Welt (Berlin)
Reinhard Wolff (Stockholm)
Charly Xaxley – UNHCR Uganda (Kampala)
Abdelbasset Zenzeri (Taboulba)

Contributors to the Migration Control research project (https://migration-control.taz.de/#en) on which this book is based:

Funding

The translation of this work was supported by a grant from the *Goethe-Institut*. The translation was also sponsored by the *Rosa Luxemburg Stiftung* with funds of the Federal Ministry for Economic Cooperation and Development of the Federal Republic of Germany. This publication or parts of it can be used by others for free as long as they provide a proper reference to the original publication.

Our thanks also to

Dr. Christian Ankowitsch – Fleiß und Mut e.V (Berlin)
Kirsten Maas-Alberts Claudia Simons – Heinrich Böll Foundation (Berlin)
Miriam Edding – stiftung :do (Berlin)
Mercator Foundation (Berlin)
taz Panter Stiftung (Berlin)
Förderverein Pro Asyl e.V. (Frankfurt)
Ruben Neugebauer Matthias Kuhnt – Sea Watch e.V. (Berlin)
Dieter Behr – European Civic Forum (Vienna)
Stefanie Kron – Rosa Luxemburg Foundation (Berlin)

Authors and Research

Inken Bartels (Hamburg)
Eric Bonse (Brussels)

Michael Braun (Rome)
Alexander Bühler (Berlin)
Tony Buyan (London)
Ali Celikkan (Berlin)
Michael Flynn (Geneva)
Katrin Gänsler (Cotonou)
Hans-Georg Eberl (Vienna)
Belinda Grasnick (Berlin)
Fabian Grieger (Berlin)
Cooper Inveen (Freetown)
Dominic Johnson (Berlin)
Susanne Knaul (Tel Aviv)
Katharina Lipowsky (Berlin)
Bernard Schmid (Paris)
Philipp Sofian Naceur (Cairo)
Andrea Stäritz (Abuja)
Nina Violetta Schwarz (Berlin)
Lea Wagner (Berlin)
Reiner Wandler (Madrid)
Paul Welch Guerra (Berlin)

Equipment

Daniél Kretschmar – taz.de (Berlin)
Laura Maikowski – Bildargumente (Berlin)
Pierre Maite – Ca Ira (Berlin)
Jürgen Neumann – Econauten (Berlin)
Gustav Pursche – Jib Collective (Berlin)
Robert Schuster – Econauten (Berlin)]

Translation

Lydia Baldwin Charlotte Bomy Anna Bodenez Nivene Rafaat – lingua·trans·fair – Netzwerk für Kommunikation (Berlin), www.linguatransfair.de
Emal Ghamsharick www.germling.com
Gaby Sohl – tageszeitung (Berlin)

University of Leeds Centre for Translation Studies School of Languages Cultures and Societies (Leeds)
Centre for Translation Studies (ZTW) at the University of Vienna

The development of this book was made possible during a period that the publisher, Firoze Manji, was Richard von Weizsäcker Fellow at the Robert Bosch Foundation, Berlin 2018-2019.

Index of place names

About the authors

Christian Jakob: Born in 1979, studied sociology economics philosophy in Bremen and Milan; global studies in Berlin, Buenos Aires and Delhi. Editor for the daily *tageszeitung* (taz) since 2006, reporter since 2014. In 2017 he won the media project award together with Simone Schlindwein and Daniél Kretschmar from the Otto Brenner Foundation for the Migration Control research project, on which this book is based. In 2016 he published 'Die Bleibenden' (Ch. Links) a history of the refugee movement in Germany. In 2018/19 he contributed to the 'Civil Society Atlas' (Bread for the World) and to the 'Atlas of Migration' (Rosa Luxemburg Foundation). In 2019 he will publish 'Angriff auf Europa' (Ch. Links) a book about the international assault on Europe from the far right with M. Gürgen, P. Hecht and S. am Orde. Christian Jakob's Twitter handle is @chrjkb.

Simone Schlindwein: Born in 1980; Eastern European studies from 2006-2008; Moscow correspondent for Der Spiegel. Based in Uganda since 2008 she has been a correspondent for the German daily *tageszeitung* (taz) from the Great Lakes region: DR Congo, Rwanda, Burundi, Uganda, Central African Republic, South Sudan. Won the 2016 journalism award 'Der lange Atem' for her research into the Rwandan Hutu militia FDLR in DR Congo and Germany and her resulting book 'Tatort Kongo – Prozess in Deutschland.' In 2017 she won the media project award together with Christian Jakob and Daniél Kretschmar from the Otto Brenner Foundation for the Migration Control research project, on which this book is based.